33

THE ECONOMY AND POLITY IN EARLY TWENTIETH CENTURY HUNGARY

The Role of the National Association of Industrialists

by

George Deák

EAST EUROPEAN MONOGRAPHS, BOULDER
DISTRIBUTED BY COLUMBIA UNIVERSITY PRESS, NEW YORK

1990

EAST EUROPEAN MONOGRAPHS, NO. CCLXXXVIII

Copyright © 1990 George Deák
ISBN 0–88033–185–2
Library of Congress Card Catalog Number 90–81156

Printed in the United States of America

Contents

Part II. The Association in National Politics

Tables

Figures

PREFACE

The National Association of Hungarian Industrialists was formed in 1902, during a cyclical downturn of economic activity. Although the recession that began around 1900 appeared formidable to the entrepreneurial elite, it turned out relatively mild, leaving unaffected a number of key industrial branches. By the end of 1904 rapid economic growth had resumed. In the decade preceding World War I the system of mechanized factories expanded into almost every branch of industry. By the outbreak of the war, Hungarian industry had gained a distinctly up-to-date character. Our investigation focuses on the last Antebellum decade.

The period was one of crises in the structure of Dualism, in the rule of the Liberal Party and in the political and social environment that had been so hospitable to economic development in the preceding decades. The forces of the Independence Party and of agrarianism, the form of *fin-de-siècle* conservatism most influential in Hungary, combined to bring thirty years of Liberal Party rule to an end in 1905. A short experiment with absolutism under the unconstitutionally appointed Fejérváry Government was followed by the so-called Coalition from 1906 to 1909. At the outset the Coalition enjoyed the broad support of the former Parliamentary Opposition, as well as much of what had been the Liberal Party, but ended its rule abandoned and isolated, having been unable to win even the slightest concession towards greater independence from the Monarch. In 1901, the old Liberal guard returned to power under the newly formed Party of National Work, an apparent restoration which, as we shall see, nonetheless contained many novel and foreboding elements.

The political struggles of the twelve years covered by this monograph affected the economic policies of the state. In sharp contrast to the deliberate policies of the 1880s and early 1890s, the policies of the several regimes that ruled between 1902 and 1914 were marked by hesitation, a reflection of the contradictory influence of agrarian and industrial pressure groups.

This study is primarily concerned with the attempts of the National Association of Hungarian Industrialists (Magyar Gyáriparosok Országos Szövetsége, hereinafter referred to as the Association) to sustain and extend in this period the policies and climate of opinion that had earlier served the development of industry. The Association pursued its goals at both the bureaucratic and the political levels. It sought not only to affect particular policy measures in the existing order but also, in a limited way, to alter the political system in which those policies were evolved. The origins, structure and aims of the Association are examined in the first part of the manuscript. The second part deals with the organization's political orientation and activities without integrating its history into a general history of organized industrial interest groups in Central Europe during the late nineteenth and early twentieth centuries.

The present work is based on my doctoral dissertation written at Columbia University in 1980. The original research and its publication owe their existence to the help and encouragement of a great many friends and mentors. My gratitude is due to numerous historians of the Historical Institute of the Hugnarian Academy of Sciences. I first became interested in the subject of the National Association through discussions of the history of the Hungarian bourgeoisie with Dr. Zsuzsa L. Nagy during her visit to Columbia University's Institute on East Central Europe in 1973. Another visitor to Columbia University, Dr.Péter Hanák, further aroused my interest in the history of early twentieth century Central Europe and supervised my researches in Hungary in 1976 and 1977. Thanks are due to the late Dr. György Ránki, Director of the Historical Institute not only for his reading and commenting upon the manuscript but also for making me feel part of the Institute during my stay in Budapest. There I benefited greatly from discussions with László Katus, Emil Niederhauser, László Varga, Antal Vörös, Károly Vörös, and other historians too numerous to mention. I am grateful also for the help given me by the librarians and bibliographers of the Institute. All of the above colleagues helped to make my stay in Hungary fruitful and pleasant both intellectually and personally. I am also grateful to Dr. Richard Plaschka and the Institut für Osteuropäische Geschichte und Südostforschung of the University of Vienna for providing me with a congenial place to work during my stay in Austria. I am most indebted to Professor Istvan Deak, my graduate advisor at Columbia University, for all he has taught me in the past, for his help in the preparation of the dissertation on which this manuscript is based. Thanks are due also to Professor Hugh Neuberger of Columbia University for reading the preliminary draft. Anna Seleny, a graduate student at the Massachusetts Institute of Technology has helped me to reorient myself to the current status of economic interest groups in Hungary, making the history of the Association all the more interesting at the time of publication.

My research was made possible by grants from the International Research and Exchanges Board, the Fulbright–Hays Commission and the Austrian Ministry of Research and Education. I wish also to acknowledge the help of the American–Hungarian Studies Foundation during the early stages of my graduate studies.

I also wish to express my heartfelt gratitude to Dr. John Komlos of the University of Pittsburgh for his kindness in helping to bring this work to the public and for undertaking the substantial editorial work necessary to make it presentable after its eight years of dormancy.

Finally, I wish to express my deep obligation to my wife, Vera, for her patience and encouragement in difficult times as well as for her typing of the manuscript. The emotional and often financial support of my parents and members of my extended family is also deeply appreciated.

Although a great many people have aided my work, the responsibility for whatever flaws it may contain are solely my own.

—George Deák

PART I

ORIGINS, STRUCTURE, PROGRAM

Chapter 1

FROM CONSENSUS TO CONFLICT: ECONOMIC DEVELOPMENT AND ECONOMIC POLICY BEFORE 1900

The National Association of Hungarian Industrialists was founded in 1902 to represent the interests of Hungarian mechanized industry. Its principal goal was to influence the economic policy of the government in a direction that would promote Hungarian industrialization. The notion of promoting industry was certainly not new in Hungary. In fact, it was the threat of a retreat of the state from its pro–industrial economic policies of the 1880s and 1890s that prompted the founding of the Association.

Because much of the discussion will be in reference to the government's economic policy, we should consider some of the traditions of that policy as they evolved in the era of Dualism. Before doing so, however, we need to survey the economic and political development providing the context of the industrializing policies of the government.

The Age of Consensus: The Policy of Modernization

After 1867, when Hungary regained its self–rule, economic policy was marked by a consensus among the Hungarian political and economic elites in favor of a policy of modernization. Except in its relations to the "constitutional question"—that is, Hungarian independence or participation in the Dual Monarchy—this consensus extended even to most of the specifics of economic policy. The social consensus over economic policy was based in the character of Hungary's economic development prior to the 1880s.

Up to that time, economic growth had been dominated by the expansion of the agricultural sector. The relative dynamism of this sector derived from the division of labor that had developed in earlier centuries between Eastern and Western Europe as well as between the Austrian and Hungarian halves of the Habsburg Monarchy. The East became a supplier of foodstuffs, especially of grains in exchange for manufactured products. A similar division of labor applied within the Habsburg Monarchy as well.[1]

Following the Napoleonic Wars the movement for the abolition of serfdom was led by a section of the Hungarian landowning class itself. The noble reformers accepted the liberal proposition that only a free market in labor and goods could provide for the increased productivity of agriculture, an increase that was needed to take advantage of the export opportunities created by the industrialization of Western Europe. The reformers were able to carry through their program for abolition in 1848, moreover, in such a way that the system of large estates was preserved. Although a part of the peasantry also received land, another part received too little land for its sustenance, thus providing the landowners with a mobile supply of labor. The abolition of the intermediate customs barrier in 1850 by the Neo–Absolutist regime which followed the defeat of the Hungarian War of Independence, gave Hungary privileged access to the expanding Austrian market for grains and other agricultural products.[2]

The expansion of agriculture provided a focal point for the development of other sectors of the economy, which in turn often directly served the interests of further agricultural growth. The clearest expression of this process can be seen from the geographical distribution of the railroad network as it developed in the second half of the century. 6353 km of track were laid between 1847 and 1873, almost two–thirds of this in the extraordinary *Gründung* fever of the years between the Compromise of 1867 and the crash of 1873. Priority was given to the transportation needs of the great grain growing areas.[3] By the end of the century, the density of the Hungarian railroads was close to that of Austria.[4] The building of the railroads provided an important market for Hungarian heavy industry and soon was able to serve the transport needs of industry as well.

Banking also developed to serve primarily the needs of agriculture. The first bank in Hungary, the *Pesti Hazai Elsö Takarékpénztáregyesület* [First Hungarian Savings Association of Pest], was founded in 1836 with capital paid in by the great landowners. By 1873 there were 637 banking institutions in Hungary. Their assets (share capital, reserves, and deposits) amounted to 548 million K in that year and grew despite the *Krach* of that year to 803 million K by 1880. By

1900, this figure reached 2.6 billion K. Mortgage loans to agriculture provided the leading branch of business absorbing 50 percent to 60 percent of the resources of the banks in the second half of the nineteenth century. At the same time, banks played an important role in the financing of commerce, railroad building, and the capital needs of the state. They were an important avenue for the entry of foreign, especially Austrian capital, into the Hungarian economy.[5]

Wholesale commerce also developed in close connection with agricultural exports. The trade in grains accounted for the largest branch of the commercial sector. It was an important source of domestic capital accumulation and one of the main sources of the capital which was to launch the first modern branch of manufacturing industry in Hungary, flour milling.[6]

The close relationship of the food industries to agricultural production is self evident. Mining, iron production, and to some extent even the lumber industry developed in connection with the building of the railroads. The growth of these industries, at least in their early stages, provided clearly visible benefits to the owners of large estates. The food industries increased the demand for agricultural products. The landlords retained a share of the profits of the lumber, mining, and iron industries. The complementary development of agriculture and the modern sectors of the economy permitted the large landholding nobility and the emerging Hungarian bourgeoisie to agree on the main lines that economic policy should pursue when Hungary returned to self rule in 1867.

The Compromise of 1867 reorganized the conflict–torn multinational Habsburg Empire into a form that it was to maintain until its final dissolution in 1918. With it, the dynasty, the court aristocracy, and the German Liberals in effect renounced their plans for a centralized Empire, and the Hungarian nobility, or at least a majority of its representatives in the Diet, renounced their struggle for complete national independence.[7] To the Emperor and his entourage the Compromise may have seemed a temporary expedient, a means towards the goal of a Habsburg–ruled Germany, until Bismarck's victory over the French at Sedan ended all illusions. However, the architect of the Compromise, the Hungarian politician Ferenc Deák, saw the new arrangements as necessary not only for the moment but for as long as Hungary's territorial integrity could be threatened by Slavic and Romanian nationalism. The Slavs and Romanians in the Empire never fully accepted the Compromise, but after the forceful intervention of the Hungarian Prime Minister, Count Gyula Andrássy, in 1871, against an attempt to grant the Czechs the sort of autonomy that Hungary enjoyed, the Emperor Francis Joseph resisted all further attempts to change the structure of the Monarchy for the rest of his long reign.

What may be considered as the constitution of Austria–Hungary was embodied in separate, somewhat divergent laws accepted at different times in 1867 by the Parliaments of the two halves of the Monarchy. These constitutional laws provided for a common ruler from the Habsburg Dynasty to be Emperor of Austria and King of Hungary. In addition, they recognized foreign policy, defense and the finances necessary to cover these as being common affairs of the Monarchy to be administered by Common Ministers appointed by the Ruler. The legislative branch of the common government consisted of two "Delegations," each composed of sixty members, appointed by the Parliaments of each state. In practice, the work of the Delegations was limited to approval of the common budget. The more important issues of foreign policy and military affairs were debated in the separate Parliaments, though the real direction of these questions, especially those relating to the Common Army, was more absolutistic than parliamentary in character.[8]

In addition to the above-mentioned common affairs, there were also a number of matters, relating to economic policy which were determined through negotiations. Though administered separately by each state, these affairs were to be coordinated by treaties concluded from time to time (in practice, decennially) along with the "quota," the proportion of the common budget provided by each state. The decennial agreements established and maintained a common bank of issue, a common currency and a common customs area.

By recognizing the constitutional Laws of April 1848, albeit with certain modifications, the Compromise of 1867 restored Hungary's autonomy. In matters other than the common affairs already mentioned, Hungary was essentially a sovereign parliamentary monarchy. Its Parliament was bicameral, with membership in the less powerful House of Lords being largely hereditary or honorific and with a House of Representatives elected on a suffrage that included about 6 percent of the population or 24 percent of adult males. The franchise laws were based on an educational and property census as well as on "ancestral rights" for those whose families had been able to vote before 1848. The king had the right to appoint all the ministers of the government. By an informal agreement he also had the right of pre–sanction by which the government could only submit legislation to Parliament that had been previously approved by the king.[9]

Did the Hungarian national movement, a product of the early nineteenth century, achieve its aims for a national state with the Compromise of 1867? Opinions among the ruling classes, the electorate, and even the broad masses of the population were divided on this issue. The "constitutional question"—meaning the question of Hungary's relationship to Austria—remained the central issue in Hungarian politics, the issue around which the major political parties were formed. Hungary's ambivalent relationship toward Austria had a long tradition that can be traced at least as far back as the death of King Louis II on the battlefields of Mohács in 1526. Ultimately the ambivalence derived from the discrepancy between the aspirations of the nobility for political independence on the one hand and the geopolitical and ethnic realities of the Carpathian Basin on the other. As in 1526, when the Hungarian "nation" had found itself between the pincers of its more powerful Turkish and Habsburg neighbors, so in the second half of the nineteenth century, after the experience of the Revolution of 1848, the Hungarian ruling circles were faced with the difficult task of satisfying their hopes for independence from Habsburg absolutism without losing their grip over the non–Magyar nationalities in Hungary and suffering territorial dismemberment at the hands of Slavic and Romanian nationalism.

A majority of the Diet had sided with Ferenc Deák, the leading proponent of a Compromise with Austria, despite the warnings of Lajos Kossuth from his exile in Italy. Although Deák's style was no match for the oratorical genius of Kossuth, his arguments prevailed not only because Deák was in Hungary while Kossuth was in exile but also because they had the logic of history behind them. Kossuth's proposals for a federation of Slavs and Magyars had little chance of realization given the insistence of the Magyars on the maintenance of Hungary's territorial integrity and for the Magyarization of Hungary—not to mention Habsburg opposition to a non–Habsburg dominated Danubian Federation. Deák's proposals, however, essentially those embodied in the Compromise, enlisted the support of the dynasty in the defense of Magyar domination within Hungary and for a Monarchic foreign policy consistent with Magyar interests. Moreover, the system of Dualism served the economic interests of Hungarian landowners by providing them with free entry into the market of an industralizing, urbanizing Austria.

Despite the advantages of Dualism pointed out by Deák and his followers, a large part of the Hungarian political elite clung to the ideals of complete, or a more complete, national independence. Thus, two major camps dominated parliamentary politics during the entire course of Dualism: the forces of 1867, which defended the Compromise, and the forces of 1848, which demanded its revision. The latter intermittently advocated Hungary's complete independence from the Monarchy. The electorate was divided mostly between these two camps which appeared at various times under different party names.[10] Between 1875 and 1906 the adherents of 1867 were found mostly in the ruling Liberal Party. The most common party of the 1848 forces was the "Party of Independence."

Both parties were led by the untitled nobility, who formed the bulk of the electorate. Although many members of the titled aristocracy adhered to one or the other of the major parties, they tended to easily dissociate themselves from each and to form their own generally short–lived parties. The gentry—that is, the part of the nobility that was no longer able to live off its land—could also be found in both camps. The Liberal Party, which ruled between 1875 and 1906 as well as its pro–1867 precursors, favored the gentry in their hiring policies for the apparatus of the new State's administration. At the same time, the gentry also found employment in the county administrations or, being dissatisfied with their loss of status and position, voted for the opposition. Among the landed peasantry and the "sandaled nobility," (who lived much like the peasantry), the Magyar peasants of the Central Plain, with their strong traditions of local political independence and anti–Habsburg sentiment, tended to favor the forces of 1848 while the non–Magyar peasantry, with fewer possibilities for local self–rule, could be swayed to vote for the Liberal Party. The Jewish middle class, having prospered under the rule and protection of dualism, was generally pro–Liberal, while the artisans, strongly resenting the competition of Austrian industry, tended to be pro–1848.

Because the government was appointed by the king, it was almost certain that the governing party would always be a supporter of the Compromise. Only once was a government appointed from a party which claimed to challenge the system of Dualism. This, so-called "Coalition" Government of 1906–09, came to power only after secretly renouncing its program before the king. At all other times it was the same party—usually calling itself the Liberal Party—which formed the government. To guarantee a comfortable majority for this party in Parliament it was necessary to create a political machine, a task carried out with great skill by Kálmán Tisza, prime minister between 1875 and 1890. Tisza perfected a system resting on corrupt public elections, rotten boroughs, and patronage. While in practice trampling on many of the tenets of liberalism, this system was nevertheless far from dictatorial. Only 160 of the 413 constituencies were firmly in the hands of the Government Party. About 200 constituencies, situated primarily in the Magyar–inhabited Great Plain, remained "open." The Party of Independence gained most of its votes there. Though the opposition was generally much weaker in numbers than the Government Party in Parliament, its influence was enhanced by the laxness of parliamentary rules. Inherited from a feudal tradition, these provided ample opportunity for filibustering. The pluralistic tendencies of the political system were further enhanced by the looseness of the structure of the Government Party, within which the Prime Minister could be voted down and from which dissatisfied groups would often defect.[11]

The political system of Dualist Hungary was relatively stable until the 1880s. This stability was based less on the corrupt but flexible methods of rule indicated above than on the general consensus in favor of modernization which existed among the ruling classes. Modernization had been an explicit goal of the national movement in the Reform Era preceeding the Revolution of 1848. In the pre–March period the greatest theorist of modernization was Count István Széchenyi who, in addition to his voluminous writings, made several practical contributions to the modernization of Hungary, including the founding of the Hungarian Academy of Sciences, the establishment of a company to construct the first permanent bridge over the river between Buda and Pest, and the building of several flour mills. With an eye towards the modernization of agriculture, he encouraged the breeding of horses by introducing the gentlemanly entertainment of horse racing into Hungary. He also founded the Hungarian National Agricultural Association [Országos Magyar Gazdasági Egyesület], which, like the National Industrial Federation [Országos Iparegyesület], founded by Széchenyi's political rival, Kossuth, functioned as a propagator of modern technologies among its members and also as an interest group.[12] Both of these organizations survived into the period of Dualism and continued to urge various programs of modernization.

Until the 1880s, agricultural and industrial interest groups as well as the two major political camps of 1848 and 1867 considered themselves the heirs of Széchenyi's generation and favored the modernization of both agriculture and industry. Though industry was in its infancy and the number of industrialists was considerably smaller than the number of landlords, economic modernization was thought of primarily in industrial terms, a reflection of the example provided by the West. The debates of the pre–1880 era centered not so much on the question of whether or not to promote industrialization but on the manner in which that should be done. Should Hungary separate itself from Austria by a tariff barrier—a program favored by the small and medium producers in the National Industrial Federation and by some 1848 politicians, or should the government promote industry by measures other than tariff protection—the preference of financial circles, some large industrialists, and the ruling Liberal party.[13]

In embracing a program of modernization the government was not simply responding to the pressures of organized interest groups or carrying forth an ideological tradition. The commitment of the government to modernization also derived from the logic of its broader political situation. Through the Compromise of 1867, the Magyar ruling classes reestablished their rule in a state in which the Magyar element comprised less than half of the population. Hungary's rulers believed that economic progress would lessen the centrifugal tendencies inherent in the movements of the nationalities.[14] Such considerations played a role in the development of a modernizing political class based in the bureaucracy and the political machine of the Government Party. The policies of this "class with a vested interest in the conditions of national power and unity" could even diverge from the particular interests of the economic class from which most of Hungary's bureaucrats and politicians were recruited—namely, the nobility.[15] In fact, however, prior to the 1880s. the modernizing policies of the ruling parties did not conflict with the aims of the bulk of the landowning nobility who were anxious to take advantage of the expanding market in agricultural products.

The traditions inherited from the Reform Era, considerations of power politics and national survival as well as the general consensus between landowners and the emerging bourgeoisie provided the foundations for the modernizing policies of the government.

In principle, governments after 1867 accepted the liberal thesis that the best way to promote economic modernization was to clear the obstacles in the way of a free market. In the area of economic policy, the commercial code was modernized and the industrial law of 1872 went far towards abolishing the remnants of the guild system.[16] Liberal reforms were introduced in public administration, justice, mass education, and the relationship between Church and State which brought practices in these areas closer to those prevailing in the more advanced countries of the West.

The makers of the Compromise continued in the tradition—followed by modernizers in the Monarchy since Joseph II—of abolishing the legal restrictions imposed on Jews. Among the Hungarian bourgeoisie one could occasionally find descendants of the old patrician class and handicrafts industrialists and with greater frequency, Christian entrepreneurs who had immigrated from Germany, Switzerland, Austria, and other lands to take advantage of the opportunities presented by developing capitalism. Yet perhaps the largest group of bourgeoisie of commerce, banking, and factory industry were Jews or converted Jews.[17] Whereas traditional Hungarian society shunned the occupations out of which modern capitalism grew, Jews, having more often plied such trades as merchants, money lenders, innkeepers, and agricultural overseers were more likely to possess the values, connections and sometimes the capital necessary for entrepreneurial activities.[18] By increasing the civil rights of Jews and encouraging their entry into middle class professions, the makers of the Compromise were helping to create one of the most important preconditions of industrialization, an entrepreneurial class. Among the actions taken in this connection between 1867 and the 1880s, the most significant was the granting of complete equality in civil rights to Jews in 1868. The trend towards Jewish ennoblement also began in this period. Through this important symbol, the Hungarian government and the Monarch demonstrated their confessional tolerance.[19] Although political anti–Semitism had some appeal among sections of the nobility, the major parties did not give expression to it, indeed ridiculed its parliamentary spokesmen in the 1870s.

Hungarian politicians were no more consistent in following a *laissez-faire* philosophy than their Western counterparts had been in the early stages of industrialization. From the start, the Hungarian government intervened directly in the development of the infrastructure, much as most continental countries had done in the early-modern era of mercantilism and even in the post–Napleonic period. Between 1867 and 1890, much of the foreign investments reached the

Hungarian economy through loans to the Hungarian state.[20]

The government also played a role in attracting investment into railroads, by guaranteeing a minimum rate of return on investments in the privately-built lines of the 1860s and 1870s. Although a policy of nationalization was not decided upon until 1880, the government already owned about one-third of the total length of track in Hungary by that date.[21] Thereafter, under the direction of Gábor Baross, the government followed a conscious policy of promoting economic development through the "tariff" or rate-schedule policies of the railroads.

The other major project was the regulation of rivers and concomitant programs of land reclamation. 6.3 million cadastral "holds," or 13 percent of all agricultural land were reclaimed as a result of river regulations, an achievement welcomed by both landowners and industrialists. Such projects were a major focus of entrepreneurial activity for the Hungarian bourgeoisie and, of course, served the interests of landowners.[22]

Direct measures for the promotion of industry were introduced in 1881 on a very limited scale with the first industrial promotion law. This law gave tax exemptions to new factories or factories undertaking new capital investments. Under the law, distilleries operated by landholders were also eligible for aid and, in fact, 55 percent of the firms to which exemptions were granted were distilleries of this kind.[23]

Prior to the 1890s, the taxation policies of the state provided little cause for conflict between industry and agriculture. Though the tax burden did rise considerably, the tax on land rose less than did taxes on other property, and direct (property and income) taxes rose at a considerably slower rate than did indirect taxes on comsumption. On the whole, the tax burden fell disproportionately on the shoulders of the lower classes.[24]

The tariff policies of the Hungarian government provided perhaps the only object of serious dispute over economic policy before the 1890s. The tariff, however, was not so much a cause for debate between Hungarian industry and agriculture as between Hungarian agriculture and Austrian industry, since tariffs were set jointly by the Austrian and Hungarian governments. Hungarian agricultural producers expressed considerable dissatisfaction only after the turn to protectionism in 1878. At this time, exports beyond the tariff barrier still provided an important market for Hungarian grain. Large landholders, fearing the retaliation of their trading partners, especially

Germany, opposed the protectionist policies demanded by Austrian industry. Many Hungarian industrialists were also dissatisfied with the fact that within the customs union the Hungarian state was unable to provide tariff protection for domestic industry against Austrian competition. Many agriculturalists and industrialists found themselves on the same side in a movement championed by the Independence Party, demanding an independent customs area for Hungary. By 1888, agriculturalists themselves became converted to protectionism as a result of the growing importance of the Austrian market for Hungary's grain exports.

In the major areas of economic policy, then, there was general agreement between industrialists and agricultural producers until the mid–1880s. This consensus was based on the fact that most of what the government did for the economy prior to the mid–1880s clearly served the interest of both industry and agriculture in a direct manner. This compatibility of economic interests was a function of the pattern of Hungary's economic development in the preparatory stage of industrialization which centered around the modernization of agriculture and the growth of agricultural exports.

The Beginning of Conflict: Agricultural Crisis and Industrial Expansion

Already in the 1880s, however, the fortunes of agriculture and industry began to diverge. Though agriculture continued to modernize, it became less and less of a profitable activity for the majority of large–scale agricultural producers. The effects of falling world grain prices since the mid–1870s were felt in the Monarchy with some delay. Hardest hit by the agricultural crisis were the large and middle–sized estates which during the decades of rising prices had specialized in the production of grains. On the whole, the crisis encouraged the modernization of agriculture through the application of more intensive methods and a transition to the production of crops, such as sugar beets, which were not affected by the depression. Agricultural distilleries, aided by the industrial promotion law, sprang up on the large and middle–sized estates in competition with the distilleries of industrialists. Yet the struggle for survival was a hard one and of a nature for which most estate owners were not prepared by the values they had inherited from the past. The debts of the landlords accumulated and many estates were ultimately dismembered.[25] Even for the survivors, the profits seemed to remain far behind those that

were being made, seemingly so easily, by those who lent the money
or those who engaged in commercial or industrial undertakings.
Industrialization had begun to gather momentum again after the
crisis of 1873 between 1879 and 1884. After a mild setback between
1884 and 1888, Hungarian industrialization once again accelerated.[26]
By 1900, 65 percent of industrial goods (by value) were produced
by mechanized industry.[27] The total industrial labor force grew from
about 489,000 to 673,000 between 1890 and 1898 and the share of
these workers involved in factory production increased from 32 to 45
percent.[28]

The increasingly modern character of industry may also be seen
in the fact that the number of industrial firms (not including mining
enterprises) employing more than 20 workers increased from 1,120 in
1890 to 2,049 in 1900. Within this category, firms employing more
than 500 workers increased from 27 to 66 and those employing over
1,000 increased from 10 to 29. Of those workers employed in firms
with more than 500 employees in 1900, 30 percent worked in mining,
23 percent in machine manufacturing, 18 percent in metallurgy and
19 percent in such food industries as sugar refining, flour milling and
brewing. The remaining 11 percent were employed in the building
materials, lumber, leather, chemical, and printing industries (Table
1.1).

During this period the importance of the food industries declined
relatively and that of the capital goods industries rose and came into
a dominant position (Tables 1.1 and 1.2). The most dynamic industries were those involved in iron and steel production, the manufacture
of railroad building material, railroad rolling–stock, and other transportation equipment, steam boilers, steam tractor and other agricultural tools, and the production of building material.

The industries associated with the "second industrial revolution"
in technology, electric power, electro–technical engineering, and several new branches of the chemical industry also showed strong development. Even non–food–related light industries which had been
driven into the background by their Austrian competitors or by relatively low demand for their output during the earlier phase of industrial development (leather, textiles, paper, and printing), began
to increase and even accelerated after 1898.[29]

Table 1.1

Employment in Factory Industry by Branch, 1884 and 1898*

Branch	In Thousands		Percent		Index
	1884	1898	1884	1898	1884=100
Metal	19.7	44.5	18.9	19.2	226
Machinery	12.6	33.0	12.1	14.2	262
Chemicals	5.2	12.1	5.0	5.2	233
Building materials	6.4	31.6	6.1	13.7	494
Electric power and gas	1.9	3.0	1.7	1.3	158
Heavy industry	45.8	124.2	43.9	53.9	271
Lumber	13.1	28.2	12.6	12.2	215
Textiles	4.8	13.7	4.6	5.9	285
Leather	0.6	4.7	0.6	2.0	783
Clothing	0.1	3.5	0.1	1.5	3500
Paper	1.6	5.5	1.5	2.4	343
Printing	2.2	6.1	2.1	2.6	277
Light industry	22.4	61.7	21.5	26.6	275
Food	36.1	46.1	34.6	19.9	128
Total	104.3	232.0	100.0	100.0	222

Sources: 1884: László Katus. "Economic Growth in Hungary during the Age of Dualism (1867–1913): A Quantitative Analysis" in *Studia Historica Academiae Scientiarum Hungaricae*, No. 62, Budapest, Akadémiai Kiadó, 1970. 105; 1898: Iván Berend, György Ránki. *Magyarország gyáripara, 1900–1914* [Hungarian Industry, 1900–1914]. Budapest: Szikra, 1955.

Table 1.2
Horsepower from Engines and Motors in Use in Factory Use in Factory Industry by Branch
1884 and 1898

Branch	1000 HP 1884	1898	Percent 1884	1987	Index 1884=100
Metals	17.5	73.1	22.8	27.9	418
Machinery	1.9*	14.8	2.4	5.7	779
Chemicals	1.7	9.4	2.2	3.6	553
Building materials	1.4	15.8	1.8	6.0	1129
Electric power and gas	0.1	31.8	0.1	12.1	31800
Heavy industry	22.6	144.9	29.4	55.3	641
Lumber	7.4	20.4	9.6	7.8	276
Textiles	2.9	12.7	3.8	4.8	438
Leather	0.1	1.9	0.1	0.1	1900
Clothing	0.01	0.2	0.00	0.00	200
Paper	3.2	10.6	4.2	4.0	331
Printing	0.2	1.2	0.3	0.1	600
Light industry	13.81	47.0	18.0	17.9	340
Food	40.4	70.0	52.6	26.7	173
Total	76.81	261.9	100.0	99.9	341

*Figure is overestimated compared to 1898 figure.

Sources: 1884: László Katus. "Economic Growth in Hungary during the Age of Dualism (1867–1913): A Quantitative Analysis" in: *Studia Historica Academiae Scientiarum Hungaricae*, No. 62, Budapest, Akadémiai Kiadó, 1970. 105; 1898: Iván Berend, György Ránki. *Magyarország gyáripara, 1900–1914* (Hungarian Industry, 1900–1914). Budapest: Szikra, 1955.

Although agriculture continued to provide raw materials and markets for many Hungarian industries, the relationship between industrial sectors was no longer as obvious as they had been previously, a condition which, as we shall see in the next chapter, was exploited by neo–conservative critics of the industrial revolution. Despite the impressive results of the "great spurt" in 1900, Hungary was still an underdeveloped country in comparison with the West. It retained its predominantly agricultural character well into the interwar period. Between 1890 and 1900 the percentage of the active population employed in agriculture decreased only from 67.5 percent to 60.1 percent.[30] In 1913, 56 percent of Gross Domestic Material Product, GDMP, originated in agriculture, 30 percent in industry and about 14 in commerce and transportation. The per capita GDMP of Great Britain was about 3 times as great as Hungary's while Germany's was about 2.5 times as great, Austria's was 30 percent greater and even Italy's was about 15 percent greater. Typically for the late industrializers, the growth of industry as well as of GDMP per capita was faster in Hungary than it had been for the early industrializers (Great Britain, France, Germany) during comparable periods of their modern economic growth. In fact, these indicators for Hungary compare well with those of other late industrializers, such as Sweden, Italy and Russia. Only in Sweden did the GDMP per capita rise at a faster rate.[31]

The Hungarian government played an important role in the industrialization drive after 1867. In approaching the history of the Association, one must keep in mind that industrialists had become accustomed to the support of the state in the last third of the nineteenth century and resisted attempts on the part of their opponents to change the course of economic policies.

The state had been instrumental in attracting capital into Hungary through direct borrowing and the guaranteeing of dividends. It was with the help of the state that railroads, waterways, and the administrative facilities of the cities had been built and the amount of land that could be cultivated greatly expanded. The state had also played a role in the improvement of education. By 1890, 53.2 percent of the population over the age of six was literate.[32]

The beginning of the 1880s saw a gradual transition in the economic policies of the Hungarian government towards an increasingly active interventionism in favor of industry. Over time a close political cooperation developed between Liberal–Party politicians and the representatives of business. Its critics called this period the era of "mercantilism," which will be discussed below.

The era opened hesitantly with the first industrial promotion law

of 1881. The government was motivated in part by the campaigns unleashed by the critics of the arrangements of 1867, who called for the
creation of an independent customs area for Hungary. Publicists, such
as Soma Mudronyi of the National Industrial Federation (Országos
Iparegyesület), claimed that independent tariff policy was necessary
if Hungary were to industrialize. The Liberal Government sought to
prove that alternative methods, such as direct industrial promotion,
could be equally effective.[33]

A further motive of the pro–industrial policies of the 1880s was
provided by the need to raise the tax revenues. Having borrowed
at relatively high rates in the 1860s and 1870s, Hungary's budget
showed a chronic deficit by the 1880s. Those in charge of economic
policy believed that tax revenues could be increased significantly and
stabilized only if new taxable wealth was created through industrialization. As József Szterényi, a State Secretary and later Minister of
Commerce, claimed, the income that was lost through tax incentives
given to new factories was more than made up through indirect and
direct taxes levied on the workers employed in the new factories.[34]
The industrial promotion law was extended to several new categories
of industry in 1890 and while the earlier law had only given tax incentives, the 1890 law permitted direct investment by the state. A
third law followed in 1899 and a fourth in 1907. In all these cases
the amounts spent were relatively modest. Even at their maximum
between 1900 and 1914 direct payments to industry amounted to only
5.9 percent of the 800 million K of new investment placed in industrial joint–stock companies.[35] Over the course of Dualism the state
granted 76 million K of subsidies to private industry. This was only 2
percent of total industrial investment in the period.[36] Although this
figure is modest, its direct and indirect effects should not be left out
of consideration. A significant portion of the funds set aside by the
industrial promotion laws was spent on vocational education. The
yields on this investment in "human capital" may have been even
greater than those granted for physical capital. The industrial promotion laws were clearly a spectacular expression of the favor with
which the state looked upon industrial activity. Sándor Matlekovits,
who reported the first industrial promotion law to the Economic Committee of the House stated in the preface to his report that the intent
of the laws was not to industrialize the country through the direct use
of state funds but primarily to induce "society" to enter more boldly
into industrial enterprises "by demonstrating, through the granting

of financial incentives, the importance that the state attached to such activity."[37] In a developing country such psychological incentives can often be effective in promoting entrepreneurship.

Despite its limited constitutional control over customs policy, the government came to the aid of certain industries by measures intended to promote foreign trade. The interests of the Hungarian milling industry were served by the so-called transit trade which gave a full rebate on the duties paid on imported wheat that was reexported as flor.[38] The government also sought to facilitate industrial exports to the Balkans and the Middle East by participating in the founding of trading companies.[39]

In the mid 1880s, the government began to promote certain sectors of industry such as sugar refining through the granting of favorable railroad tariffs.[40] by the 1890s under the ministry of Gábor Baross these practices had spread to a large number of industries.

A very important policy was initiated by a ministerial decree in 1886 giving preference to Hungarian producers in the purchases of the state. Between 1890 and 1914 the state, which owned most of the railroads, several mines and large modern factories producing about 12 percent of the country's total industrial output in 1913, as well as real estate equal to 11 to 12 percent of the national wealth, placed about 2.4 billion K worth of investment into its various facilities, or 20 percent of the total investment made in the period.[41]

To supplement its own direct industrial–promotion activities, the government obtained passage of a law in 1890 to aid the creation of industrial investment banks by the granting of tax incentives. In the same year a joint–venture bank was set up by the government and private enterprise. The aim of the Hungarian Industrial and Commercial Bank was to assist in the founding of new industries and in the enlarging of existing ones by providing long–term capital. Though this bank was short–lived because of its imprudent investments, it provided a clear expression of the alliance that had developed between the ruling circles of the liberal Party and the leading members of Hungary's business community. The president of the bank was István Tisza, son of Kálmán Tisza, and eventual heir to the leadership of the Liberal Party. On the Board of Directors were found the leaders of the Party's economic policy, such as Ambrus Neményi and Károly Hieronymi along with such industrialists and bankers as Sándor Hatvany–Deutsch, Emil Ullmann, and Berthold Weisz.

The close cooperation between the government and the business elite led to the cementing of the political ties between the bourgeoisie and the Liberal Party. As we have seen, Hungarian governments after 1867 had been willing to accommodate the rise and assimilation of the Jews who were helping to modernize the country. When a popular anti–Semitic movement, led by certain members of the gentry, broke out in the early 1880s and revived the ancient myth of ritual murder, Kálmán Tisza and the ruling Liberal leadership (as well as most of the Independence Party) came to the defense of the Jews during the Tiszaeszlár case. Tisza also obtained the reform of the Upper House of Parliament in such a way that the entry of Jews into that body was facilitated. After Kálmán Tisza resigned from his fifteen–year tenure as Prime Minister in 1890 not all his Liberal Party successors were equally dedicated to carrying forward his liberal anti–clerical program. Nevertheless, under Sándor Wekerle's Prime Ministry, civil marriage was instituted and Judaism became a "received," religion, that is, granted equal rights with the Protestant denominations.[43] (Catholicism was the religion of the Habsburgs and continued to maintain certain symbolic privileges.)

The members of the bourgeoisie reciprocated the support they received in economic policy matters and—insofar as they were Jews—in the area of civil rights. They not only voted for the Party, or belonged to it in Parliament (their numbers there were still few), but also supported it financially. The issue of illegal campaign contributions, which were used to finance the increasingly costly process of electioneering in Hungary and most often involved members of the bourgeoisie, provided a point of attack for opposition party spokesmen and for critics of the government's pro–industrial politics.

Compared to the spectacular and, in their entirety, quite significant efforts of the government on behalf of industry in the 1880s and 1890s, the aid given to agriculture lagged somewhat behind. Certainly, the government did not ignore agriculture. The industrial promotion laws themselves ought to encourage the development of small agricultural distilleries even at the expense of the existing large industrial ones. Attempts were made to promote agricultural modernization by state projects for soil improvement, the setting up of agricultural experiment stations and model farms, the improvement of livestock and the providing of veterinary services. The tariff policy of the railroads had been framed in the first place with the needs of grain exporters in mind. These measures, however, had little effect in shielding landowners from the effects of the agricultural crisis.

The divergent fortunes of industry and agriculture led also to divergent perceptions of interest and to conflicting demands of government economy policy.

The pro–industrial economic policies of the government had helped to launch Hungarian industrialization which, by the end of the century, had led to the development of a large–industrial sector. The agricultural crisis helped to intensify a conflict born of the divergence of agricultural and industrial development. The conflict was reflected in the political realm, destabilizing the system of rule designed by Kálmán Tisza and eventually shaking the very foundation of Dualism. The spread of industrialization, however, also brought with it a crisis in the handicrafts trades. Many small industrialists felt themselves to be the victims of the conquering factory system. And with that conquest there also developed an industrial labor movement. In the next chapter we examine the contribution of these conflicts to the formation of the Association.

Chapter 2

ORIGINS AND FOUNDING OF THE NATIONAL ASSOCIATION OF HUNGARIAN INDUSTRIALISTS

The impressive growth of Hungarian industrial production and the diverging interests of industry and agriculture go far to explain the emergence of an organization seeking to represent the interests of large industry. Yet, by themselves, these factors are not sufficient. The pioneer of industrialization, England, did not have an organization comparable to it at the turn of the century, though most industrialized countries did.[1] Besides the general developments traced in Chapter 1, there were a number of other factors at work motivating Hungarian industrialists to organize. Only with the help of these factors can one account for the timing of the founding of the Association and for the aims that the organization set for itself.

To a great extent, the foundation of the Association was a defensive reaction to what were perceived as adverse changes in the economic and political climate at the turn of the century. At the very time that the Hungarian economy was in a recession, a neo–conservative movement, agrarianism, was proving effective in undermining the political position of industrialists and in undoing the economic policies that had promoted Hungarian industrialization. Though competition with Austrian industry seemed more damaging than ever, Hungarian politicians were too preoccupied with questions of national prestige related to the Common Army to deal with the demands of industrialists for some form of protection. Although there was a calm in labor relations during the downturn in economic activity, the working class was relatively well organized. Finally, it was the economic and social conflict between small and large industry that made cooperation impossible within the already existing industrial interest groups. Taken together, these factors prompted an overwhelmingly favorable response from large–industrial circles to the call for the creation of a National Association to represent their interests.

Economic Recession

One can hardly understand the sense of urgency with which industrialists reacted to the problems and conflicts to be described without reference to the recession experienced between 1899 and 1904.

Bringing to a close a long, uninterrupted advance of industrialization that had begun around 1887, the recession coincided with a general downturn in the international economy.[2] Signs of an economic slowdown were already visible towards the end of 1898 with complaints of high interest rates soon to be followed by a rapid decline of stock prices. In 1899 there was a considerable decrease in the activity of the housing industry and railroad construction. By 1900 the same could be said of most branches of industry. Most severely affected were the industries closely linked to housing and railroad construction, e.g., the housing–materials industry on the one hand and the iron mining, steel milling and machines on the other. Hurt by the increased importation of goods which could not find buyers in the similarly depressed Austrian market were such light industries as paper, beer, and alcohol. Flour milling experienced the worst fate among the light industries, for its plight was also affected by the increase of the price of its inputs by the revised tariff regulations of 1900. The newly developing textile industry and the robust sugar industry were the least affected by the depression. In fact, their expansion continued during these years (Figure 2.1).

It is hardly a coincidence that the worst year of the recession, 1902, was the year in which the Association was founded. The economy did not fully recover until 1904 and 1905 when a new expansion that lasted until 1913 took hold of Hungarian industry and raised it to a new level of maturity.

Hungarian businessmen had come to expect the government to support industry even in periods of prosperity. Their expectations were naturally heightened in adverse times, particularly since it appeared to industrialists and, probably not without reason, that the depression had been stimulated by a decline in government support for business.[4] Both the building industries and the construction of local railroads had been promoted by the government in the early 1890s. By the end of the decade, however, tax incentives for these

Figure 2.1.
Selected Indicators of Economic Activity
1898–1905

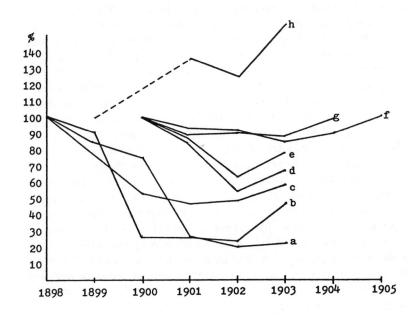

a: Dwellings build in Budapest
b: Km of new railroad track laid
c: Building material entering Budapest
d: Sales of machines by Danubius Machine, Wagon and Ship Works
e: Sales of machines by Ganz and Partner
f: Iron ore production
g: Steel production
h: Sugar exported by weight

Source: Based on: Iván Berend and György Ránki, *Magyarország gyáripara, 1900–1914* [Hungarian Industry, 1900–1914] (Budapest: Szikra, 1955, 18–28.

activities had been phased out on the grounds that supply had met
effective demands.[5] The recession began, in fact, with these industries. Of course, if effective demand had actually been "met," as
dropping rents and increasing vacancies in Budapest's middle–class
housing market would in part indicate, the slowdown in these industries would have occurred even with the maintenance of government
programs. Though industrialists generally realized that some effects
of the downturn were inevitable, they resented the fact that the government had apparently lost its concern for the well–being of industry.
Instead of replacing programs whose aims had been fulfilled, the government was cutting back altogether just when industry needed its
support the most.

Ferenc Chorin, one of the key industrialists behind the foundation of the Association, expressed the dissatisfaction with the economic policies of the government in face of the depression as follows:

> The inevitable consequences of the present depression have
> to be endured by Hungarian industry. There is no denying,
> however, that the industrial downturn we have been expe-
> riencing is not simply a natural product of the economic
> situation but a phenomenon that can be traced back to the
> mistaken actions of the legislature and the government.

Chorin went on to suggest what many industrialists who had responded to the call for the formation of an Association no doubt
felt: that it was the duty of the state to take up the slack in demand
through a massive program of government contracts. Needless to say
the recession mobilized businessmen to look to the government for
support and to form an organization which could effectively transmit
their demands to the centers of power.

Austrian Competition

The economic depression and its coincidence with the negotiations over the Decennial Economic Agreements intensified the conflict
between Austrian and Hungarian industry. Chorin referred to the
Austrian threat in his opening speech at the founding meeting of the
Association.

> By themselves the fact that in every country the economic
> forces are being organized and concentrated and that inter-
> est groups are taking their place beside the legislature as
> important factors of public opinion attest sufficiently to the

righteousness and public utility of our movement. But the
indispensability of our organizing is even more evident if we
look at the position of Hungarian industry within the peculiar context of our constitutional and economic status within
the Monarchy. . . . As long as the common customs areas
exists, our industry can benefit from the industry–promoting
effects of tariff protection only to a very limited extent, or
not at all, because in accordance with its nature, the protective tariff will serve primarily the interests of the older
and tremendously powerful Austrian industry. Even in that
narrower area where our state has the right to practice its
industrial promotion policies, the government's energies and
activities are tied down by the struggle it must wage against
the jealousies and transgressions of the nations with which
we share an economic community.[7]

The possibilities of conflict, as Chorin indicated, arose in part out
of the disparity between the levels of development of the industries of
the two halves of the Monarchy. Austria's industry was considerably
more developed than was that of Hungary. While the proportion of
population engaged in industry in 1910 in the Austrian and Czech
lands was 26 and 34 percent respectively, for Hungary this figure was
18 percent. Per capita industrial product in Austria was 189 K and in
Hungary 110 K in 1913.[8] Similar results can be obtained by comparing
the metallurgical industries of the two halves of the Monarchy. In
1900 the Austrian half produced 10.0 million tons of raw iron while
Hungary produced only 4.6 million.[9] Their trade was characterized by
Hungary's exports of agricultural and industrial raw materials, while
Austria's exports to Hungary were mostly manufactured goods.

As Chorin also indicated, the constitutional relationship between
Austria and Hungary was another source of conflict between the industries of the two halves of the Monarchy. The fact that the Monarchy was a common customs area meant that Hungarian industry could
not be protected from its more developed Austrian rivals by the means
most frequently used by independent states. Many industrialists saw
th severance of the common customs union as a necessity. Though the
actions of the Association were ambiguous in this regard—indicating a
split within the organization—its official position soon after its founding, maintained throughout the period under discussion, favored the
establishment of an independent customs area.[10]

Conflicts of interest with Austrian industry also arose in connection with the decennial economic agreements that were negotiated between the two halves of the Monarchy according to the constitution. The matters for negotiation included: the determination of the quota, (the proportion of the common expenses contributed by each partner); the determination of the Monarchy's "autonomous tariff," which applied to imports from countries with which the Monarchy had no bilateral trade treaties; the charter of the Common Bank; the taxation of goods traded between the two halves of the Monarchy; and since the nationalized railroads were used by both sides as a means of promoting their respective industries, reciprocities in railroad tariffs also had to be negotiated. In all these areas the interests of Hungarian and Austrian economic groups could and often did clash.

The conflict inherent in these arrangements was somewhat dampened by the fact that the two governments had been unable to reach agreement or obtain acceptance of their agreements by the respective Parliaments. Nationality conflicts in Austria, as in the case of the Badeni decrees, and debates over the constitutional question in Hungary held up approval of the agreements renegotiated several times after 1896. The agreement due for renewal in 1896 could not be settled until 1907.[11] Under these circumstances industrialists in both halves of the Monarchy came to prefer almost any settlement to the continuing uncertainty in the relations between Austria and Hungary and therefore moderated their claims.

In fact, with the exception of the general complaints of industrialists about the common customs area, there were few, though important, issues over which Hungarian and Austrian interests clashed. Significantly, however, the most conspicuous of such issues—relating to the flour milling and alcohol industries—also involved a conflict of interest between Hungarian industrialists and agrarians.

The Austrian and Czech milling industries objected to the practice of the milling transit trade. Prior to 1900 the Hungarian government had permitted the duty-free importation of grain from the East that was to be reexported as flour by the Hungarian mills. The Austrian government demanded that the ban, already in effect, be incorporated into the decennial economic agreement.[12]

Industrialists had to contend with a similar combination of opponents in its fight for a more favorable distribution of the "alcohol contingent." The alcohol industry was encouraged by the governments of both Austria and Hungary through tax exemptions. The quantity of production to which the exemptions applied was fixed for the Monarchy and it was divided between Austria and Hungary in the decennial agreements according to the stated principle that the production of each country should cover its domestic consumption. The Hungarian government further divided its contingent between industrial and agricultural distilleries, the competition of which provided a source of conflict between agriculture and industry. During the recession, the export of Austrian alcohol to Hungary increased dramatically—over 300 percent between 1900 and 1901—as a result of a unilateral increase in the Austrian tax.[13]

The numerous conflicts of interest between particular Hungarian and Austrian industries, often of artisanal but occasionally also of large industrial character are evident in the annual reports of the Budapest Chamber of Commerce and Industry prior to 1903. As the reports indicate, Austrian imports increased in the years prior to 1902, intensifying the effects of the cyclical downturn in economic activity in Hungary.[14]

The industries of the two countries clashed also on matters outside the scope of the decennial agreements. Most noteworthy in this regard is the issue of public contracts provided by the Common Army and the common ministries. Hungarian industrialists complained that they were not receiving contracts in the same proportion that Hungary was contributing to the common expenses. This issue became increasingly relevant after 1900 as Hungarian industry developed the capability to fulfill more of those contracts.[15]

Austrian industry may have given its Hungarian counterpart an impetus towards organization not only through competition but also by example. The first non–official nation–wide Austrian organization claiming to represent the interest of large industry in general was the *Zentralverband der Industriellen Österreichs*, founded in 1892. In fact, this was a rather loose federation of already existing specialized industrial interest groups. Until 1896, meetings were held only once a year and a member association was elected for a one–year term to try to implement the decision of the annual meeting. Though a permanent bureau was set up in 1896, the federal structure of the organization and its financial weakness prevented effective action.[16] Dissatisfaction with the limitations of the *Zentralverband* led in 1897 to the foundation of a more centralized *Bund Österreichischer Industrieller*. According to an account written for the tenth anniversary of the organization, one of the reasons for the founding of the *Bund* was to safeguard the interests of Austrian industry in the negotiations that were then getting under way for the decennial economic agreements. The *Bund* saw itself as a more militant organization, in contrast to the weakness of the *Zentralverband*.[17] Its militancy was directed also against the labor movement; one of the *Bund's* major innovations was that it sought to function as an employers' association.[18]

The Hungarian economic press made much of the ill effects of Austrian competition; and industrialists like Chorin also voiced these concerns at the time of the founding of the Hungarian Association. Yet, Austrian competition, which Hungarian industry had always experienced, does not seem to have been as significant a motive in the founding of the Association as were changes in the domestic political economy. While the need to counter the influence of the *Bund* may have been a motive in the founding of the Association, a new industrial interest group would not have been necessary if the resolve of the Hungarian government to promote industrialization had not weakened. Another contributing factor was the fact that conflict within the industrial sector in Hungary rendered the already existing industrial interest groups ineffective representatives of large industry.

The Advance of Agrarianism

The gains in the political influence of agrarianism by the turn of the century posed the most serious threat to the continued support of industrialization by the Hungarian government. While in the 1890s the benevolent intervention of government could generally be taken for granted by industrialists, this was no longer so in the era of agrarian political revival.

The ideological roots of Hungarian agrarianism can be traced to similar West European movements which Hungarian noblemen had encountered during their travels. Neo-conservative thinkers, who had managed to gain a considerable following in France and Germany after the disastrous crash of 1873, differed from their early nineteenth century predecessors by adapting some of the principles of nineteenth century socialism to their critiques of the capitalist system. While in exile for his participation in the Revolution of 1848 Count Sándor Károlyi, one of Hungary's greatest landowners and subsequently a leader in the agrarian movement, discovered the conservative Catholic thought of the French sociologist, Le Play. Le Play was an advocate of credit and consumer cooperatives as alternatives to both socialism and what he saw as the "predatory capitalism" of his day. Károlyi became the leader of the cooperative movement in Hungary. Another

aristocrat–intellectual, Albert Apponyi, transmitted the thinking of
the German conservative social reformers, Roscher, Rodbertus and
Schmoller. The publicist Rudolf Meyer, one of the early figures of
German political anti–Semitism, made a strong impression not only
on Apponyi, who was to become the leader of the dissident National
Party, but also on two other aristocratic agrarians, Géza Andrássy
and Imre Széchényi, who participated in 1881 in a tour of the United
States to study the Homestead Act, the transplantation of which
became a favorite demand of the agrarian movement in Europe, including Hungary.[19]

The ideas of Western neo–conservatism found fertile soil in the
economic and social problems of Hungarian rural society. The response of the nobility was motivated by such economic factors as
declining prices for its main products, grain and wool, and by the
inability of the landowners to attain sufficiently high productivity to
meet the challenge of foreign competition. The social crisis of the nobility had two aspects. In the first place, the nobility felt its economic
failure intensified by the patent success of the bourgeoisie not only
in commerce, banking and industry but even in agriculture. This
challenge of the bourgeoisie predisposed the Hungarian nobility to
conservatism.

Yet agrarianism would probably not have adopted the character-
istics of neo–conservatism without the existence of a second conflict
in the countryside, that between landlord and peasant. The outbreak
of peasant–socialist riots in the first half of the 1890s provided a
dramatic reminder of this problem. Although the Social Democratic
Party had been ambivalent in its attitude towards the peasantry, socialist ideology was spread in the countryside by a dissident wing of
the Party. Marxism mingled with a sort of Christian Millenarism in
the minds of certain segments of the peasantry to produce a powerful
ideological mix feared with good reason by the landlords. The ideology spread most rapidly among the seasonal laborers and navvies of
the Great Plains whose ranks had been swollen in the 1890s.

The modernization of agriculture itself had played an important
role in this process. The long–term decline of wheat prices had stimulated both an intensive and extensive expansion of wheat production
on the large estates. The introduction of machinery for certain phases
of wheat cultivation, such as plowing and threshing but not reaping,
created seasonal demand for labor so that a short intense period of
relatively high wages, for which peasants migrated great distances,

was followed by periods of massive unemployment.[20] Dislocations of rural labor were also occasioned in the early 1890s by the completion of the great public works projects of river regulation and land reclamation. Unemployed agricultural laborers congregated in the large peasant towns of the Great Plains which functioned as focal points of peasant socialism.[21]

Riots by agricultural workers demanding higher wages and the right to organize had broken out in towns such as Oroszháza, Békéssaba and Hódmezővásárhely in connection with the May Day celebrations during the summers of the early 1890s. What started out as peaceful demonstrations often led to bloody clashes with the gendarmerie. The unrest was also expressed in strikes and work stoppages on the latifundia.

Agrarian ideology sought to find a response more sophisticated than simple repression to the problems of the peasantry by linking these to the problems of the other traditional classes, namely the artisante and the nobility—all, according to the agrarians, the victims of the depredations of "mobile capital."

To the initiates of the movement, the prime target of criticism was subsumed under the unclarified term of "mercantilism." "Mercantilism" was used by agrarians in the first place to denote anything pertaining to "mobile capital," that is, the capitalism of merchants, bankers or industrialists, the "impersonal" capital of "stock jobbers" and speculators.[22] More generally, "mercantilism" stood for the economic policies of *laissez-faire* liberalism as well as pro–industrial interventionism that the Hungarian governments had followed after 1867 and which had been instrumental in bringing about the industrialization of the country. As the opposite of "mobile capital," agrarians saw "fixed capital" *kötött tőke*), the best example of which was land. Presumably the capital of the artisan also belonged in this category as long as it remained within a traditional pattern of ownership and did not expand at too fast a rate. The concept of "mercantilism" allowed agrarians to uphold the principle of private ownership while attacking those aspects of capitalism which had proved disadvantageous to the classes of the great landlords, to the gentry and to the artisanate.

The distinction between "mobile" and "fixed–down" capital was seen not so much from the point of view of an economic theory as from a cultural one.

Agrarian politics is everywhere national and nation–supporting. Mercantilism is international, spawned by the world economy which tramples across nation, country, God and religion in the interest of high profits.[13]

It is at this point that the anti–Semitism of agrarianism gained its greatest expressions. "Mobile capital" was generally considered Jewish, while "fixed capital" was assumed to be "national" or even "Christian."

One agrarian pamphlet went so far as to argue that the Jew, even if a landowner, is still a mercantilist.

> The property of the Jew carries a smaller debt and is greater; it can therefore better take advantage of market forces which the Jewish landowner himself crates. When in the fall the poor landlord who had let his debts pile up finds himself in a pinch and is forced to sell at any price, then the Jew is not a landlord but a "knight of the bourse." He keeps his wheat on storage and throws immense quantities of paper wheat onto the market thereby lowering prices to a minimum. The Christian landowner, especially the owner of small or medium–sized properties, is forced to part with his crop at whatever miserable price. In this way, his crops end up in the silos and mills of the Jew . . . [who sells them in the spring when again through speculation he has raised prices].[24]

It was assumed that a Christian agrarian landlord, even if he had the means, would not engage in the type of manipulations of which the Jewish "mercantilist" was accused.

Though agrarians frequently declared themselves critics of liberalism, it should be noted that by liberalism they meant either the economic system of competitive capitalism or the Liberal Party which had permitted the ascent of "mercantilism." Parliamentarian government, deeply ingrained in the political culture of the nobility and still an affair of the few in turn–of–the–century Hungary, was not rejected, as it was to be in the interwar period. Nor were the civil liberties associated with liberalism rejected except in their extension to socialists, though in this respect, the government did not remain far behind agrarian wishes. It was primarily economic liberalism, especially the removal of restrictions on entry into trades and on the circulation of land that agrarians criticized. These "liberties," practiced, as one agrarian had put it, without the two other aspects of the liberal creed of fraternity and equality, had led to the tyranny of the strong over the weak and threatened to lead Hungary to the brink of a socialist revolution.[25] By freeing competition, the freedom to compete had itself been destroyed. Agrarians attributed determining economic powers to speculators and cartels, so that in their view, the economy and society were in the hands of an "oligarchy" consisting of "mercantile" businessmen and the politicians supporting them.[26]

The society pictured by the agrarians as an alternative to mercantile capitalism was primarily agricultural. By reversing the government's policy from helping the "mercantile" sector to helping the modernization of agriculture, an economy and society could be created in which all traditional classes found their rank and place. Between the large landlords and the landless peasantry there would be a healthy class of middle landowners, below whom there would be the landed small-holders. In this way, a leading agrarian activist suggested, the values of the genteel classes could be transmitted downward by example.[27]

In place of large industry, the growth of the artisante should be promoted. Agrarians were not opposed to the modernization of agriculture or even to the development of some industry but they proposed to accomplish this in an "organic" way, that is, without the hectic pace that they felt had been imposed by the methods of mercantile capitalism. Economic progress must be allowed without the destruction of the livelihood of the classes which, for the agrarians, had carried the essence of the nation through the centuries. First among these classes was the nobility (and agrarians neglected the cosmopolitan past of the aristocracy, so that it was the greatest landowners who stood at the apex of the agrarian's organic pyramid). Yet, characteristically, important roles were attributed also to the artisanate and to the peasantry. According to agrarian writers these traditional classes had always provided a reservoir for the social and biological rejuvination of the nobility into which they had been allowed to rise in Hungary in contradistinction to "the blue-blooded feudalism of Western Europe."[28]

As an alternative to the competition of liberal capitalism as well as to the exploitation of the consumer by cartels, agrarians proposed a system built on economic cooperation. In fact, the agrarians played a leading role in the creation of a rather extensive system of consumer, credit and marketing cooperatives in the Hungarian countryside.[29] The National Central Credit Cooperative was formed in 1898 by the government in response to agrarian pressure. In the first year of its existence it coordinated 712 local credit cooperatives with a total membership of 141,623. By 1908 these figures had jumped to 2,098 cooperatives with 551,514 members. The agrarians also took the lead in forming a National Association of Consumers Cooperatives in 1898. In 1901 this organization boasted 171 member cooperatives with 30,664 individual members. In 1918 there were 2,140 such consumer cooperatives with about 658,000 members.[30] The cooperatives were the basic structural unit of the agrarian, indeed of all neoconservative movements in Hungary. They provided a mean for the local landlords who adhered to the agrarian creed along with the local clergy to play important roles in the life of the cooperatives, to spread the neo–conservative doctrine to the members and to recruit support in elections and political protest actions.[31]

The dominance of the constitutional question in Hungarian political life did not permit the successful development of a neo–conservative political party. Nevertheless the movement had a serious impact on parliamentary policies. An Anti–Semitic Party had been formed in 1882 under the leadership of Győző Istóczy, who had attended the international anti–Semitic congress held in Dresden that year. Although it won 17 seats to the Lower House in the elections of 1884, internal dissention led to the dissolution of the Party.[32] Neo–conservatism became somewhat less virulently anti–Semitic and more concerned with the agrarian crisis after the mid–1880s. Agrarians were to be found in both major political camps. In the Liberal Party they directed their criticism against the "mercantilist" policies of Kálmán Tisza. The Party of Independence began to lean towards the agrarian economic demands. Agrarianism and the Independence movement reinforced each other in their attack against the rule of Kálmán Tisza, whose resignation in 1890 signalled the beginning of the crisis of the Liberal Party and of the system of Dualism that it had upheld.

Tisza's more conservative successor, Count Gyula Szapáry, (1890–1892), sought to avoid a clash between neo–conservative and liberal forces. His cabinet, however, which he had inherited largely from Tisza, contained a number of powerful ministers, Dezső Szilágyi, Count Albin Csáky, and Sándor Wekerle, who were committed to carrying forward the liberal, modernizing reforms that had been started in the 1890's. The last years of the 1880s and the first half of the 1890s were in fact the heyday of modernizing leadership. It was in this period that Hungary's finances were put in order, and the currency of the Monarchy was placed on the gold standard. It was then that Gábor Baross' system of using railroad–tariff policy as an instrument of economic development was perfected.

The most controversial measures of reform involved the relationship of Church and State rather than economic policy. Szapáry lost his position in the Party leadership because of his unwillingness to support the efforts of his Minister of Justice, Count Albin Csáky, to introduce the institution of civil marriage, to take over from the Church the registry of births, marriages, and deaths, and to declare Judaism one of the received religions—that is, the granting of certain corporate political rights to Jews, such as representation in the Upper House, which Catholicism and the major Protestant religions already enjoyed. These reforms were carried through under the Prime Ministry of Sándor Wekerle in 1894. However, they called forth the strong opposition of neo–conservative elements to which had been added a dimension of political Catholicism. The liberals had won the battle but the resignation of Wekerle in the same year signalled the turn of their fortunes. Under the succeeding Prime Minister, Baron Dezső Bánffy, himself a rather colorless bureaucrat known for his brutal repression of the nationalities, the agrarians gained a great concession by securing the Ministry of Agriculture for Ignác Darányi who, while primarily interested in the modernization of agriculture, also supported some of the social–conservative demands of the agrarians.[33]

In 1895, the agrarians gained a dominant position within the main interest organization of the landowners which until then had been largely under the control of the Liberal Party. The increasingly popular agrarian movement used its strength to overthrow Bánffy in the hope of further excluding the "mercantilist" forces from the Liberal Party even though Bánffy had succeeded in negotiating a common tariff that was highly favorable to the Hungarian agricultural interests. Their efforts were in part successful. The next Prime Minister, Kálmán Széll, tried to maintain a balance between the agrarian and mercantilist wings of the Party, but was forced to make serious concessions to the agrarians—concessions that had a direct effect on prompting industrialists to found the Association.[34]

Although they did not form a political party, the agrarians created a novel type of interest organization with political and economic aims. Founded in 1896, the Association of Hungarian Landowners (MGSz), grew rapidly, reporting 30,000 members by 1906.[35] Its structure, style and methods were very different from those of its predecessor, the OMGE. While the OMGE limited itself to voicing the demands and grievances of landholders, the MGSz sought to organize politically and socially for the realization of agrarian goals. Beside the traditional demands of the agricultural interests, the MGSz agitated for programs such as the homestead act, the cooperative movement, and after the turn of the century, even for land reforms—programs which were intended to reach an audience outside the class of great landowners, and to attract to the movement the peasantry, the gentry and the artisanate.

The agitation paid off for the agrarians in the Parliamentary elections of 1901. Count Sándor Károlyi, one of the leaders of the MGSz and himself a member of the Liberal Party, called on Hungarian landowners to vote for agrarian programs regardless of the candidates' party affiliations.[36] The Liberal Party lost over 40 seats to the opposition mostly to the detriment of the "mercantilist" Liberal old guard. Kálmán Tisza himself lost his seat.

Thus, the agrarian movement was in the ascendent when the National Association of Industrialists was formed. In several important cases its demand had already been met.

The demand for the raising of agricultural tariffs was the oldest of agrarian demands, voiced already at the agricultural congress of 1879. The demand made little economic sense at the time, for Hungary and the Monarchy were still net agricultural exporters. Nonetheless the tariff on wheat rose from 0 to 1.19 K per ton in 1882 and to 3.57 K in 1887, reflecting the general increase in international tariff rates after the brief experiment with free trade in the 1860s and early 1870s.[37] As population growth in the Monarchy started to catch up to the output of agricultural products around the turn of the century, the protectionist demands of agrarians were heard even louder. The realization of these demands in the tariff structure of the Monarchy was prevented only by the inability of the Austrian and Hungarian governments to renegotiate the decennial "economic compromise" until 1906, so that until then the tariff of 1887 remained in effect. In 1906 the tariff on wheat was raised to the prohibitive level of 6.30 K in the so-called "autonomous tariff," that is, the unilateral tariff which applied to those trading partners of the Monarchy with which it did not have bilateral trade agreements.[38]

There was constant bickering between the agricultural and industrial interests over the fact that the tariffs of one raised the costs and worsened the export prospects of the other. Industry, however, was not strongly opposed to the raising of agrarian tariffs. It, too, was basically protectionist and was in no position to claim the right exclusively for itself.

One aspect of tariff policy, however, one which agrarians and industrialists had clashed with full force was the so-called milling transit-trade. The transit trade was very important for Hungary's large flour mills which were equipped to serve an international market. On the other hand, the bourgeoisie involved in milling was a main target of agrarian attacks. The Hatvany–Deutsch, the Beck and the Herzog families were some of Hungary's most successful entrepreneurs who stood almost as symbols of "mercantilism" for the agrarians. It was the large mills and their agents who, according to agrarian propaganda, manipulated the grain market through the so-called "paper wheat." While the demand for prohibiting speculation in grain futures was somewhat of a propaganda slogan, the demand for the cessation of the milling transit-trade was realizable. The restriction of the trade in 1897 and its abolition in 1900 under the Prime Ministry of Kálmán Széll was a major agrarian victory and a blow from which the Hungarian milling industry never completely recovered. For the rest of the pre–War period, its capacity was greatly underutilized.[39]

The agrarians gained a similar victory in the area of alcohol production. Alcohol for industrial use was produced by both specialized industrial firms and by landowners. In the 1880s, the legislature had exempted a fixed amount of the annual output of the industry from taxation as a means of promoting alcohol production. The "contingent" was divided by the state between agriculture and industry. This was naturally a source of competition—with the agrarians demanding a greater share. In 1900, the agrarians were victorious in this regard as well.

Undoubtedly the greatest victory in the agrarian campaign against the advance of the bourgeoisie was the law of incompatibility passed in 1901. This law declared any individual with close ties to a firm that was doing business of a certain amount with the state as ineligible for a seat in the Lower House of Parliament. In the case of agricultural enterprises, the law was extremely lenient, so that in practice it was only the industrialists and bankers who were barred from the Lower House by this measure. As a result of the purge all prominent businessmen were forced to resign their seats.[40]

Agrarian victories in politics and in economic policy between 1897 and 1902 provided the most important external stimuli to the organization of the Industrial Association. Industrialists began to perceive a profound reorientation in the attitude of government to their economic interests. Ferenc Chorin referred to this change in his opening speech at the founding meeting of the Association on May 29, 1902.

> While in the 1840s the incipient social movement for the creation of industry was directed by the best men of the nation and the idea of support for industry, while still in its infancy, was embraced by the nation with indivisible enthusiasm and a willingness for self–sacrifice, today, in sharp contrast, the currents that are coming to the fore not only begrudge the sacrifices required by industrial promotion but wish even to deprive existing industries of the foundations on which their existence rests.[41]

If agrarian victories put industry on the defensive, the agrarians also indicated to industrialists the importance that organized interest groups, capable of formulating consistent programs and of effectively agitating for them, would have in future political struggles. As the Association pointed out in its first annual report: "It was agriculture that provided the example for the joining together of forces when it united in a single extensive organization."

The Organization of the Working Class

The founding documents of the Association, while replete with references to agrarianism and the Austrian threat, make no mention of the working class movement that might indicate that this, too, had a role in the founding of the organization. In other countries there was no such reticence on this score. In the words of its Secretary General, Friedrich Hertz, the *Bund Österreichischer Industrieller* had been founded in 1897 in part to deal "with the rapidly growing socialist menace" and to "defend industry from the working class movement." Its function as an employers' association—that is, an association of employers organized to counter the activities of labor unions through lock–outs, black listing, etc.—was central to the work of the *Bund* from the start.[42] The German *Zentralverband* saw its function in a similar light. Already in 1879, its emphasis shifted from tariff policy to social policy and continued to move in that direction throughout the pre–war period.[43] Hungarian industrialists did not yet react with such concern to the growth of the Social Democratic Party and of unionism. Yet it is inconceivable that the Association founders would have overlooked the organization of the working class.

The foundation of the Social Democratic Party in 1890 was the major milestone in the development of the organized representation of the interests of the working class in Hungary. Breaking with the purely political long–range aims of its predecessors, the originality of the Party lay in its efforts to bring the developing trade unions under its wings, to promote further unionization and, thereby, to make place in the work of the Party for the immediate economic and social–policy concerns of the workers. The reorientation of the socialist movement to the unions in 1890 gave the Social Democratic Party the character of an organized interest group.[44]

Yet, the size of this movement was rather small at the time of the founding of the Association. Hungarian trade unions had less than 10,000 members in 1899 and about 16,000 in 1902. The latter figure was about 7 percent of the labor force in large industry and only about 2.7 percent of all industrial workers. The fastest growth in union membership took place in the years after the founding of the Association. The improvement of the economy after 1903 and the chaotic political climate of 1905–06 brought union membership to a pre–war peak of 135,000 in 1907. The most highly unionized trades were those where the proportion of skilled to unskilled workers was highest. Thus, printing and the iron and machine trades were the best organized while in the textile trades, the level of organization was very low.[45]

About 50 percent of the labor union members also belonged to the Social Democratic Party and an even greater proportion were members of the normally secret "independent organizations." The latter were local intermediary organizations between the Party and the unions. They were made necessary by the fact that Hungarian law forbade both the setting up of local networks by the Party and the organization of strikes or participation in political activities by the unions. Despite the law, the connection between the unions and the Social–Democratic Party were rather close.[46]

One factor contributing to industry's complacency towards the working class around 1902 may have been the low level of strike activity during the years of the depression. The only noteworthy strikes of the period 1898–1902 took place in the iron and machine industries. The conflicts had an effect on the attitude of industrialists in these branches that was not shared by all industrialists. The Iron and Machine Manufacturers was the only group to dissent from the Association's support of the enfranchisement of the working class. The notion of forming an employers' federation within the Association aimed at combatting the strikes of the unions was first brought up only in 1906 when industrial conflicts were at a peak.[47] In contrast to the Austrian *Bund*, the Association did not consider itself an employers' federation from the start and such activity remained peripheral to its activities in the period covered by this study.

Its enforced political isolation and relative weakness did not permit the working class to exercise nearly as much influence on economic and social policy as agrarianism. Government social policy with regard to the industrial working class progressed very slowly. Maximum hours of work were set at 16 hours per day by the industrial law of 1872, though by 1901 only 10.1 percent of industrial firms in Hungary had longer than 12–hour shifts and these were generally small firms. Safety standards were set by the industrial law of 1884, and a corps of factory inspectors was set up to enforce the law.[48] Although industrialists resented the interference, this was a relatively minor complaint.[49] The major aspect of social policy in which the government was planning significant new legislation was that of health and disability insurance. Hungary, following in the footsteps of Bismarckian paternalism, was fairly advanced in this regard. Since 1891, the providing of health insurance in private industry was mandatory. Though the health insurance itself was quite liberal in comparison to several Western countries, it did not provide any benefits, outside of the usual medical care for disability. At the turn of the century, the Ministry of Commerce was considering a broad revamping and extension of the system.[50] These efforts show that the government was not totally unresponsive to the demands of the workers. Some aspects of the reforms were urged by the employers themselves, who were often held liable by the courts for losses suffered by workers as a result of industrial accidents.[51]

Although grave conflicts existed between the working class and industrialists in the areas of economic and social policy, industrialists could justifiably believe that government strongly favored their side even without the special pleading of an organized industrial interest group. The fact that the Social Democrats and the unions were giving clear expression to the demands of the workers may have given an incentive to the organization of the Association of Industrialists. Yet, judging from the records, it was a less forceful push than that provided by the agrarian movement or even by the competition of Austrian industry.

The Conflict of Large Industry and the Artisanate

If the growth of Hungarian industry, the occurrence of an economic crisis at the turn of the century, the pressures of agrarianism, Austrian competition and the movement of the working class help to account for the willingness of industrialists to organize, one should also ask why they considered it advisable to create a new organization rather than to work through and to strengthen the already existing representatives of industry. Specifically, what prevented the Chambers of Commerce and Industry, which functioned as the official representatives of commercial and industrial interests, or the National Industrialists' Federation, with its venerable past as a spokesman for industry, from meeting the requirements of the new situation?

Certainly, in the case of the Chambers, their decentralized organization, their need to represent both commerce and industry and their semi–official status which made them more susceptible to government manipulation worked against their ability to satisfy the need for a forceful representation of large–industrial interests. These factors did not exist for the Federation, and yet that organization fared even worse in its ambitions to become the leading representative of industry. Ultimately, a more important problem common to both contenders was the incompatibility of the goals and ideologies held by the mass of small industrialists and artisans on the one hand and the fewer but disproportionately powerful large industrialists on the other who participated jointly in these organizations.

The most common explanation for the hostility between small and large industry rests on the notion of a one–sided competition between handicrafts and the modern factory system which, according to the spokesmen of small industry, was leading to the "extinction" of the artisanate.[52] Contemporary statistics, however, support neither the theory of the harsh competition between small and large industry nor the claim of the extinction of the artisanate in the period between 1890 and 1913. The decennial censuses of 1890, 1900, and 1910 show an impressive growth of small industry both in terms of the number of enterprises and in terms of the number of employees. (Table 2.1).

Table 2.1
Development of Small Industry in Hungary
1890–1910

Year	(a) No. of Enterprises* (in 1000s)	(b) No. of Employees (in 1000s)	(a+b) Approximation of Population active in small industry (in 1000s)
1890	352	280	632
1980	424	334	758
1910	476	440	916

*This gives us an approximation of the number of independent artisans (owners).

Sources: 1890: Iván Berend and György Ránki, *Gazdaság és társadalom* [Economy and Society] (Budapest: Magvető, 1974), 178–179; 1900 and 1910: *A Magyar Szent Korona Országainak 1910. évi népszámlálása* [1910 Census of the Lands of the Holy Hungarian Crown] (Budapest: Statisztikai Hivatal, 1923), Part VI, 244–247.

A breakdown of the aggregate figures by branches does, however, indicate the existence of a few problems (Table 2.2). While most crafts experienced growth in the decade of the 1890s, a few were declining. No doubt the troubled conditions of the shoemakers, belt and saddlemakers, potters, tanners, furriers, coopers, and milliners were one cause of the discontent in the artisans and of their hostility towards large industry. Yet, it should be noted that it was not so much the competition of Hungarian factories that was the source of small industry's difficulties as the imports from Austria. As the last two columns of Table 2.2 show, Hungarian large industry was rather undeveloped in the declining small industrial trades. The balance of trade vis-à-vis Austria, however, was highly unfavorable in these branches (Table 2.3). In many cases, as in the confectioned goods, shoes and furs, it was the better organized Austrian handicrafts industry which provided the damaging competition.[53]

Table 2.2
Percent of Change of Population Active in Selected Occupations
1890–1900

Occupation	No of Small Industrialists in 1900	Percent Change 1890–1900	Factories (more than 20 Employees) in Declining Trades in 1900	
			No.	Workers
Brick makers	17,687	+88.2		
House painters	6,546	+76.4		
Masons	58,756	+45.6		
Tinsmiths	8,843	+44.1		
Locksmiths	20,596	+32.9		
Bakers	18,926	+27.2		
Carpenters	50,502	23.3		
Tailors	74,352	+21.8		
Distillers	5,816	+11.0		
Rope makers	5,256		+ 8.1	
Butchers	29,093	+ 7.4		
Carriage makers	25,027	+ 6.7		
Blacksmiths	56,773	+ 4.7		
Building carpenters	25,582	+ 4.1		
Millers	45,665	+ 0.1		
Shoemakers and bootmakers	111,476	- 0.2	24	823
Belt and saddlemakers	5,982	- 1.1	2	49
Seamstresses	26,369	- 4.4	–	–
Potters	7,376	-10.3	3	637
Tanners	7,368	-12.4	30	2,305
Furriers	8,332	-20.0	2	53
Coopers	7,699	-23.3	6	190
Milliners	4,016	-23.6	5	362

Sources: István Salgó, *Kisipari vállalkozások a tőkés Magyarországon* [Small–industrial Enterprises in Capitalist Hungary], (unpublished Diploma Essay, Karl Marx University of Economics. Budapest, 1976), 143; For number of factories in 1900: *A Magyar Szent Korona*

Országainak 1900. évi népszámlálása [1900 Census of the Lands of the Holy Hungarian Crown] (Budapest: Statisztikai Hivatal, 1906, 98–102; József Szterényi, *Emlékirat a hazai kis- és gyáripar fejlesztésztéséről* [Memorandum on the Promotion of Domestic Small and Large Industry] (Budapest, Állami nyomda, 1909), 72.

Table 2.3
Hungarian Foreign Trade in Selected Articles
by Weight (in quintals) 1890, 1900

Goods	Imports		Exports	
	1890	1900	1890	1900
Shoes	9,501	20,049	1,622	2,455
Belts and saddles	3,338	3,524	554	962
Leather goods	16,796	28,618	3,048	4,028
Confectioned goods	44,908	61,552	15,049	11,269
Men's garments	15,660	17,990	7,386	5,253
Ladies' garments	7,974	8,806	3,441	2,879
Linens	10,356	15,433	2,017	2,427
Metal pots and pans, tin vessels	4,128	22,171	850	12,286
Tanned goods	78,137	106,561	18,205	43,522
Furs and pelts	2,618	3,084	1,197	1,980
Hats	6,070	11,703	924	1,597

Sources: *A Magyar Szent Korona Országainak 1882–1913 évi külkereskedelmi forgalma* [Foreign Trade Statistics of the Lands of the Holy Hungarian Crown, 1882–1913], Magyar Statisztikai Közlemények, Új Sorozat, Vol. 63, (Budapest: Statisztikai Hivatal, 1923), 217–281.

Most of the industries that could be displaced by the advanced technologies of the pre–World War I period, were already displaced by 1890.[54] The presence of more small industrialists of course did not necessarily mean more wealthy small industrialists. While nominal income figures for the period 1900–1913 show some increase (27 percent), the existence of inflation meant that real income was stagnating at best after the turn of the century (Table 2.4).

Table 2.4
Nominal Income in Small Industry[a]
1900, 1910/1913

Year	Active in Small Industry	Income in Small Industry in Million Crowns	Per Capita Nominal Income in Small Industry in Crowns
1900	758,000[b]	200[d]	264
1910	916,000[b]	269[e]	294
1913	995,000[c]	335[d]	336

[a] We have not made the conversion to real income, lacking meaningfully precise figures for measurement of inflation.

[b] Table 2.1.

[c] In our calculations for the small industrial population of 1913 we assumed that the growth between the 1900 and 1910 figures really took place between 1903 and 1910 (allowing for the depression between 1900 and 1903) and extrapolated on the basis of this 2.8 percent annual rate of increase.

[d] Iván Berend and György Ránki, *Gazdaság és társadalom* [Economy and Society] (Budapest: Magvető, 1974), 56.

[e] The income figure for 1910 is extrapolated back from 1913 assuming a 7 percent annual growth rate between 1910 and 1913. The actual growth rate was probably less than 7 percent so that our estimate of per capita income is quite conservative.

Discontent was greatest among the independent artisans, whose "independence" was becoming more and more of a fiction. According to one estimate, at least 20 percent of the artisanate, though nominally independent, was actually in the employ of a commercial or industrial entrepreneur.[55] The situation was especially common among tailors who often worked for the large clothing stores or tailoring establishments.[56] These tailors were dependent on those who gave them work in much the same way that factory workers were dependent on their employers; a situation conducive to the development of resentments against the larger entrepreneurs quite apart from the question of incomes. Ironically, the very forces that made small industry flourish in number also destroyed its independence. Working for distant markets with materials derived from an increasing variety of sources and often bought on credit, small industry became ever more dependent on middlemen.[57] Similar dependencies were typical also in the several branches of the building trades, one of the professions which experienced growth during our period. These artisans resented their plight, for which they blamed the large entrepreneurs, despite the fact that their incomes were relatively high.[58]

The popularity of marketing and credit cooperatives, at least in the literature of the artisanate, is an indication of the desire of many artisans to break out of their dependence on merchants. In this area the thinking of small industrialists met with the promises of agrarianism—mostly by the design of the latter—who sought to turn small industrialists' discontent to their own political advantage.

The market conditions of small industry had become thoroughly capitalistic in the classical sense, being characterized by a high degree of competition and the rapid introduction of innovation in products, technologies, and organization—these being the only ways of earning more than a minimum profit. Judging from the volume of complaints in the publications of small industry as well as from the internal history of the older industrial interest organizations, it is evident that much of small industry was unable to adapt to the dizzying pace set by a regime of free enterprise. It thus came into conflict over the course of economic policy with large industry, which by that time had to a great extent protected itself from the harshness of competition through cartels, a high degree of concentration and government support. Through the industrial interest organizations, small industry sought to secure the aid of the government for limiting entry into trades, for the creation of cooperatives, the distribution of funds and tax credits for the protection of small industry, as well as a radical breaking away from the common customs area. Large industry opposed such programs. Conflicts over these demands between small industry and other members of the existing interest organizations prevented such organizations from concentrating with sufficient energy and unity on the representation of large–industrial interests.

The Chambers of Commerce and Industry

The Chambers of Commerce and Industry had been centers of conflict ever since their creation in eleven districts in 1850. They were a form of government–regulated self-administration typical of the nineteenth century Habsburg bureaucracy. Subordinated to the Ministry of Commerce, the most important tasks of the Chambers were: (1) to report yearly to the Ministry and to the public on the conditions of business in their districts; (2) to collect relevant statistics; (3) to transmit grievances and petitions and to make recommendations to the Ministry in questions effecting their constituency; and (4) to issue permits and maintain standards in the trades. The Chambers were elected by a constituency composed of all independent merchants and industrialists—regardless of guild membership—in the territorial district of the Chamber.[59]

The most persistent source of conflict about the Chambers was their commitment to industrial freedom. Their creation was an attempt to bypass the decaying but recalcitrant system of guilds and to set up a more modern and "liberal" method for the regulation of business. Simultaneously, this was an incidental recognition of non-guild industrialists who were probably in a majority by mid–century among the craftsmen of Pest and Buda.[60] The conflict over industrial freedom was won, at least administratively, by the liberal forces, which included the Chambers, when the industrial law of 1872 finally abolished the guilds. Yet the demands for greater regulation were not to be silenced even after the industrial law of 1884 made certain small concessions, and the opposition to "industrial anarchy" remained strong even after the turn of the century.

From the start, the representatives of large business, who at that time were also the most adamant advocates of industrial freedom, held key posts in the Chambers, especially in the most important one, that of the capital. The first president of the Pest–Buda Chamber was Antal Valero, owner of a silk factory which employed 340 workers.[61] With the increasing divergence of the character as well as interests of large and small business, the dominance of big business was increasingly contested in the Cameral elections. Feeling their position threatened, the secretaries of the Budapest and Miskolc Chambers presented a memorandum to a National Congress of Commerce in 1896 demanding a revision of the cameral electoral law. The memorandum warned that the existing law which provided for "universal" and equal suffrage presented the danger that "the large mass of small industrialists and merchants could completely dominate and exclude from representation in the Chambers the factory industrialists and large merchants who, though a numerical minority, made the greatest financial contribution to the Chambers." The memorandum goes on to say that

> In the past this law did not work to the disadvantage of large industry and trade, which were not excluded from

proper representation. Recently, howeer, there are signs
which point in the opposite direction.

As a remedy, the memorandum proposed a system of voting by *"cu-
rias"* based on the size of firms. Though the Commercial Congress
adopted the resolutions of the memorandum—one would suspect through
undemocratic practices—and forwarded them to the Ministry of Commerce, the reform was not carried out.[62]

Small industrialists and merchants protested to the Ministry of
Commerce the fraudulent methods by which their opponents were
elected to the Chambers. In 1904 they protested the election of
Leo Kirszhaber, "a man who in the recent past put the beggar's
stick into the hands of nearly 2,000 small industrialists," as well as
of Tivadar Wolfner, owner of Hungary's largest and most modern
leather factory (over 600 workers) on the grounds that he had bribed
the electorate.[63] As contemporaries observed, the days of peaceful
elections to the Chambers vanished sometime in the 1890s and these
elections began to resemble the boisterous, corrupt Hungarian parliamentary elections.[64]

Only through such practices was big business able to maintain
its dominance in the Chambers of Commerce throughout most of our
period. In 1893 Leó Lánczy, president of the powerful Hungarian
Commercial Bank also became president of the Budapest Chamber
of Commerce and Industry, a post he would fill without interruption
for the next quarter century. Still, the dominance of big business was
rather uneasy and unstable. Most Chambers, including the Budapest
Chamber, passed resolutions in favor of the independent customs area,
though Lánczy was a strong supporter of the common customs.

Such circumstances provide the background to Chorin's com-
ments at the founding meeting of the Industrial Association.

> It is true that it is within the authority of the legally con-
> stituted Chambers of Commerce and Industry to represent
> also the interests of large industry. But the existing elec-
> toral system, which restricts the representation of industry
> into the narrowest confines or even completely excludes it,
> as well as the fact that these bodies can only act within
> the confines of the law pertaining to them, place insupera-
> ble obstacles before the intensive representation of industrial
> interests [through the Chambers].[65]

The National Industrial Federation

The inability of existing organizations to act effectively as spokesmen for all industry can be seen also in the case of the National Industrial Federation. It was a voluntary organization for the promotion of Hungarian industry. It was founded by Louis Kossuth and other nobles in the reform era of the 1840s. In existence nearly fifty years before the coming of age of large industry in Hungary, it was natural that its membership and target constituency—those whom it sought to organize, for whom it published its weekly newspaper, and out of whom it wished to build a modern industry—should have been small industrialists. Yet, its leadership did not simply reflect the wishes of the craftsmen who formed the bulk of its membership. In fact, part of the organization's problem was the lack of consensus between its leaders and small industrial members.

Lóránt Hegedüs, executive secretary of the Association between 1905 and 1912 pointed this out in his reminiscences.

> The Federation was in the peculiar situation that its president, Sándor Matlekovits, one of Hungary's most outstanding and perhaps most learned economists, avowed in all his works his belief in free trade, the common customs area of Austria–Hungary and the victory of big business and big industry, while—contrary to this—the organization itself was oriented towards the independent customs area, isolation, the protection of handicrafts, and the guild–like intervention of government. . . . Gradually, the Federation became the spokesman for the interests of the handicrafts industry.[66]

Neither small nor large industry shared the views or the organization's president whose election can be attributed to his close ties to the government bureaucracy and to his reputation, as well as to the fact that his views placed him outside of the major factions of the Federation.

It seems that in the majority of cases, the Federation took positions favorable to large industry. As a representative example we may paraphrase an article of Mór Gelléri, editor of the Federation's newspaper, *Magyar Ipar* [Hungarian Industry]. A group of cobblers from Nagyvárad feared that the planned establishment of a shoe factory in their town would increase the hardship of the craftsmen. Gelléri answered their complaints by stressing his own personal preferences for shoes produced by hand and by sympathizing with the hard lot of small industrialists who must be saved from ruinous competition. His

conclusion was nonetheless in favor of the factory for he claimed that
on the basis of import–export figures the factory would only displace
imports from Austria. Rather than providing competition to the cobblers of Nagyvárad, it would provide employment for the unemployed
cobblers. Such a factory, he concluded, "could only be a blessing for
the city as well as for its environs."[67] Similarly in 1898, in response to
a request by the Ministry of Commerce for an opinion on the necessity of legislation to regulate the activities of cartels, the Federation
concluded that "cartels [were] indispensable and so far have played
only a beneficial role in Hungary. Anti–cartel legislation is, therefore,
unnecessary."[68] Even in 1910 when the movement against cartels had
gathered considerable momentum not only among small industrialists
but among the public at large, the Federation still refused to change
its position.

Still, the traditionalist, anti–big–business attitudes of small industry could not be totally silenced in the Federation. This position
was represented most forecefully by Endre Thék, the owner of a furniture factory, who, despite his wealth, remained true to his roots
as a craftsman. In his speeches one can see signs of the incipient
alliance between agrarianism and small industry. Responding to a
lecture on economic policy by Sándor Wekerle, the former Liberal
prime minister, who claimed that the problem of immigration must
be solved by industrialization rather than by government support for
small industry and agriculture, Thék declared:

> The physical power possessed by those 40,000 patriotic in-
> dependent small industrialists who have been forced to emi-
> grate because of the competition of large industry surpasses
> by far the value of the 2,545 smoke stacked factories we have
> in Hungary. The first shocks to the nation can annihilate the
> development of our factories. But the industry developed in
> the hands of the 40,000 patriotic families cannot be swept
> away or halted in its vigor unless we destroy it artificially.
> Your Excellency errs, therefore, in stating that at all costs
> we must promote large industry; on the contrary, it is the
> 40,000 industrialists along with their workers who are im-
> portant. . . . It cannot be a wise promotion of industry
> and commerce or a correct economic policy that turns the
> last penny of the earning capacity of the defenseless landed
> property to guaranteeing the capital invested in industry
> and industrial firms.[70]

Large industry could justifiably feel the hostile spirit of "agrarianism" even within such a "liberal" organization as the Federation. Sensing that under such circumstances, the intensive advocacy of their interests could not be achieved, most large industrialists turned a deaf ear to Gelléri's attempts to maintain the unity of the "industrial classes." Although the Federation tried to reform and strengthen its various occupational sections, including its division for large industry, the reorganization of the Federation met with little success. Gelléri was forced to admit at the time of the formation of the Association that the general tendency was towards more and more specialized organizations outside the framework of the Federation. "I myself," complained Gelléri, "who have devoted my entire life to the representation of the interests of all industry, was not even invited to the founding meeting of the Association."[71]

The Creation of the National Association of Hungarian Industrialists

From the point of view of the Chambers of Commerce and Industry and the Federation, the foundation of the Association represented a differentiation of interests. In fact, however, a differentiation into interest groups representing particular branches of industry had already taken place in the previous decade and from their point of view the formation of the Association represented a new synthesis. The most prominent large industrial branch organizations were: (1) the National Association of Hungarian Iron Works and Machine Factories, founded in 1899 from a similar "Club" which had been in existence since 1890; (2) the National Association of Hungarian Mines and Forges, founded in1901 by Ferenc Chorin; and (3) the National Association of Hungarian Sugar Manufacturers, founded in 1894.[72]

The shift in political life and social movements described above, along with the concommitant economic depression at the end of the century, forced the leaders of large industry to consider the general interests of their "class." The issues touching the interests of all of large industry, such as the passage of the law of incompatibility and the need for increased government support through public orders, industrial promotion, and reduced railroad rates, had grown in number and significance. The needs of particular industries also required stronger representation than what the branch associations could provide. In response to these conditions the leaders of the branch associations, especially of the three most significant ones, took the initiative in organizing the Association.

The events of the founding are mostly shrouded in obscurity. By all accounts the lead for organizing the Association was taken by Ferenc Chorin, president of the Salgótarján Coal Mines and of the Hungarian National Association of Mines and Forges, and by Sándor Hatvany–Deutsch whose family owned Hungary's largest sugar refineries and who himself was founder and president of the Hungarian Association of Sugar Manufacturers.[73] The names of Ferenc Aich, president of the Hungarian Brewers Association, and of Nándor Förster, president of the National Association of Iron and Machine Manufacturers, are also mentioned among the founders of the organization.[74]

The first discussions took place in January 1902. Chorin was entrusted with the task of inviting "other outstanding representatives of Hungarian industry" to a meeting on February 5th for a "confidential and in–depth discussion of plans for the founding of a National Association."[75] The resulting meeting, attended by fifty large–industrialists, decided upon the foundation of the National Association of Hungarian Industrialists. Other meetings followed in the same month. An executive committee met for the first time on February 19th and elected Chorin as its president. An appeal was drafted "To Hungary's Industrialists" calling upon them to join the organization. This document explained the reasons for the founding of the organization. "Hungary's industrialists deserve to be heard and respected by the nation and given a position in public life commensurate with their economic importance." It stressed the need for industry to organize on its own behalf since the government had not done enough to relieve the effects of the recession. It justified the creation of an organization encompassing all the branches of industry on the gorunds that the smaller associations were unable to represent the general interest with sufficient force and were open to charges of representing special lobbies. (Implicit in this formulation is the notion that the Association could represent the general interests of the country.) The aim of the projected organization was "to debate, clarify, and initiate action in all those questions which touch upon the flourishing of Hungarian industry in the areas of tariffs, transport, social policy, legislation and, in short, all economic matters." The document was signed in the name of the executive committee by the leaders of Hungarian industry.

The response to the appeal was so great that, within a week of its issuance, the founding of the organization was assured. Twenty meetings of the executive committee were held between February and May and its members also travelled the country recruiting members and collecting dues. The inaugural meeting took place on May 29, 1902, in the Hall of the Budapest Chamber of Commerce and Industry, a courtesy arranged by Leó Lánczy, despite his disapproval of the dissipation of industrial forces that might result from the proliferation of industrial interest groups.[76] Láncy himself did not join the Association in the year it was formed. He, nonetheless, appreciated the challenge faced by the new group to create an organization that would be recognized as the representative of large industry, an organization that would make industry speak with a more coherent voice and one that would promote the evolution of a pro–industrial economic policy.

Chapter 3

STRUCTURE AND MEMBERSHIP, 1902–1914

So far we have considered the environment of Hungarian industry and the conditions which provided the impetus for the founding of the Association. We now consider how the organization was structured, who its leaders were and whom it represented. In doing so, we gain a basis for understanding the economic demands and political activities of the Association.

Formal Structure and Actual Functioning

A preliminary version of the By–Laws was drafted at the founding meetings before May 29, 1902. This draft was reworked after the founding and the revised version was accepted by the General Assembly at its first annual meeting in April 1903.[1] The formal structure of the Association combined features of centralization with decentralization which permitted the affiliation of a broad range of firms in terms of size, geography, and industrial branch without sacrificing the manageability of the organization by those at its center. The Association was divided into a central organization, a network of provincial branches and a series of affiliated industrial branch interest groups (Figure 3.1). These distinctions have to be made from the outset because membership in a provincial branch or in an affiliated interest group was not equivalent to full membership in the central organization.

The central organization consisted of a series of several assemblies and committees representing varying degrees of authority and executive functions.[2] Ultimate authority resided in the General Assembly which was composed of all members of the central organization of the Association, including representatives of the affiliated industrial branch interest groups and one–third of the members of the regional branches. It had the right to modify the constitution and dissolve the organization. It also elected the President and two Vice–Presidents,

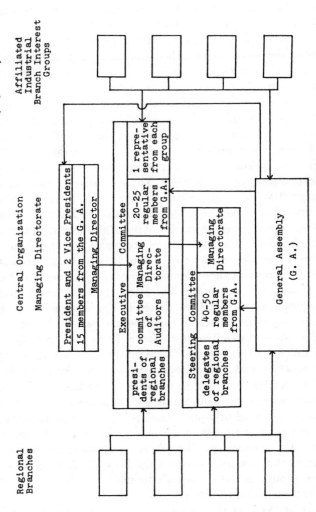

Figure 3.1
Organizational Structure of the Association (GyOSz)

Based on: GyOSz, *A Magyar Gyáriparosok Országos Szövetségének Alapszabályai* (By-Laws of the National Association of Hungarian Industrialists), (Budapest: Pesti Lloyd Társulat, 1903).

the Managing Directorate, and the members of the Executive and Steering Committees; it approved the disposition of the previous year's finances and of the coming year's budget, and discussed proposals initiated by the members of the Association. The General Assembly had to be convened at least once annually. Acting as a representative of the General Assembly was the Steering Committee which consisted of 40–50 delegates from the General Assembly, delegates from the provincial branches, and the Managing Directorate. It could approve proposals placed before it by the executive organ and had to be convened at least twice annually.

The most inclusive of the executive organs of the Association was the Executive Committee. It consisted of 20–25 members elected by the General Assembly, the Presidency of the Association, the Managing Directorate, the Board of Auditors, representatives of the affiliated interest organizations of particular industrial branches, and the presidents of the regional branch. The Executive Committee had to be convened at least three times annually, but, in fact, it was convened much more frequently. Only five members had to be present at a meeting to make a decision. The duty of the Executive Committee was to administer the affairs of the organization and to execute the decisions of the General Assembly and Steering Committee. It also elected the Managing Director and decided on matters placed before it by the Managing Directorate. The Managing Directorate, consisting of the Presidency, 15 members elected by the General Assembly, and the Managing Director was to supervise the day–to–day administration of affairs and to administer those matters not expressly claimed by the Executive Committee. The Managing Directorate met at least once a week. At least five members were necessary for a valid decision.

The Presidency, consisting of the President and two Vice–Presidents, represented the organization before the government and public authorities, presided over and convened all meetings and guaranteed the proper implementation of the resolutions brought by the various organs of the Association. The actual job of administration was carried out by the Managing Director and his staff. As we shall see, this position, though in theory purely administrative, had great influence in the determination of policy.

Besides the central organization, provincial branches could be set up in any area of the country where at least 10 local industrialists called for one. An industrial firm, an interest organization representing a branch of industry, or an individual could be affiliated with the

Association in several ways. "Regular membership" in the central organization was possible for firms and Hungarian industrial–branch interest organizations. Only regular members could vote in the General Assembly and run for office. Like any other regular member, interest organizations had only one representative with one vote in the General Assembly. The representative was, however, automatically a member of the Executive Committee. Regular members had to pay a nominal annual fee of 100–500 crowns, depending on the size of the firm. Affiliation with the central organization was also possible through honorary, supporting and corresponding membership so that prominent industrialists whose firms were already represented by someone else, or politicians and bureaucrats who were close to industry but not the representatives of a particular firm could also take part in the meetings of the General Assembly. They could make proposals but could not vote. Applicants for membership in the central organization had to be considered by a meeting of the Executive Committee and approved by at least two–thirds of those present. Members of the provincial branches were not automatically members of the organization, though they could apply for membership individually. Every three members of a provincial branch could delegate one of their number to the central organization where he could exercise the rights of a regular member. Like the industrial branch organizations, the provincial branches were also represented by their presidents in the Executive Committee.

In the actual functioning of the organization, quite naturally the smaller, more administrative organs of the Association exercised greater influence than the larger assemblies from which authority supposedly derived. The Managing Directorate generally initiated policy which would be discussed by the Executive or Steering Committee. In almost all cases the recommendations of the Managing Directorate would be accepted, as one may gather from the minutes of the various organs published in the periodical *Közlemények* [Bulletins], until the end of 1910 and thereafter in the biweekly *Magyar Ipar* [Hungarian Industry]. Only in a few cases were disagreements in the Managing Directorate taken for resolution to the Steering Committee.[3] If disagreements existed between the Managing Directorate and groups outside it, they were probably ironed out through informal discussions. Unfortunately, we know little about rivalries within the Association, though we do know that there were conflicts of opinion, most prominently on such issues as the customs union with Austria and the extension of suffrage to industrial workers. Whenever conflicts could not be resolved, the views of the dissenting minority were also made known in the official position. The only important such case, however, was that of suffrage reform.

It seems that elections were also uncontested. The nominations of the Managing Directorate for the officers of the Association were placed before the General Assembly and most often accepted without so much as the nomination of contenders from the floor. The members elected to the governing organs were generally the representatives of the most prestigious firms in their fields, though some smaller firms were also represented.

Figure 3.2
Growth of Association Membership

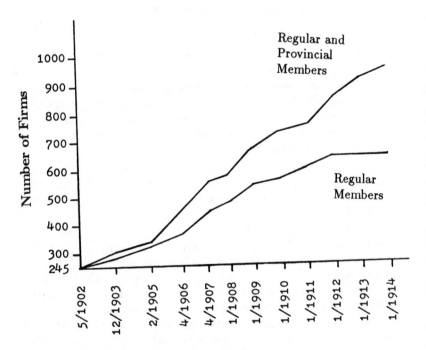

Sources: GyOSz Annual Reports, 1903–1914.

The Membership of the Association

At its founding meeting on May 29, 1902, the Association reported a total membership of 245 firms and 11 interest groups.[4] By the end of 1913, its regular membership had reached 666 firms and 22 industrial–branch interest groups, an average annual increase of 7 percent (Figure 3.2).

These figures may be compared to the 2,500 strong membership of the *Bund Österreichischer Industrieller* in 1908 which represented about 20 percent of Austrian "large industry" (defined the same way as the broader membership in Hungary).[6] Both the Association and the *Bund* represented about the same share of total industrial enterprises (Table 3.1).

Table 3.1
Percent of Large Industrial Firms (more than 20 workers) Represented in the Association 1902, 1910, 1913

Year	Industrial Firms in Hungary	Regular Membership of GyOSz	Broader Membership of GyOSz	Percent for Regular Membership	Percent for Broader Membership
1900	2329				
1902	2329*	245	256	10.5	11.0
1910	4025	595	712	14.8	17.7
1913	4931*	640	931	13.0	18.9

*Approximations.

Sources: Industrial firms, 1900 and 1910 from Iván Berend and György Ránki, *Magyarország gyáripara, 1900–1914* [Hungarian Industry, 1900–1914] (Budapest: Szikra, 1955), 74; Membership, see Figure 3.1.

These percentages seem rather small because we are comparing the Association's membership to a broad definition of large industry used in the period. To evaluate the large–industrial character of the Association one might ascertain its share of all really large industrial firms. Although data for such calculations are not readily available, at least joint–stock companies were listed in the *Magyar Compass* [Hungarian Compass] along with the par value of their capital stock.

Of course, not all members of the Association were joint–stock companies. Only about half of the regular members were joint–stock companies in both 1903 (135 companies) and in 1913 (305 companies).

These represented 32 percent of the total of 419 joint–stock companies in 1903 and only 19 percent of the total (1,623) in 1913. Yet in 1903 the 32 percent of companies represented 48 percent of the capital stocks issued by all joint–stock companies in Hungary (227 million K out of 496 million) and in 1913 the 19 percent represented 52 percent of the total capital (717 million K out of 1,374 million K).[7] This means that the larger industries were more heavily represented in the Association than the smaller ones at the beginning of the period and even more so at its end.

Figure 3.3
Percent of Association Members Among Joint Stock Companies with Headquarters in Budapest (by sextiles) 1903, 1913

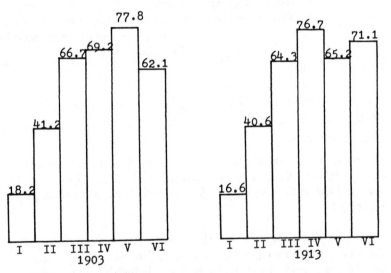

Calculated from: *Mihók–féle Magyar Compasz* 1902/1903, 1912/1913; GyOSz, *1903. évi jel,* (1903 Annual Report), GyOSz, *1914. évi jel.,* 256–275.

It becomes evident that Association membership was more frequent among the largest firms, with 62.1 percent of the top sixth of Budapest listed joint–stock companies regular members of the Association in 1903 and 71.1 percent regular members in 1913 (Figure 3.3).

Having considered the size of the industrial firms in the Association, let us look at the branches of industry that were represented, confining our attention to joint–stock companies headquartered in Budapest (Table 3.2).

Table 3.2

Association Membership Among Budapest–based Industrial Joint–Stock Companies by Branch 1903, 1913

Branch	Total	1903 GyOSz	Percent	1913 Total	GyOSz	Percent
Milling	8	8	100	14	10	71
Food	19	9	47	28	11	27
Lumber	10	2	20	75	20	35
Coal mines	15	5	33	20	8	40
Other mines and forges	6	2	33	37	8	22
Metallurgy and machines	33	12	36	106	35	33
Construction, materials	11	1	9	40	12	30
Construction, real estate	0	0	0	53	2	4
Leather	3	3	100	18	3	17
Paper	4	1	25	20	8	40
Printing	22	1	5	79	4	5
Textiles and clothing	6	3	50	33	1	33
Glass porcelain	6	2	33	18	3	17
Chemicals	22	11	50	66	24	36
Electric	10	5	50	36	11	31
Total	175	65	37	643	170	26

Source: See Figure 3.3.

Flour milling and (in 1903 only) the leather industry led the highest participation rate. The case of flour milling may be explained in part by the fact that this industry had been most severely hurt by agrarian–inspired legislation. Moreover, flour milling like the leather processing sectors were the sectors in which the Hungarian bourgeoisie had matured the most. In some other areas, such as sugar refining and in brewing, we find a similarly high concentration of Association members (eight out of eleven Hungarian joint–stock sugar refineries were members and three out of the four large breweries of Budapest). All these firms had prominent members of the Hungarian bourgeoisie associated with them.

The low degree of representation of some industries, such as construction, printing, glass, and porcelain may be explained by the craft nature of many firms in these industries (even among joint–stock companies). Some branches, such as metallurgy may have been well represented in their respective industrial branch organizations which were themselves members of the Association.

Other industries may have had close ties with the Industrial Federation and the Chambers of Commerce which they did not wish to "desert" for the Association. This may have been why a number of very important Hungarian firms such as the Ganz Machine Industries, perhaps the largest and most modern firm in all Hungary, or the Armaments and Machines Factory, the Fiume Rice–Refinery, the Franklin Press (the second largest in the country) did not join the Association until the 1910s. These companies and several other non–members were all connected to the Magyar Hitel Bank and its president, Zsigmond Kornfeld.[8] Most of these firms were members of the Industrial Federation in which Kornfeld played an active role. It is a measure of the ultimate victory of the Association that by 1912 most of these firms, too, had become its members.[9] This transition was eased by Kornfeld's death in 1909. His successor, both at the Hitel Bank and in the Federation was Adolf Ullmann. Unlike Kornfeld, Ullmann seems to have had a more positive attitude towards the Association. At the celebration of the Tenth Anniversary of the Association, Chorin's son, Ferenc Chorin, Jr., then its vice president (and its president after his father's death in 1925), toasted Ullmann as "the newest ally of the Association to whose decision may be gratefully attributed the fact that today the whole of Hungarian factory industry joins as one united phalanx."[10]

The formal membership of the Hitel–Bank–associated companies was in fact only a recognition of a relationship that had existed earlier. The Ganz concern, for example, participated in the pre-founding meetings of the Association and its chairman of the board, Emil Asbóth, had been a signatory of the call for its formation.[11] Though by not joining the Association in 1902 he may have deferred to Zsigmond Kornfeld whose bank owned a controlling share of Ganz stock, the Ganz concern participated in the activities of the Association through the affiliated National Association of Iron and Machine Works. In fact, Asbóth represented this organization in certain committees of the Association.[12] By 1914, the son of Zsigmond Kornfeld, Baron Mór Kornfeld, was a member of the Managing Directorate of the Association.[13] These steps were not compensated by similar moves on the part of Association members to join the Federation. They may, therefore, be taken as signs of the recognition of the importance of the Association compared to the decline of the Federation.

We have noted above that large firms were more likely to be regular members of the Association than were smaller firms. Budapest was also more heavily represented than were the provinces. Nevertheless, it should be noted, that firms from cities such as Arad, Brassó, Debrecen, Fiume, Győr, Losonc, Pécs, Pozsony, Szeged, Temesvár, and Zenta were also to be found among the membership.[14] Often the firms from these cities, for example the Rózsahegyi Cellulose and Paper Company, were owned by minority nationalities against whom the Association does not seem to have discriminated.[15]

The Association also urged the founding of a separate association for Croatia. The Croatian National Association of Industrialists was formed in 1903 and, like the regional branches, was represented on the Steering and Executive Committees and the Managing Directorate of the Association.[16] We might note that this Croatian organization had a generally critical attitude towards those Croatian nationalists whose political demands disrupted normal relations between the Hungarian government and Croatia.[17] The members of this association, therefore, seem not to have been typical of the bourgeoisie of the nationalities.

Finally, we should mention that occasionally the subsidiaries of foreign-owned companies, such as A-G., Nobel Dynamite, Vacuum Oil, and the Telephone Manufacturing Company, (*Telefongyár*), were also members of the Association.[18]

The Personalities

We have so far considered the institutions that made up the membership of the Association. Let us now shift our attention to the men who represented these institutions. The representatives of most of the firms in the Association were either the owners, founders or descendants of the founders of firms. We begin with a description of the career of the organization's founder and first president, Ferenc Chorin, Sr., even if that career was not typical in many ways.[19] Chorin, born in 1842, was the son of a medical doctor in Arad, a town in the Hungarian Plain from which many of Hungary's leading industrialists originated, and the grandson of Rabbi Áron Chorin who had been born in Moravia and settled in Arad in 1789. The grandfather had been one of the leaders of Jewish assimilation to the German culture of the Habsburg Empire. Like Moses Mendelssohn in Germany, he called for the modernization of Jewish ritual, for the adoption of the German language and also for participation of Jews in handicraft and agriculture. The grandson not only lived up to these expectations, but exceeded them to an extent that would have been unimaginable and certainly uncomfortable for the reformer rabbi. Ferenc Chorin not only became a captain of industry but, in order to obtain entry into the Upper House of Parliament in 1903, converted to Catholicism. Even his grandfather had begun to realize towards the end of his life that in view of the subsequent rise of Magyar nationalism his advocacy of an identification with German culture had been misplaced. The grandson, though of course learning German, grew up an ardent Magyar nationalist. He was trained in Vienna as a lawyer, became attracted to a political career and used as his vehicle towards that end a newspaper in Arad which he had founded and edited. Before 1867 Chorin's newspaper was ardently Kossuthist, that is, opposed to the Compromise advocated by Deák. His opposition was, however, moderated subsequently by the fact that among the earliest acts of the new government were measures further promoting the emancipation of the Jews. Still, it was as an opposition deputy that Chorin entered the lower House of Parliament in 1869. In the words of William McCagg, "the religious zeal of his grandfather flamed in him in the secular form of Magyar nationalism."[20] Yet Chorin never joined the most extreme parliamentary group of the independence movement. By 1884, the anti-Semitism that found a haven in the independence camp drove Chorin to reenter Kálmán Tisza's Liberal

Party. He had earlier broken with this party over the issue of the establishment of an independent Hungarian national bank which, he believed, had been insufficiently pressed by Tisza in the decennial negotiations of 1876–1877.

In 1890 Chorin became executive director of Hungary's largest coal mine, the Salgotarján Hard Coal Company. Perhaps Chorin was invited to assume this position because of his lobbying activities in favor of industry. Chorin's career can be seen as representing something unusual in the history of the Hungarian managerial class. While most managers at Chorin's level were either entrepreneurs from the start or had a technical education, Chorin came to business by way of journalism and politics. This transition, the details of which are unfortunately obscure, is a good reflection of the social barriers shaping Jewish careers in Dualistic Hungary. Clearly a politician by inclination and temperament, Chorin found that the path to social advancement for Jews led through the boardroom rather than the halls of Parliament. It was a sign of political disintegration at the end of World War I that a Jew, József Szterényi,became prime minister. The Association presented Chorin and other Jewish entrepreneurs with an alternative way to participate in the political arena.

While Chorin's Kossutist sentiments and political past set him somewhat apart, Sándor Hatvany–Deutsch was a more typical member of the Hungarian bourgeoisie among the founders of the Association. The Hatvany–Deutsches were perhaps Hungary's wealthiest, most powerful and illustrious industrialist families.[21] They, too, originated from Arad. Already in 1822 Ignác Deutsch, Sándor's grandfather founded a "grocery" shop in Arad which prospered so well that in time the father became a money lender to the local grain producing aristocracy. Subsequently he moved his business to Budapest, entered into the insurance business and was active in industry. Along with a number of families of similar backgrounds as grain merchants, his son participated in the creation of the Hungarian milling industry in the late 1860s and early 1870s. The Hungarian flour mills were equipped with the most modern technology of the time. Through innovations by the Ganz firm which supplied their equipment, the Hungarian milling industry became the most successful in Europe. These modern mills were founded as joint–stock companies since the capital required for such a venture exceeded the resources that most grain merchants were willing or able to provide.[22] Thus, the few families who had amassed enough fortunes in the grain trade, becoming thereby the upper crust of the Hungarian economic elite, shared among themselves the boards of most of the mills. They were to extend their activities into new industrial branches as well as into banking in the 1880s and 1890s.

For the Hatvany–Deutsch family, the most important new branch was sugar milling. It was already the generation of grandsons who guided the family fortunes in these enterprises. This generation had received a modern economic education in the large banks of Berlin and Budapest, where Sándor Hatvany–Deutsch, too, spent his youth in such schools as the Viennese, Hochschule für Bodenkultur, a school which was also attended by his cousin Jószef. As the fathers had done in milling, their sons applied the most modern technologies to the failing sugar mills which they purchased. One of the main problems of earlier attempts at sugar refining had been the scarcity of the supply of sugar beets. The Hatvany–Deutsches solved this problem by undertaking the production of the beets themselves.

The Hatvany family developed close connections to the ruling Liberal Party which promoted the Hungarian sugar industry through subsidies, export premiums and the revision of the tax laws which, until 1888, had favored the Austrian industries and Austrian government. In this way the Hungarian sugar refiners, with the Hatvanys at their head, became equal bargaining partners to their Austrian colleagues. In their view, their success showed that the ruling Liberal Party and the *Ausgleich* framework that it supported permitted sufficient leverage for the satisfaction of Hungarian interests. In the Association, too, the Hatvany–Deutsches were the leaders of the faction—in opposition to Chorin—which saw no need to revise the customs relations between Austria and Hungary.[23] Sándor Hatvany–Deutsch was one of the two founding vice–presidents of the Association.

The other vice–president until his death in 1910, was Ferenc Aich, president of the Association of Hungarian Brewers and part owner and manager of the prominent Dreher Brewery in Budapest. Unlike the majority of the Association, Aich was not a Jew, a fact that the Jewish community's newspaper, *Egyenlőség* [Equality] was quick to point out as evidence of the Association's non–denominational character.[24] Only after World War I did the anti–Semitic press stress the Jewish nature of the Association, and only in the late 1930s did a conflict between Jews and non–Jews become noticeable within the organization.[25]

In the organs of the Association above the level of the Steering Committee, one encounters the names of most of the families that had been prominent participants in the boom of the agriculture–related industries of the sixties and seventies: from milling, besides the Hatvany–Deutschers there were the Brülls (changed to Bíró), the Kohners, the megyeri Krauszes, Baron Péter Herzog, Izidor Déri, Ede Langfelder, Konrád Béláváry–Burchard; from brewing and alcohol, Vilmos Leipziger, Aurél Münnich, Imre Linczer, Arthur Deutsch, Samu Neumann, Ferenc Aich, and the Tószegi Freuds; from sugar refining, Károly Kuffner and Dániel Rothermann, and from lumber, Gyula Vuk and several members of the Neuschloss family. The Wolfners and Mauthners, pioneers in the modern tanning industry in Hungary as well as two members of the Weisz clan (Berthold Weisz and Manfréd Weisz), who started in the tinned–food business and were also among its prominent members. Manfréd Weisz, who built one of the largest industrial empires and the major armaments works in Hungary, was one of the initiators of the founding. His brother, Berthold, is credited with the writing of the original constitution of the Association and continued to play a vital role in the Executive Committee as the representative of the National Association of Textile Manufacturers.

Although those whose families had started out in the agriculture–related industries formed the largest group, other important industries—such as machine manufacture, iron milling, coal mining and chemicals—were also represented in the Association's leadership. Among them we find such engineer–entrepreneurs as István Popper, the founder, along with the internationally known inventor, Tivadar Puskás, of the Hungarian Telephone Company, and Nándor Förster, President of the National Association of Iron and Machine Works.[26]

Most of the men we have named were, by the time of the founding of the Association, prominent industrialists and bankers. Most of them sat on the Boards of Directors of at least one bank and often of several banks. Though the Hatvany–Deutsches, the Weiszes and Chorin were involved with the largest bank in Hungary, the Kereskedelmi Bank, the most frequent connections were with the medium–sized banks such as the Hazai Bank (seven members), the Belvárosi Savings (six members), the Országos Központi Savings (five members), the Budapest Lipótvárosi Savings (four members) and the Magyar Bank (three members), for a total of forty–six board memberships among the fifty–two officers surveyed.[27] This fact might warrant a reassessment of the role played by the medium–sized Budapest banks in industrial financing. It would seem that in the case of the industrialists in the Association, their influence on banks was as strong as the more frequently noted influence of banks on industry.

For its domestic sources of investment, Hungarian industry had to rely to a great extent on the business and personal wealth of the few hundred families who made up the Hungarian upper bourgeoisie. This reliance was true also in the case of entrepreneurial talent. In this way, most of the men we have been discussing, sat on the boards of several firms, sometimes in quite dissimilar industries. To mention only the most prominent examples, Ferenc Chorin and his son of the same name shared between them seats on the boards of two banks and of eighteen industrial firms. The Hatvany–Deutsches were involved with four banks and seventeen firms, and Manfred Weisz, with one major bank and six firms.[28] Thus, unofficially, the men in the Association represented many more firms than appeared according to their official mandate in the organization. They were a most important section of the Hungarian bourgeoisie. Typically they were second generation industrialists born in the 1850s who had developed, modernized and expanded the industries and wealth inherited from their fathers. Many had also inherited or acquired noble rank by 1902 or were to acquire it because of their economic prominence, political loyalties and services by 1914. Of the forty–four members of the Executive Committee of 1905, eighteen were ennobled Jews.[29]

The largest firms of Hungarian industry—and hence their above-named representatives— were in a minority among the members of the Association. Yet, the representatives of the smaller firms played a minor role in the more influential organs of the Association. Occasionally one encounters there the voices of men like Endre Thék, the furniture and piano manufacturer; Kálmán Szabó, president of the Debrecen branch of the Association and a local banker and mill owner; or Traugott Copony, a Transylvanian Saxon paper manufacturer and president of the Brassó branch. While such men may have been important in transmitting the sense of the majority to the leadership, policy in the Association generally evolved through the councils of Hungary's greatest industrialists.

Among the men whose personalities made a strong imprint on the Association one must also mention its manaaging directors. Acting as a chief organizer of activities, directing research into issues, presenting the results of the various committees of the organization and drafting memoranda to the government, the managing director was able to exercise considerable influence. The choice of managing directors, therefore, was a good indication of the general political and ideological orientation of the leadership.

During the period covered by this study, the three managing directors of the Association were Ambrus Neményi (1902–1905), Lóránt Hegedüs (1905–1912), and Gusztáv Gratz (1912–1917). Gratz was followed by Miksa Fenyő, who had been on the Association staff since 1904 as an editor of its *Közlemények* and of the *Magyar Ipar* after its founding in 1910.[30] It is significant that all these men leaned towards social reform and the latter three were even critics of the Hungarian political establishment, though, as we shall see, they too belonged to it. Neményi was a Liberal member of the Lower House and a journalist. Trained in economics, he had been a strong supporter of the industrialization policies of the Liberal government.[31] His performance in the short time that he served until his death in 1904, leaves one with the impression that Neményi was more of an administrative expert than a strongly individualistic character.

Not so with Lóránt Hegedüs, whose personality made a strong imprint on the organization. Hegedüs, whose father had served several times as minister of commerce in Liberal governments, belonged to a younger generation than Neményi or most of the Association's founders. His education and sensibility brought him into contact with Hungary's so–called "second reform generation" which manifested broad discontent with the political and esthetic life of Hungary. Although he was unwilling to follow the main body of this movement's pro–socialist orientation after 1905, he did share its anti–agrarianism and certainly subscribed to its esthetic tastes. His dynamic personality helped to impose his progressive views on certain policies of the Association, especially on that of suffrage reform.

Yet the appointment of Hegedüs was certainly no accident. As the case of Miksa Fenyő shows, some of the founders of the Association were also attracted to the "reform generation": if not so much to its politics then certainly to its esthetics. In 1908, Fenyő founded the literary magazine *Nyugat* [West], which became the main organ of Hungary's modernist writers and their poet laureate, Endre Ady. In many cases, as in that of Ady, modernist literature in Hungary was highly critical of the anti–democratic elements of Hungarian political and social life. When Hegedüs praised Ady to István Tisza in 1913, the then Prime Minister said of Ady that he was a "vermin on the palm leaf of Hungarian culture."[32] Nevertheless, it was the founders of

the Association who financed the *Nyugat*.[33] Its three founding share-
holders were, besides Fenyő, Ferenc Chorin, Jr., and Lajos Hatvany,
who were both sons of the Association's founders. Ferenc Chorin,
Jr. was also a prominent member of the Association by that time
and was to become its president after his father's death in 1925. Of
the 150 shares of *Nyugat* stock, Sándor Hatvany–Deutsch held 20 and
his brother Béla, 5. Altogether, the family owned 85 shares. Other
prominent Association members who owned 5 or 6 shares each were
Manfréd Weisz, Leó Goldberger and Alfréd Brüll (the banker Leó
Lánczy and Wolf Kohner, the son of an Association member, also
owned stock).[34] We shall have further occasion to discuss the political orientation of the Association and encounter situations where the
organization or its members took positions that were most unpopular
in the circle of the *Nyugat*. The points of contact between the Association's staff and the reform movement of the turn of the century
should be kept in mind.

   Already at the beginning, and all the more so at the end of our
period, the size of the Association membership, the amount of capital it represented, the high percentage of large firms that were its
members and the identities of the men involved in the organization
guaranteed that it would be recognized as an important spokesman
for Hungarian large industry. Yet its success as an interest organization depended on several further factors besides its membership. The
ability of the organization to recruit and maintain its membership
was ultimately dependent on these factors. They can be grouped into
two categories: those aimed at increasing the influence of the Association by developing relationships with the economic ministries of the
government at a bureaucratic level and those aimed at increasing its
influence by virtue of its place in political life. The first of these is
discussed in the next chapter, and the second will be the theme of
the second section of the monograph.

Chapter 4

PROGRAM AND INFLUENCE OF THE ASSOCIATION

In the earlier stages of industrialization, from the 1870s until the early 1890s, the government had occupied a most important position in the development of Hungarian industry. The government shouldered a considerable portion of the costs of industrialization through its railroad policies, public works projects, industrial promotion laws and tax policies. One could even argue that in the period preceding this study the truly significant modernizing policies of the state originated within the ministries and among professional policy makers rather than from the associations of businessmen such as the Industrial Federation or the Chambers of Commerce and Industry. The policies advocated by these associations were often based on simple protectionist notions designed to shield Hungary's small industrialists from Austrian competition. On the other hand, economic ministers, such as Gábor Baross, pursued policies most notably in the area of railroad–promotion and in the building of infrastructure, which encouraged the development of large industry.[1]

As we have seen, the "mercantilist" policies of the government came under serious attack around the turn of the century, an attack which led to their curtailment at a time when Hungarian industry, suffering from a recession, believed that it needed them most.

One of the primary aims of the Association was to restore the momentum to the government's promotion of industry. The Association was first of all an interest group rather than a political organization aiming either at the attainment of power or the reorganization of society. Certainly, ideological convictions could be found among the Association's leadership, and, as we shall see, the organization gave expression to such views on certain issues such as taxation and suffrage reform. Yet on the whole, ideology was subordinate to specific policy demands. Such a separation of policy demands from politics was a conscious goal. On the occasion of Chorin's fortieth birthday, Hegedüs praised the President for freeing industry's struggle for economic policy "from the necessity of supplications in the anterooms of the ministeries" and for giving industry the ability to "pursue its pioneering work independently from the favors of any particular government."[2] This statement should not be taken to mean that the Association was not partisan. However, the organization itself made a distinction between its partisan (political) goals and its economic ones.

Tariffs, Foreign Trade, and Imperialism

Hungarian industry came of age in an era characterized internationally by protectionism and the "new imperialism." The industrialists of the developed countries urged their governments to erect barriers to industrial imports by means of high tariffs and at the same time to promote the export of goods and capital through means ranging from the granting of export premiums to the acquisition of colonies. In the West, policies connected with foreign trade were perhaps the most important aspects of economic policy. In Hungary there were a number of significant digressions from this pattern—due to Hungary's peculiar constitutional position and the comparatively low level of her industrial development.

As already mentioned in Chapter 2, many industrialists were concerned that the customs union between Austria and Hungary exposed Hungarian industry to the full fury of Austrian competition and thereby stifled the development of many industrial branches. A sentiment for an independent customs area had existed with varying degrees of support ever since the formation of the common customs area in 1850. After 1867 movements for an independent trade policy flourished most when the decennial economic agreements were being renegotiated.[3] The movement was especially strong between 1897 and 1907. The failure of the Austrian and Hungarian governments to renew the decennial agreement in 1897 led the Party of Independence to claim that Hungary had thereby been absolved of its obligation to remain in the customs union. The provisional nature of the arrangements in force until 1907 kept the issue on the agenda for the full decade.

The most vehement supporters of the movement were the small industrialists and their interest organizations, such as the Industrial

Federation. The Chambers of Commerce and Industry, more dependent on the government and, some of them, dominated by representatives of large industry and banking, generally restrained their members from supporting a position that was considered in opposition to the ruling 1867 Party. After 1897, however, a number of provincial Chambers came out in favor of an independent customs area and in 1905 even the Budapest Chamber, voting against the recommendations of its president, Leó Lánczy, declared itself for an independent customs area.[4]

It is somewhat enigmatic that the so–called "finance bourgeoisie" should have been able to restrain the Chambers for so long while the Association, which has generally been viewed as the representative *par excellence* of the interests of the finance bourgeoisie, declared itself in favor of an independent customs area from the start.[5] The traditional generalizations about the "finance bourgeoisie" and the Association have to be modified if we are to explain this enigma.

First of all, the concept of a finance bourgeoisie is itself only an "ideal type." It is meant to characterize the most powerful men of business whose activities are divided between industry and banking. However, since these activities at times were in conflict on such matters as industrial tariffs and different men combined these activities to varying degrees, one should not expect to find a uniform set of attitudes on the question of the independent customs area. It does seem that those primarily involved in banking were opposed to customs independence. They tended to be more aware of the factors that determined Hungary's international credit standing, such as its balance of trade. Whatever its long–term effects, in the short run, a separation would probably have resulted in a decrease in Hungarian agricultural exports and hence a negative balance of trade which would have increased the risks borne by foreign lenders. Separate customs area would have also caused complications and uncertainties regarding the maintenance of a common central bank and currency. Hungarian bankers seem even to have feared the reprisals of Austrian banks protecting the interests of their own Austrian clients. Although the nature of the dependence of the Hungarian banks on those in Austria is not yet clear, evidently there was a certain degree of dependence if only that derived from Austria's position as Hungary's principal "foreign" creditor.[6] Thus, bankers like Leó Lánczy were outstanding critics of the independent customs area movement.

From the narrower, market–oriented point of view of industrial interests, the independent customs area had greater attraction. It would have provided protection to those industries which were net importers rather than exporters via Austria. Except for flour milling and certain other food industries, this included every industry in Hungary. Hence a number of the members of the "finance bourgeoisie," who may have nevertheless been closer to the marketing function, favored an independent customs area. The most outstanding example of men belonging to this category was the Association's President Ferenc Chorin, who was also president of the Salgótarján Coal Mines (one of Hungary's largest firms) and a member of the board of several large banks, including the Kereskedelmi Bank. Other members of the "finance bourgeoisie" who supported the movement for an independent customs area were Mihály Mauthner, partner of the First Hungarian Paper Products Company, and Adolf Kohner of the Hungarian Petroleum Company.[7]

Some industrialists, even apart from the perspective they may have gained from their banking connections or from simply possessing a broader vision, may have favored retaining the common customs area because their firms were competitive on the Austrian market and may have come to terms with Austrian competition through cartel agreements. The Ganz Electrical Company provides the prime example of firms in this category. The company, one of the international leaders in its field at the time, negotiated a cartel agreement by which it was granted 46 percent of the Austrian market and 68 percent of the Hungarian.[8] The sugar industry was in an even more special position. The state helped to maintain the cartel agreement that fixed the quantity of sugar Hungary and Austria might export to each other by collecting a surtax at the border—that is tariff—on quantities traded above the quotas.[9] This may help to explain the strong advocacy of the status quo by Sándor Hatvany–Deutsch, a vice–president of the Association and the leading figure in Hungary's internationally competitive sugar industry.[10]

While we find both proponents and opponents of an independent customs area among the representatives of the largest industries, we should remember that most firms belonging to the Association were relatively small or medium–sized firms rather than the "giants" associated with the "finance bourgeoisie." The representatives of these firms judged their interests primarily from the point of view of the market for their goods—and from there, an independent customs area seemed to make sense.

Although the official position of the Association favored customs independence, the organization did not undertake any major efforts to realize its alleged aims. The issue actually presented the Association with a dilemma in the early years of its existence. Negotiations were going on in 1902 between the Hungarian Széll and Austrian Koerber Governments for the decennial economic agreement. For the Association to take a position in these negotiations on the questions of the autonomous tariff and other traditional issues meant an abdication of the possibility of rejecting the traditional arrangements altogether. Yet this is what the Association did in practice, explaining that it was in no position to prevent an agreement desired by the government and of vital interest to agricultural exporters, and that under the circumstances, it should at least have some say in the agreement that was to come about. In fact, by 1905 the minority within the Association in favor of the status quo had convinced even Chorin that a number of problems would have to be worked out before Hungary could embark on an independent customs policy. Among the problems mentioned by Chorin in a speech to the Steering Committee were financial and credit considerations, the export difficulties of the milling industry and agriculture, the need to work out a tariff in order to train workers to fill the jobs that proponents of independence claimed would be created, and the need to promote new industries that would decrease Hungary's reliance on imports.[11] Chorin's argument seems to contradict the declaration at the beginning of the speech that "the Association sees the independent customs area as the only means of creating a powerful industry in Hungary." Nevertheless it is evident of a developing trend within the leadership of the organization to consider an intermediate solution between the status quo and the demand for full independence.

The idea of a compromise was expressed in a pamphlet in 1905 by Endre Scheiber, a publicist on economic matters who was later closely associated with the Association. As an alternative to both the "common customs area" and the "independent customs area," Scheiber proposed a "Hungarian customs area" which would have maintained the common customs of the Monarchy with regard to third countries but would have also permitted certain, more modest tariffs between Austria and Hungary. Thus Hungarian industry would have gained some protection from Austria while Hungary's products, including its agricultural ones, would still have had privileged entry in comparison to those coming from third countries.[12] In the same year, the

Association held an inquiry into the question of Hungary's economic relations with Austria in which the declared guiding principle was that "Hungarian industry must be protected in such a way that the interests of agriculture are also taken into account."[13]

The Association put up no resistance to the conclusion of the decennial economic agreement in 1907 renewing the common customs area for another ten years. However, it viewed this period as one in which preparations for a more satisfactory solution should be made. In 1908, the Association urged the Ministry of Commerce to work out a plan for an eventual customs barrier between Austria and Hungary.[14] Apparently it had in mind an "intermediate" solution similar to Scheiber's. The concept was discussed by the Coalition Government (1906–1909) but was rejected by the Party of of Independence which wanted a clean break.[15]

In 1913 or early 1914 Chorin suggested a serious study of the possibility of a separation. He envisioned a 20–25 year period in which restrictions on tariffs would be gradually lifted until finally Hungary could act with complete independence in its tariff policy towards Austria. The plan would have permitted the simultaneous, gradual raising of Austrian tariffs on Hungarian agricultural exports.[16] An editorial in the *Magyar Gyáripar* contained a veiled attack on Chorin's "fanatical defense" of the concept of the independent customs area which has "become an article of faith," even a "dogma" of the President.[17] Nevertheless, just after the outbreak of World War I, the Association submitted a memorandum to the government outlining the reasons and means by which an intermediate customs barrier should and could be set up in the next decennial agreement due to be concluded in 1917. The memorandum claimed that Hungary would never be able to occupy an equal position with Austria economically unless it could protect its own market. It argued that landowners had wasted the opportunity for modernizing their holdings provided by the common customs area and should no longer be indulged at the expense of industry. The alternative to the common customs area favored by the Association was a moderate one, showing that it did not wish to disrupt the economic community altogether but merely to alter it to serve better the interests of Hungarian industry. The method it favored most was an extension of the surtax system already used for sugar to other products.[18]

Prime Minister István Tisza, a staunch adherent of the arrangements of 1867, was inclined—along with the Ministry of Commerce—

to support the demands for an intermediate customs barrier at the coming negotiations, though primarily out of fiscal and tactical considerations rather than those having to do with the promotion of industry.[19] At the same time, the Ministry of Agriculture was adamantly opposed.[20] However, the negotiations between Austria and Hungary never took place, the two governments having agreed to extend the existing arrangements until the end of World War I.[21]

The demand for an independent customs area, or even its more moderate forms, though important slogans, were never pursued with full determination by the Association. They conflicted with the wishes of some of the most prestigious industrialists and bankers associated with the organization as well as with other, more immediate aims such as the reestablishment of stability in the relations of Austria and Hungary, disrupted by the political crises of Dualism in the early twentieth century. Nevertheless, the sentiment for an independent customs area seems to have been genuine among the majority of the members.

With regard to the external tariffs of the Monarchy as a whole, the Association often claimed that in the absence of an independent customs area, the autonomous tariff or the trade treaties with the West did not have much significance for Hungarian industry. To a great extent this claim was mere rhetoric for it implied that Hungarian industry was making a sacrifice in favor of the interests of Hungarian agriculture and Austrian industry. The fact of the matter was that the protectionism demanded by Austrian industry also served to protect Hungarian industry, especially those branches which exported to Austria. Lajos Láng, Hungary's chief negotiator on tariff matters, noted in his reminiscences that a change took place in the attitude of Hungarian industrialists after 1902. Originally only the iron and machine industries favored protection from third countries. By 1903, most of Hungarian industry had come around to the Austrian view.[22] The Association admitted in a confidential memorandum of 1914 that "the protective tariffs on industrial goods undoubtedly served the interests of Hungarian industry, too." Nevertheless, it proposed to the government that for tactical reasons it demand lower tariffs in some areas such as raw materials so that Austria could be forced to make concessions outside the issue of the autonomous tariff.[23]

While the Association favored high tariffs towards the West, it favored low tariffs towards its Balkan neighbors. In this area, its interests clashed with those of agriculture. The Association saw the role that Hungarian industry should play in international trade to be the processing of raw materials from the Balkans and reexporting them to the West. Thus it demanded the reinstatement of the 'milling traffic" and generally low tariffs on Balkan agricultural products. The constant tariff wars unleashed by the agrarian interests and politicians against Serbia and Romania prevented the import of livestock from these countries for the purposes of fattening, processing and reexport. The Association blamed the development of food industries in the Balkans, which, it feared, were becoming competitors to Hungarian industry, on such tariff wars.[24] It complained in 1910 that industrialists were forced to watch passively while foreign powers conquered the Balkan markets because the governments of Austria and Hungary concerned themselves more with the agrarian interests and with power politics than with the interests of industry.[25] Largely because of agrarian–inspired policies and the Monarchy's political conflicts with Serbia, the share of the Balkans in Hungary's foreign trade fell steadily after 1900. In the 1890s one–third of Hungary's imports had originated from the Balkans; in 1913 only one–seventh did.[26] The export figures showed a similar trend.

The Association worked for the improvement of Hungarian industry's foreign–trade prospects in several ways. Already in its first year of existence it called on the government to organize and promote Hungarian exports to the Balkans and overseas by researching market conditions and giving financial support to exporters.[27] The Association also complained that the diplomacy of the Monarchy was an affair of aristocrats who were insensitive to business interests.[28] It demanded a reform of the personnel and training policies of the Ministry of Foreign Affairs and urged the setting up of a corps of economic attacheés whose tasks would be the promotion of economic contacts.[29]

With regard to Serbia, the attitude of the Association was considerably more conciliatory than that of the common Ministry of Foreign Affairs. When the Ministry tried to justify its opposition of Serbia's attempts to gain a port on the Adriatic by alluding to the industrial interests of the Monarchy, the Association protested vigorously that the industrial interests of the Monarchy warranted trade based on mutually advantageous commercial treaties and were not well served by a belligerent policy on the part of the Monarchy that prevented trade.[30]

It would indeed be a mistake to try to trace the Monarchy's

foreign policy leading to the outbreak of World War I back to the interests of the Monarchy's industry. In 1909 and 1910 when the Monarchy's military spending was steeply increased, the Association complained that the economic benefits of military spending were not commensurate with its cost. It raised the costs of labor and other inputs without spreading its benefits widely to the domestic economy.[31] In a 1911 editorial, the Association urged West European industry to turn against the rapid growth of military spending.[32] Even later, when the economic benefits of rearmament were already evident to many industrialists, the Association complained that the state preferred to supply its military needs from the cheapest possible sources, either foreign or state–owned industries.[33] The complaint shows that in this respect the state was acting out of concerns other than the economic interests of industry.

While it would be a mistake to trace the foreign policy of the Monarchy back to the demands of industry, Hungarian industry was not entirely free of all imperialistic tendencies. Although Hungarian industry played no part in the annexation of Bosnia–Herzegovina in 1908, after the fact, the Association competed vigorously with Austrian industry for the division of the spoils. The complaints of the Association against the "artificially forced" industrialization of the province by the Common Ministry of Finances which administered Bosnia–Herzegovina, and the demand that 50 percent of the raw materials, especially the iron, found in the province should be made available to Hungarian industry, shows that the Association too wanted to take advantage of the situation.[34] Its demands, however, remained unsatisfied.

Hungary's lack of independence in customs policy, the deference of the government to agricultural interests in its dealings with the Balkans and the traditional political rather than economic orientation of the common foreign policy denied Hungarian industry of the full benefits associated in the West with protective tariffs and imperialism. Frustrated in these respects, the other aspects of economic policy were all the more important to the Association.

Government Contracts and the Fourth Industrial Promotion Law

Already in the 1880s and 1890s the Hungarian government pioneered a mix of economic policies which were meant to compensate to some extent Hungary's infant industries for the protection precluded by the common customs area. Prime among such policies was industrial promotion through direct government subsidies and tax exemptions. An updating and expansion of the industrial promotion laws of 1881, 1890, and 1899 was demanded by the Chambers of Commerce and Industry and the National Industrial Federation. One of the most prominent supporters of the concept was József Szterényi, State Secretary in the Ministry of Commerce who presented to the public a draft for a fourth law in 1902. Interestingly enough, the Association was only lukewarm in its support of a new industrial promotions law.[35] It mentioned the issue only rarely in its annual reports, *Közlemények* [Bulletins], before the actual passage of the bill in 1907. Large industry was apparently somewhat apprehensive with regard to certain aims of the bill.

In part, the skepticism towards such means of industrial promotion derived from past experience. The three predecessors of the 1907 law, though ostensibly designed to aid industry, made significant concessions to Hungary's agricultural interests by distributing large sums for the development of agricultural distilleries.[36] This was much regretted by the industrial distillers whose industry suffered from the subsidized competition. They saw their fears justified in the law passed in 1907 and the Association voiced its objections to the aid proposed to agricultural distillers. Similarly, in the case of the handicrafts industry, the Association feared that a new law, like its predecessors, would make concessions which were not beneficial to large industry. In particular, the Association demanded that only those products of handicrafts industry should be supported whose production by large industry would also be eligible for support. The general fears of industry may be seen from a third demand raised in connection with the 1907 law, namely, that no new plants should be subsidized in industries where their competition might "damage" already existing firms.[37]

If fear of competition prevented the Association from giving high priority to the passage of an industrial promotion law, it nevertheless supported the bill once it was under discussion. In several ways it tried to extend it to the support of existing industries: it demanded that existing firms experiencing serious problems through no fault of their own should be given financial aid; that all new firms should be exempt from the assessment of the costs of the building of industrial railroad tracks; and that the expropriations law should be "modernized" to make transportation more efficient. Despite dissatisfaction in these areas, the Association favored industrial promotion for a number of reasons. It realized that the equipping of new industries would create a demand for the products of existing capital–goods industries. In this connection it asked to be advised by the government of impending subsidies in sufficient time to permit it to bring the prospective entrepreneur into contact with possible domestic suppliers of his needs.[38] The intermediary role that the Association could play was a strong attraction of the bill stipulating an Industrial Council of which the Association was to be a member. The Council was to be consulted by the government regarding the approval of petitions for aid. The Association hoped that such a role would enhance its position both within industry and toward the government bureaucracy. It was to be disappointed in these expectations for the Industrial Council was rarely convened.[39]

Though the Association did have its reservations, the principle of industrial promotion was basically in line with its "ideology." It strongly supported the concept of an active government role in the process of industrialization. Chorin claimed:

> The most important factor in the development of every country's industry is the support of the legislature and government, which, through customs, regulations, trade treaties, colonial policies and, finally, through great programs of government purchases guides, the development of industry and insures that the industrial products not sold at home will find markets abroad.[40]

Finally, it was the inclusion of the regulation of government purchases in a manner favored by the Association that made the industrial promotion law irresistible to the organization. A law which would place Hungarian industry at an advantage over "foreign" (including Austrian) firms in the awarding of government contracts and the simultaneous undertaking of public works projects to spur the need for government contracts had been two interrelated major demands of the Association since its foundation. These, rather than government subsidies or tax exemptions to fledgling industries were the means of industrial support preferred by the Association.

Public works and government contracts had been considered tools of an industrial policy already by Gábor Baross. In 1890 Baross claimed:

government contracts are a tremendously potent tool of industrial promotion, one which provides the contractor firm
with a secure foundation and enables it to pursue industrial
goals which otherwise, at least at the outset, would entail
certain risks.[41]

The first ministerial decree regulating government contracts was pro-
mulgated according to Baross' conceptions in 1891 and the first such
law was passed in 1897. A related law of the same year contemplated
a number of public works projects some of which had not yet been
constructed in 1902 when the Association was founded and it strongly
urged their completion.[42]

Furthermore, the Association demanded an increase in government purchases immediately after its founding. The arguments it
used demonstrated an awareness of such a policy's countercyclical effects. After describing the economic, social and political dangers of a
continuing depression, which, the Association observed, had affected
Hungarian industry through no fault of its own, the policy is set forth:

A successful resolution of the crisis is possible only if the
state intervenes with its own initiating forces and provides
the private sector with quick, strong impulses. By placing a
number of large–scale orders and undertaking public works
projects above and beyond those that are standard, it can
provide work for the presently underutilized branches of industry until the point is reached where private enterprise
can once again create a new level of demand.[43]

The Association claimed that all the projects it proposed were
ultimately profitable investments for the state aside from their immediate effects on the economy. Most of them pertained to the modernization of the railroads—which, as the 1904–1912 boom proved,
would indeed have been worthwhile—and the construction of government buildings and other infrastructure in both the capital and the
provinces. The program would have involved spending an additional
300 to 500 million K by the state over a three to four year period.[44]
The efforts of the Association met only with limited success with the
passage of Law II of 1904 under the first István Tisza Government,
when the economy had already begun to recover without the aid of
the law.[45]

Nevertheless, the Association continued to agitate for a revision
of the method of distributing public contracts in a way that would

benefit Hungarian industry. The amounts of money involved in government contracts exceeded by far the amounts given by the government as subsidies or tax exemptions in the industrial promotions laws. According to the Association, the Hungarian government alone spent about 100 million K per year on industrial goods in 1900.[46] This represented about 18 percent of the 567 million K's worth of total industrial output in 1900, to which one would have to add the purchases of local governments, a proportion of the purchases of the common ministries, and, especially, of the common army and navy, to arrive at the total extent of government expenditures.[47] By comparison, the government spent only 1.27 million K on the average annually between 1900 and 1906 on subsidies to factory industry and an annual 4.7 million K between 1907 and 1914.[48] It is understandable, therefore, that the Association paid greater attention to the securing of government contracts than it did to the other aspects of industrial promotions.

The methods used in the campaign for the regulation of government contracts clearly set the Association apart from the older representatives of industrial interests and go far towards explaining its success. In a conscious imitation of British interest organizations, it supported its demands for a new regulation by presenting the economic ministries with a complete legislative proposal. By doing much of the work of the ministries, the Association hoped not only that more of its views would be incorporated into a new law, but that the inertia which at times characterized the Hungarian political process, especially with regard to economic affairs, would thus be overcome.[49]

The final draft of the proposal was based on extensive research and deliberations at all levels of the Association. Preliminary drafts were published in the *Közlemények* so that the membership could comment on them. Surveys of opinion were taken and discussions were held in the various councils.[50] When completed, the proposal stipulated the principles as well as the mechanics of the awarding of government contracts.

The foremost principle of the proposal was that domestic government contracts, including those of the local authorities, should be given whenever possible only to Hungarian producers. The Association rejected the principle of the existing law according to which domestic producers would be given preference only if they were able to equal the offers of their foreign competitors. This gave Austrian industry the chance to underbid Hungarian products, they thought, even when this involved a temporary loss "in order to prevent Hungarian industry from developing."[51]

Furthermore, the Association wished to use the law on government contracts as a means of inducing Hungarian industry to use domestic inputs by requiring the fulfillment of this condition for all goods purchased by the government. In this case, however, the proposal was less severe. It gave the Minister of Commerce the power to waive this requirement in certain cases.[52] It appears that the machine industry was especially interested in this principle while other industries, such as textiles which used foreign machines, were opposed to it.

Another important innovation in the proposal was the creation of a regulatory agency within the Ministry of Commerce to monitor the compliance of governmental bodies with the law and to prepare an annual registry of goods purchased by the public sector.

Finally, the Association insisted that no preference should be given to government–owned industries in the awarding of contracts. The government was itself the owner of several large industrial firms. Most prominent among these were the Hungarian State Iron, Steel and Machine Works (MAVAG), whose main product was locomotives, and the State Iron Works (whose main product was rails), both of which were the second largest firms in their respective branches. The state also owned a number of coal mines which accounted for 7 percent of the total coal production in 1914.[54] The state–owned industries (including ore and salt mines, mints, presses and tobacco factories) employed 11 percent of the industrial labor force and produced 12 percent of total industrial output.[55] The state had acquired many of its holdings in the 1870s or earlier. Most grew into modern industries through the building of the state railroads and other government projects.[46]

The Association opposed the government's operation of those industries which competed with the private sector. It was especially concerned about competition with the state–owned firms for government contracts since the government did have a tendency to favor its own factories run by the Ministry of Commerce. Therefore, one of the demands of the Association was that the proportion of certain government contracts be fixed at the ratio of 75 to 25 in favor of private industry.[57] Another possible solution for controlling competition between the private and public sector was embraced by the Association with the demand that the Army's planned second cannon factory be constructed in Hungary by converting one of the state iron works to this purpose.[58] It is interesting to note that the Association was then more concerned to supply the government with civilian rather than with military goods. By 1914, however, it opposed the setting up of another arms factory by the state, claiming that private industry should be assigned the work.[59]

Hegedüs' previously quoted statement about the independent pursuit of economic policy objectives from politics seems to be borne out by the history of the legislation regulating government contracts. The Association began the drafting of its proposal in 1904 under the rule of the Liberal Party to which it could well have expected to present it. The upheaval in 1905 which swept the Liberal Party from power after thirty years of uninterrupted rule and the installation of an immensely unpopular government by the King did not deter the Association from presenting its completed draft to László Vörös, Minister of Commerce of the new Fejérváry Government. A close cooperation developed between the Ministry of Commerce and the Association with the ministry's effort to work out its own proposal.[60] Elements of the Association's draft were finally incorporated into the industrial promotion law of 1907 under the Coalition, a regime with which the Association was less than comfortable.

Although dissatisfaction with the Liberal Party had helped the Coalition achieve power, the Government sought to attract a broad base of support, including the agrarias, the artisanate, and the industrial bourgeoisie. Thus the industrial promotion law of 1907 substantially raised subsidies and spread them over a broader spectrum of industries including more small industrial firms, agricultural distilleries as well as large industry.[61] Whereas the government had spent an average of 2.3 million K annually between 1899 and 1906, the amount increased to 6.8 million annually between 1907 and 1914, although of this figure only 4.7 million was spent on large industry. The rest went to the artisanate and agriculture.

Though it was more inclusive than the Association would have liked, the law met many of its demands. Most important of all, the law accepted the proposals for the regulation of government contracts. According to Szterényi, by 1913, 89 percent of the government's industrial purchases were produced at home.[62]

A final issue of the question of government contracts to consider related to the orders of the common ministries. Beyond its economic importance, which was considerable, this issue provided the Association with an opportunity to demonstrate to the public its commitment to Hungarian nationalism. Not surprisingly, it was one of the favorite issues of Ferenc Chorin, the one to which he devoted his greatest attention after the initial work of organizing the Association was complete. As a politician turned industrialist with a long history of nationalism somewhat to the "left" of the Liberal Party,[63] Chorin was the appropriate man for the task. After 1905, Chorin was also in a good position to lead the campaign, for as a member of the Upper House he was appointed to the Hungarian Delegation, the legislative organ where the budget of the common ministries was debated.[64]

Basically, the Association demanded that Hungary's share of the common orders be equal to Hungary's share of the "quota," that is, the proportion of the common budget contributed by Hungary. The Association argued that between 1901 and 1904 it had received 53 million K less in military orders than it should have according to the quota, though the Austrians had accepted the principle of common purchases being in the proportion of 34.4 to 65.6.[65] The correction of this disparity, as Chorin pointed out, would mean considerably more to Hungarian industry than the 3 to 4 million K given annually to industry in subventions under the industrial promotions law.[66]

By 1908, Hungarian industry's share in the deliveries to the common army had risen to 35.7 percent. This was still below the new quota, which had been raised in 1907 to 36.4 percent, but considering the annual 6 percent increase in military spending, Hungary's position had greatly improved. In its 1909 annual report the Association proudly announced that its previous efforts were beginning to bear fruit, and domestic industry was achieving parity with Austrian in military contracts.[67]

Thus, the Association was instrumental in increasing substantially the share of Hungarian industry's public contracts at all levels of government. In 1909 the Association central office praised the provincial branches for their contribution to this effort at the local levels, also.[68] Clearly, government purchases played an important role in Hungary's industrialization, and the Association deserves much credit for obtaining a large part of these contracts for Hungarian industry.

Railroad Policy

One of the most important means by which the state promoted industrialization was through its railroad policy. The state had attracted capital into railroad building after 1867 by guaranteeing a minimum return on investment. In the 1880s and early 1890s, following the German example, the state embarked on a program of nationalization of the railroads which on the whole were unprofitable for private capital. Recognizing the importance of the railroads to both agriculture and industry, the government was willing to assume the burden of running them. As it turned out, by unifying the system and extending it, the government was able to make the Hungarian State Railroads (MÁV) a profitable operation by the 1890s.[69]

Under these circumstances, the railroads could be used as a form of economic promotion and as a substitute for tariff protection towards Austria. At first, preferential rates were given to agricultural exports as a compensation for the falling international prices. After 1887, under the leadership of Baross, the system was extended to sugar and then to a number of other industrial goods.[70]

In the 1890s, the government added more than 500 km of railroad track yearly to the main lines, so that by 1896, there were 14,876 kilometers of track in Hungary (including local lines).[71] However, by the turn of the century the state railroads turned out to be not profitable. In 1902, therefore, the government announced its plans to raise the rates for the first time since 1891. The proposed increase would have added 5 percent to all fares.[72]

The matter was discussed at the first meeting of the Association's Executive Committee on November 12, 1902. The Managing Directorate presented the Committee with two alternatives: either to oppose the hike altogether, or to ask the Ministry of Finance, which administered the railroads, to arrange an inquiry to study the elaboration of an economically more "appropriate" scheme that would differentiate between the freight on which rates should not be raised. While some leaders such as Sándor Hatvany–Deutsch were not opposed to a hike so long as it was not general, the executive committee nonetheless decided that the Association should oppose any hike altogether regardless of its structure, and if this were rejected, it should demand the holding of an inquiry.[73]

It is not clear whether it was the arguments of the Association concerning industry's inability to bear a rate hike in the midst of a depression that finally deterred the government from its plans. Undoubtedly the political instability within the ruling classes in the early years of the decade had much do to with the government's decision. Be that as it may for the time being, industry escaped a hike.[74]

In the period of recovery following 1905, the growth of the railroads did not keep up with the demands generated by a rapidly expanding economy. Even though the total length of track increased from 14,876 km in 1896 to 21,840 km in 1913 and the number of locomotives increased from 2,436 to 4,451 in the same period, businessmen continued to complain about chronic deficiencies in the transport system.[75] During the peak season there was a serious shortage of wagons which was an impediment to the expansion of the Hungarian mining sector.[76] Complaints about this shortage were voiced constantly.[77] The Association even set up a mechanism for collecting and transmitting specific complaints about railroad service to the government.[78]

A week–long strike of railroad employees, traditionally supporters of the opposition Independence Party, took place in April 1904. Though the leaders were arrested and many participants were inducted into the Army by the Tisza Government, the Coalition, which came to power in April 1906, granted a considerable increase in wages and improvement of working and living conditions for railroad employees.[79] Higher wages, further modernization of the railroads and the generally inflationary tendency made the raising of railroad tariffs imperative.

In 1908, the National Association of Iron and Machine Manufacturers even recognized the necessity of the rate hike "to pay the costs of the higher wages granted after the strike," though they opposed the amount of the hike proposed by the government.[80] In the following year, the Association also came around to accept the necessity of an increase but demanded that the government differentiate between various industries according to the ability of each to pay and remain competitive with their Austrian rivals.[81] The following year the Association reported success in their lobbying efforts. On the whole, long distances were favored over short ones and the tariff on coal was kept relatively low. A number of other industries were also promised exemptions. Considering that the general price level had increased about 23 percent since 1891, even the government's proposed hike of 5 to 7 percent was moderate, indeed. In all likelihood, the Association was able to reduce the expected added revenue of 8 million K still further through its bargaining. Except for a conflict between the provincial mills and those of the capital, which the Association failed to resolve, most other groups accepted the arrangements worked out by the Association.[82] The new rates went into effect on January 1, 1910.

The slight increase in tariffs achieved under the Coalition by the State Railroads failed to meet its needs. After the return to power of the men previously associated with the Liberal Party and after 1910 functioning under the label of the Party of National Work, the new government announced its plans for a further round of fare increases. It also refused to renew past 1910 most of the exemptions granted by the Coalition. This time the Association protested vehemently but the government would not even consider its recommendations.[83]

The Association complained bitterly about the party that it had helped to bring to power.[84] Yet, the behavior of the government is understandable. It was in a much more secure position politically than the Coalition had been. It could afford to treat the issues relating to the State Railroads on their own merits and given the deteriorating financial situation of the railroads and the needs for its modernization, which the Association freely admitted, a further round of fare increases was in order.

Though after 1910 the Association was less successful in this regard than before, it should be noted that transportation costs were still relatively low in Hungary and the modernization of the railroads was ultimately more important to industry than the maintenance of low rates during an inflationary period.

The adamant refusal of the government to grant an extensively differentiated rate hike in 1912 might indicate a shift in at least one aspect of the former railroad policy. Austrian industry had never ceased to complain about the Hungarian government's use of preferential railroad rates as a means of substituting for the absence of a tariff barrier. The new Austrian railroad tariffs which took effect on January 1, 1910, adopted the methods pioneered by the Hungarians. The Association complained that some of the new rates would have the effect of a prohibitive tariff against Hungarian goods and that on the whole, Hungarian industry's annual transport costs would be raised by 10 million K.[85] It seems possible that the negotiations which ensued between the Austrian and Hungarian State Railroads made both governments less willing to structure railroad rates so as to function as a substitute for a tariff barrier.

Can the course of action followed by the railroad administration be construed as a retreat altogether from Baross' policy of using the railroads to promote economic growth? A statement made by the Minister of Finance, János Teleszky, might support such an interpretation:

In the beginning, when our country was faced with the problem of actually having to create a modern economy, it was the government that had to take the lead and assume the role of an initiator, commander and supporter while the society could only begin to move slowly indeed and only with the help of the crutches offered it by the government. But, gentlemen, this had to be so and already we can observe the fortunate results. Society began to gradually emancipate itself from the crutches and support of the government. . . . The past ten years have been extremely bright and I don't think any of us would have foreseen that our industry would prosper as well as it did in these ten years. . . .. I think the time has come for society to take the lead and for government to merely follow (lively interjections: ah, not yet!) because the government, even with the best intentions, will not be in a position to support the functioning of society with as much force as the various factors of society are able to muster through their own energies.[86]

Clearly, the policies that were appropriate at the beginning of industrialization could not be followed without alteration at a more mature state of development. Yet, the government did not turn against industrialization. Teleszky, like most of the leaders of the 1910–1914 period, had worked personally with Baross before the turn of the century and shared his aims. At the same time, as Minister of Finance, his primary responsibility was to the solid foundation of state finances. It was clear that the Association would henceforth have to fight hard for support that used to be given almost as a matter of course some twenty years previously. Despite the rate increases, it should be kept in mind, that the government did continue to use the railroads as a means of supporting the economy. The profitability of the railroads was never high enough to make it an attractive private investment. The dispute between the government and the Association concerned the extent to which the government should assume the burden of subsidizing the railroads.

Cartelization

The determination of the Association to maintain and expand the government's active participation in the economy has been evident in the issues we have discussed so far. Arguing that industrialization was necessary if Hungary were to keep pace with the more advanced nations both culturally and politically and pointing out the difficulties of industrialization in the face of Austrian and foreign competition, the Association could demand and to a large extent obtain such policies as direct industrial promotion through subsidies and tax incentives, an increased level of public contracts through an expansion of government–sponsored infrastructural and other building programs, and reservation of public contracts for Hungarian industry, and the maintenance of low rates on the State Railroads.

In other areas of economic life, however, the Association, on the basis of very similar arguments, opposed government intervention. Governmental regulation of safety standards, hours of work, certain environmental issues, and cartel policy belonged to this category. In 1906, for example, the Association demanded that the government should repeal a Law dating from 1875 banning the use of tar–based dyes in the food industries. "It is necessary [to change the Law] if our candy and liquor industries are to be competitive [abroad]."[87] Similarly, the Association opposed the prohibition of nightwork for women, stringency of sewage disposal regulations and numerous similar issues.[88]

The arguments advanced by the Association are fairly obvious. Regulations would raise the private costs of industrial production and, would thereby adversely affect industrialization, a national priority. In most instances, the government complied with the wishes of industry, which it could well afford to do since opposition was largely confined to the unenfranchised and still poorly organized working class.

The issue of government control of cartels presents a more complex set of questions. In this case, too, the Association claimed that cartels were necessary for the maintenance of industrial progress. The Association argued that in the era of free competition prior to the 1870s, firms sought to increase their profits by decreasing their average costs of production. They therefore tried to produce in ever greater quantities. This led to overproduction and caused the depression of the 1870s. Industrialists were forced to recognize the necessity of coordinating their activities to protect their investments. To counter the accusation that cartels restricted economic development, the Association pointed to the case of Germany where "in the era of cartels, the output of raw iron grew from 3 million tons in 1880 to over 10 million in 1903, which was more than the production of Great

Britain."[89] They warned that "those who oppose cartels forget that the flourishing of industry serves not only the interests of industrialists but also of the many workers . . . and the nation as a whole. In the final analysis, it benefits the consumers as well."[90] As in so many other instances of economic policy the case for cartels was presented also in terms of the Austrian threat. "Our industry, unprotected by tariffs against Austria, is forced to rely upon sane agreements between producers."[91]

The validity of these arguments was contested by broad segments of the politically active population. Though cartels existed in such industries as metallurgy, sugar, petroleum and flour milling already since the late eighties and early nineties, the few years following 1900 saw the mushroom–like growth of at least 82 cartels encompassing most branches of Hungarian industry.[92] Agrarian propaganda on the right and socialist propaganda on the left helped to inflame the natural passions of consumers against the cartels which allegedly either directly or indirectly raised the prices and restricted the supply of many consumer goods.[93] Cartelization, claimed the agrarian publicist István Bernát, was one of the evils of a "mercantilist" economic policy and one of the main causes for the emigration of the Hungarian poor.[94]

> The lumber cartel's effects on prices are felt throughout the economy. It raises the costs of production, for wood is used in every branch. It raises the cost of housing by making construction more expensive. As with all cartels, its effects pass like a wave through the entire economy . . . to the ultimate detriment of the workers,

wrote Jenő Varga, a socialist critic, in his 1912 pamphlet on "The Hungarian Cartels."[95] Criticism of cartels was widespread also in the press oriented towards small and medium sized business. The newspaper of the smaller financial institutions, *Hungarian Finance*, claimed that support of the Hungarian iron cartel, which in 1902 had agreed with its Austrian counterpart not to introduce any new products for ten years and to prevent the establishment of new firms in the industry within the Monarchy, was "incompatible with the aims of the Association to promote the development of Hungarian industry."[96] Occasionally, opposition to cartelization was voiced by some of the lesser members of the Association itself, though this was never reflected in the organization's official policy.[97]

A cartel is an arrangement between several firms in an industry to coordinate price or production policies in an attempt to extract monopoly profits. The motive to form cartels derives from the fact that an industry that is monopolized can obtain a greater profit than one which is competitive. In the long run, under a regime of perfect competition, profits, exclusive of rent, are at the minimum normal level, that is, at what might be considered zero for the industry as a whole. If the existing firms, however, can join together to keep new firms out of the industry, they can maximize industry profits by restricting their output.

While the motive to form a cartel or, even better, for one firm to monopolize the industry may be generally present, cartels can only be formed under certain circumstances. The major impediments to the formation or survival of cartels are the entry of "interlopers," and the actions of "chiselers." Interlopers are new firms which enter the industry and by adding their output to that of the cartel, they end up lowering the cartel price. If they can, interlopers will enter until all monopoly profits disappear. "Chiselers" are firms within the cartel that do not adhere to the cartel rules. By slightly lowering their prices, these firms can greatly increase their share of the market and, thereby, their profits. If, in response, other firms follow suit, the cartel will break down and monopoly profits will disappear. Thus cartels can be formed effectively only when barriers to entry can be erected and when the number of firms in an industry is small enough so that "chiselers" can be relatively easily detected.

Economies of scale led to the emergence of large firms in such industries as metallurgy, coal mining, electrical equipment, railroad-wagon production, petroleum refining and even brewing. The level of concentration was quite high in several of these industries already by the turn of the century and even increased thereafter (Table 4.1).

In 1900 the top .5 percent of industrial firms produced 5 percent of the total industrial output and in 1910 .9 percent produced 70 percent.[98]

Economies of scale deriving from technology do not by themselves account for the high level of concentration. In Hungary, as in Austria, financial factors also played a part. Two recent studies have described the manner in which Austrian banks encouraged joint stock companies whose stock they held to enter into cartels.[99] Contemporary observers made similar observations.[100] Banks wished to prevent

Table 4.1
Concentration in Selected Hungarian Industries

Industry	No. of Top Companies	c. 1900 Controlled % of Industry	c. 1913 Controlled % of Industry
Coal mining	5	63.3	70.7
Metallurgy	3	63.9	95.0
Brewing	4	53.9	62.8

Source: Iván Berend and György Ránki, *Magyarország gyáripara, 1900–1914* [Hungarian Industry, 1900–1914], (Budapest: Szikra, 1955), 81–82.

competition among "their" several companies and wished to benefit from the monopoly profits earned by the industry as a whole. Certain banks concentrated on gaining influence in particular industries. For example, the Pesti Kereskedelmi Bank [Commerce Bank of Pest] held a dominant position in the machine tool and brick industries.[101] Rudolf Sieghart, who became President of the Austrian Boden Creditanstalt in 1910 expressed similar aims, stating that while his predecessor, Taussing had been interested in large industries whatever their product, "he forgot that the industrial policy of a bank must . . . follow definite goals towards the creation of groups which complement each other . . .[102] Clearly, a bank that held stocks in the firms of a cartelized industry would stand to gain from their increased profits. Furthermore, bank lending policies, with their high aversion to risk, made entry into an industry more difficult since a prospective entrepreneur would generally need the support of banks to raise the necessary capital for a venture.

Another factor promoting cartelization in Hungary was the existence of cartels in Austria. The absence of tariffs between Austria and Hungary meant that cartel agreements could have meaning only if they incorporated competing firms in both parts of the Monarchy. Thus, Austrian cartels would strive for the cartelization of Hungarian industry, often with the intermediation of the large banks. As in the case of the iron cartel, generally a separate cartel would be formed in each country and the two would agree upon the amount that the one could export into the territory of the other.[103] The more rapid rate of growth of Hungarian production occasionally led to conflicts between the two cartels. In 1900, the Rimamurányi Iron Works unleashed a price war against the Austrian cartel through a number of subsidiary firms which were not cartel members. With the mediation of the Austrian and Hungarian banks a new agreement was reached in 1902 raising the Hungarian export quota to Austria by almost 50 percent.[104] At least twenty-seven Monarchy-wide cartels existed not only in such concentrated branches as metallurgy or petroleum but also in glass manufacture, candle making and even whip handles.[105]

Of course cartels in competitive industries were extremely unstable as the history of the glass cartel demonstrates. The organization, which had been in existence as a division of the Association since 1902 under the name of the National Organization of Glass Manufacturers was dissolved as a cartel (though it continued to function as an interest group) numerous times and generally reformed with the inclusion of smaller manufacturers. In 1914 the agreement between the Austrian and Hungarian glass cartels was again in force.[106] The survival of such cartels, however tenuous, would tend to indicate that considerations of security outweighed the attractions of a short-term increase in profits for most cartel members. This guild-like mentality must also be taken into account when considering the prevalence of cartels in Hungary, especially among the more traditional industries. The relatively slow appearance of interlopers on the other hand might indicate that the monopoly profits extracted by such cartels were quite low.

The role of the Association in the process of cartelization may be divided into two aspects: that which sought to coordinate the activities of the cartels within the industrial sector; and that which faced outwards, defending cartels from government intervention and hostile public opinion.

The Association, whose most active members were often prominent men in the affairs of cartels as well, saw itself as the mediator of inter-industrial and intra-industrial disputes arising from the operations of cartels. A Cartel Committee was set up in 1905 on a permanent basis for the task of "extending, perfecting and administering existing agreements" and of insuring that these are consonant with the general interests of industry."[107] The Committee's first president was the industrialist, Sándor Hatvany-Deutsch, and the membership was a roll call of the most illustrious names in Hungarian industry. The first agreement worked out by the Committee was an arrangement for providing a preferential price by the iron cartel to the Hungarian ship–building industry, (understandably enough, since the ship builders were in a better position to obtain substitutes than most other consumers).[108] This agreement was well publicized to demonstrate the nationalist tendencies of the Committee. Unfortunately, the Association decided thereafter to keep the details of the work of the Committee secret, as it later reported in 1910.[109] The Committee was evidently quite active between 1906 and 1910 in an effort to smooth out differences between the coal producers and their customers who complained about the cartel's assigning of customers to suppliers as a means of enforcing its quota system.[110]

Alongside the Cartel Committee which could deal with cartels that were independent of the Association, the industry–specific divisions of the Association also sought to "improve the prices forced down by competition."[111] In 1914, there were six such divisions, representing the brandy, yeast, lumber, central heating, paper and alcohol industries. Finally, the formally independent but institutionally "associated interest groups" of the Association also functioned at times as cartels or promoters of cartelization. There were twenty–two such groups associated with the Association in 1914.[112] In addition to the cartels formed by the Association of Glass Manufacturers, the National Association of Iron and Machine Manufacturers prepared a plan in 1908 for the cartelization of the machine industry. The plan envisioned a greater degree of product specialization for each firm and the determination of production quotas.[113] However, the projected cartel did not materialize. The machine industry proved too deconcentrated and unspecialized for cartelization despite the renewed efforts of the Association and the Kereskedelmi Bank in 1912.[114]

The determination of the Association to act as a promoter of cartelization may in part be explained by the overlapping industrial and banking connections of its leaders. Men like Chorin, Leó Lánczy, Manfréd Weisz, Pál Elek and numerous others occupied important positions in both worlds. Generally, they were presidents or members of the boards of several banks, including the large ones, and of several industrial firms. Moreover, the coordination of potential conflict within the industrial sector was deemed important to the functioning of the Association as a potent political interest group. The less open conflict there was within industry, the more effectively the Association could function and the more convincing could be its case for a benevolent government cartel policy.

The political issue was joined in December 1905 when a court, the Royal Curia, refused to enforce a cartel agreement on the grounds that such agreements, though not illegal, "violated proper morality and were opposed to the public interest."[115] After debating the matter in a meeting of the Steering Committee, the Association decided that the issue should be fought in the courts or through personal channels without attempting to gain passage of a cartel law in Parliament "as the strength of the agrarian forces in the political parties is well known."[116]

The principle on which the Association based its demand of government non-intervention was that

> cartels are necessary and justified if during the favorable part of the business cycle prices rise to a level at which a decent profit can be earned so as to balance out the losses that might be incurred during a depression. Only in cases involving the most flagrant and persistent violation of this principle would government action be justified."[117]

The official position of the government by 1913 was similar. Though it differed slightly in tone, it too defended the right of cartels to exist and indicated a *laissez-faire* attitude on condition that cartels behave decently. Finance Minister János Teleszky, replying to an agrarian critic in the Lower House of Parliament in 1913, declared:

> A cartel can be good or it can be very bad. . . . A cartel should not be condemned as such, but rather it should be judged according to its effects. Insofar as it brings about the organization of a branch of production, enabling that branch to stand up to foreign competition, and insofar as it prevents overproduction and lowers the costs of production, the existence of a cartel can only have fortunate effects. However, if it results in the extraction of a tribute from the consumers by the producers, if it levies a tax on the consumers, this is naturally a harmful formation from which we must protect ourselves.[118]

The propaganda and political efforts of the Association were aimed at maintaining the status quo, which on the whole was a favorable one of benign neglect. Except for the refusal of the Royal Curia to enforce cartel agreements, there seem to have been no instances of an unfavorable action on the part of government towards cartels. In fact, by 1912 the Association reported a favorable change in the attitude of the courts as well.[119]

In certain cases the Association asked for government support for the formation of a cartel or for regulating entry into a cartelized industry. Such help was granted in the case of the alcohol industry in 1913 when the licensing of alcohol producing industrial firms was instituted.[120]

To what can we attribute the generally favorable cartel policy of the government in the period between 1902 and 1914? This is noteworthy in light of the fact that the various administrations were all dependent to a significant extent on the support of the agrarian forces critical of cartelization. What balanced the impetus to regulate coming from these forces? Part of the explanation lay, no doubt, in the fact that the Hungarian government, following in the footsteps of Germany and Austria, judged the effects of cartels to be efficacious for economic growth; that is, it accepted the basic argument of the Association.

Cartel behavior is generally associated with fairly stable prices while competition within an oligopoly tends to cause great fluctuations. Price stability can enhance economic growth by permitting firms to plan with a greater degree of certainty. Cartelized firms in Hungary seem to have enjoyed fairly high and stable profits.[121] This, in turn, attracted foreign capital into the country. About one–third of the capital invested in Hungarian factory industry was imported.[122] This was a major source of economic growth.

Cartels are often also credited with stimulating research and innovation. Funds for research are made available from the increased profits and cartels generally tolerate the competition of new products. This theory is much debated in the economic literature and the data we possess for Hungary do not suffice to test a hypothesis in this regard. In the electrotechnical industry Hungary was at the highest international level and contributed many innovations in electrical rail traction, electrical generation, transformation, motor construction and incandescent lighting, most of it associated with the Ganz Electrical Company, which was a prominent leader of cartelization. On the other hand, cases can be cited, as in the iron industry, where cartel members agreed to forego the introduction of new products.[123] It may also be significant that the average number of patents granted annually in Hungary during the boom of 1906–1910 was 31 percent lower than the average number granted in the 1891–1895 period, though of course this earlier period coincided with the great boom of industrialization.[124]

Without further study one cannot conclude whether by promoting cartelization, the Association and the government were serving the best interests of industrialization or only the interests of industrialists. Unlike the Austrian Ministry of Commerce, which in 1912 held an exhaustive inquiry into the workings of cartels, (which, however, did not lead to changes in policy) the Hungarian government seems to have accepted the Association's position without reservation.[125]

The stance of the government should be viewed from a political perspective. Though agrarians opposed cartels, it was not a question of vital importance to them but, as the Association pointed out, merely a tactical weapon.[126] Other opponents of cartels—such as small industrialists, consumers or socialists—did not yet have much influence in Hungarian political life. However, to the great industrialists and bankers whose support was critical to the government, the unhindered operation of cartels was a matter of the most serious concern. The Association helped to transmit this concern to the government whose unequivocal support of cartels demonstrated the influence of large industry in this issue.

Social Policy

Government policy with regard to the social welfare of the working class can be seen as another aspect of economic policy. It affects labor costs, making it either more or less expensive to the employer depending often on who is to pay for the costs of a particular policy. Social policy can also improve the quality and, therefore, the productivity of labor, a consideration that ought to have and sometimes did enter into the calculations of industrialists. Finally, social policy can improve the relations between labor and capital, thus reducing the frequency of disruptive industrial conflicts and the threat of political upheaval.

The nature of the Hungarian labor market impelled many industrialists to consider seriously these connections between social policy and industrialization. The labor market was characterized by both high unemployment and a shortage of workers.

Although national unemployment statistics were not yet collected, one can get a sense of the degree of industrial unemployment from the figures of the Employment Service of the City of Budapest.

Of the approximately 84,000 workers who reported for employment in 1901 only about 36 percent were actually placed.[127] In depressed years such as 1901, the number of unemployed industrial workers reached about 100,000 in Hungary or over 15 percent of the industrial labor force. Even in years of high employment there were about 35,000 to 40,000 unemployed workers or 4 or 5 percent of the industrial labor force. Generally, the unemployed were found in the unskilled trades for which the vast pool of the rural underemployed provided a source of supply.[128]

In many trades, however, there was a critical shortage of skilled workers, which was especially severe in the years of prosperity characterizing most of our period. Labor shortage was a problem for many of Hungary's most important industries, such as iron and metallurgy, machines, electricity, glass, stone, cement, furniture, leather, textiles, milling, sugar and printing industries. The disparity in the conditions of supply and demand for the skilled and unskilled trades is shown by the fact that while the wages of unskilled workers were extremely low, those of the skilled workers were quite high. In 1910 about 18.8 percent of industrial employees earned less than 10 K per week while 5.8 percent earned more than 40 K. Those earning the lower figure lived in the squalid conditions typical of the worst urban areas, while those earning the higher figure shared in the comforts of lower management.[129] At the lower end of the scale, wages tended towards those prevailing in agriculture, while at the upper end they were influenced by the level of wages in the countries to which labor tended to emigrate, such as the United States.

Emigration exacerbated the problems of training and supplying a labor force and of building an industry that would be competitive with those of the more advanced countries of the West. Emigration from Hungary had been increasing gradually ever since the 1890s. At the beginning of that decade the annual figure stood only around 100 persons. In the course of the 1890s the figure reached 20,000 to 30,000 per year and then increased suddenly at the end of the 1890s to 90,000 to 100,000. By 1907 about 200,000 people were leaving Hungary annually.[130] Between 1899 and 1913 about 1.2 million people left the country (exclusive of Croatia) and about 86 percent of these emigrated to the United States.[131] About 13.4 percent of those who emigrated in 1905 had been employed in industry and mining, but the bulk of the emigrants had been employed in agriculture, yet the loss to industry and mining was proportionately greater. About .5

percent of the agricultural labor force left in 1905 but 5.2 percent of those who had been engaged in mining and industry emigrated in that year.[132]

The concern of the Association with the problem of emigration and the labor shortage was highlighted in 1907 when it organized a five–day–long inquiry into the subject. The Association considered the preparations for this inquiry and activities connected with the issue to have been the central theme of its work that year. In addition to Association members, the participants of the inquiry included government officials, representatives of other industrial interest organizations, economists and other "experts," some mildly "radical" journalists as well as a few agrarians. However, no workers (or representatives of workers) had been invited.[133]

The analyses offered to account for the origins of the problem and the suggestions proposed for its correction spanned a broad spectrum of attitudes. The study of emigration had been a concern of Lóránt Hegedüs, already before his connection with the Association, indeed before the founding of the organization. In his sociological studies Hegedüs focused on discovering the causes of emigration in general rather than on studying its effects on industry. He found these causes to lie primarily in the problems of the countryside, specifically, in the barriers to social mobility and to the acquisition of land by the peasantry created by the institution of *main morte*. Hegedüs' concerns were expressed to the inquiry and gave a somewhat more anti–agrarian tone to the proceedings than that held by some industrialists.

Zoltán Lázár, speaking on behalf of the Rimamurány Iron Works, pointed out that Hegedüs' concerns did not necessarily serve the best interests of industry for if it were to become easier for the peasantry to acquire land and if social mobility in the agricultural sector were increased, wages in industry would rise even further. Indeed, workers preferred to work on the land even at lower wages than what they could get in industry. Typically, the spokesman of the Rimamurány urged the most authoritarian measures for dealing with the problem. He wanted the government to make emigration more difficult by refusing to grant passports to youths liable to military service, by abrogating the contract of the Cunard Line which shipped many emigrants to the United States from the Monarchy's ports, and through similar measures considered draconic by many industrialists and government officials at the time.[134]

At the end of the inquiry, the Association summarized the demands and proposals with which the majority of those present had indicated an agreement. These measures consisted of two categories: recommendations for action by the government and those considered the responsibility of industrialists. Generally the demands emphasized positive social policy rather than restrictions on freedom of movement. The tasks assigned to the government were that the institution of government emigration officers who had served to give guidance to those wishing to emigrate be abolished, that secret emigration agents be ruthlessly prosecuted and that anti-emigration propaganda be spread to the population. Income taxes should be reformed, giving tax relief to workers and instituting a progressive income tax applied equally to all sectors of the economy (meaning also the large landlords). Costs of food consumed by workers should be lowered by abolishing or lowering tax on certain meats and beer and raising tax on distilled alcohol. Institutions of welfare—such as state-run old age pensions—should be expanded, industry should be fully promoted, free public education extended, and land reform implemented. To "society" (as opposed to government) the Association recommended that employers should insure clean, healthy dwellings and set up consumer cooperatives for workers, raise wages as far as economically possible, and provide workers with welfare institutions such as schools, hospitals and vacationing institutions.[135]

Along with these proposals we should mention the support given by the Association to the principle of compulsory health and accident insurance for workers and to the extension of the suffrage. These two issues were not mentioned in the resolutions of the inquiry on emigration because of a lack of concensus on how best to deal with them. Though the Association had supported the reform and extension of the existing health insurance laws, there was some debate over the reform passed in 1907.[136] Judged by the standards of the time, the new law created a progressive system of health and disability insurance. Medical benefits included twenty weeks of free medical treatment and medication for workers and their families plus twenty weeks of sick pay at a rate of 50 percent of the regular wage. In case of industrial accidents, free medical care was available after the eleventh week of an injury, and after the fourteenth a monthly payment was made for the duration of the disability. For a full disability, the annual payment was 60 percent of the yearly earnings. In case of death, the widow received 20 percent of annual income and children under sixteen received 15 percent for a maximum of 30 percent. If the deceased was the supporter of older parents, they also received 20 percent annually.

The premiums for the health insurance were set at 2 to 4 percent of salary and were to be contributed equally by the employer and the employee. The premium for the accident insurance was to be paid in full by the employer; its amount was to be determined by the central administration of the insurance on the basis of a danger index of the firm.

The administration of the insurance was carried out by the National Worker's Insurance Office and the National Worker's Health and Accident Insurance Fund. These had district and company branches which were run on a parity basis by workers and employers.[137]

Some industrialists objected to the increased burdens placed on them by the insurance. What opponents of the reform resented most, however, were not so much the increased costs for the employers as the administrative organization of the insurance. Many felt that the centrally determined premium payments would lead to high administrative costs and to "injustices." Industrialists also criticized the "politization" of the insurance through the joint worker–employer administration, especially of the Central Fund. While pointing out that cooperation with labor in such matters as insurance was the best weapon against the excessive demands of the socialists, the Association also warned the government that if the insurance were to be "saved" those aspects inspiring the strongest antipathy of industrialists would have to be corrected.[138] Conflicts between the various views within industry persisted on this question throughout the period, reflecting the different attitudes that existed within industry on the social question. The Association tended to side with the more liberal camp as well as to try to mediate between the two.[139]

There was a similar conflict within industry concerning the movement for the extension of suffrage to the working class. The Association did not take an official position on this matter in 1907 at the time of the inquiry on emigration. Later, it was to lend its support to this movement with certain restrictions and reservations. This issue will be discussed at greater length in Part II. At this point we should merely note that the Association's proposals on the problem of emigration, its position on the extension of the suffrage and on health and disability insurance show that in many ways it sought an accommodation with the working class by recognizing the legitimacy of its demands for an improved standard of living, greater security and political rights.

On financial issues, however, the attempts of the Association to translate its theoretical support into action received little support from industry. When, at the initiative of Manfréd Weisz, owner of one of Hungary's largest metallurgical and munitions firms, the Association helped to set up a joint–stock public utility for the building of workers' dwellings, investors showed little interest in the company.[140] Eventually, the Association transferred the responsibility for the housing problem from private industry to central and local governments.[141] This attitude of the Association was typical of its social policy. It recognized the necessity for social policy but wanted government to bear most of its costs.

Despite its often progressive attitude and actions, the Association also supported the specific conservative demands of its members. It opposed the "interference" of government factory inspectors.[142] It fought for the repeal of certain health codes such as those connected with the processing of animal furs.[143] It supported the demand of the Association of Iron and Machine Works for the revocation of discount local–railroad passes to workers who quit their jobs.[144]

While recognizing the rights of workers to unionize, the Association voiced its support after 1906 for the formation of employers' associations as a counterweight to the unions. In the words of Hegedüs: "All signs indicate that in the present century the economic system of societies will rest on this dual organization of labor and capital."[145] In 1907, in two rather important cases, the Association succeeded in defeating strikes by showing the way to the organization of the employers.[146], and in 1908, it formed a Section for Employers' Associations which, nevertheless, remained inactive during the year— supposedly "because of the relative calm in labor relations traceable to the effects of the depression in America."[147] Indeed, the section seems to have remained inactive for the rest of the period. In 1908, the Social Democratic Party daily, *Népszava*, even praised the Association for not supporting the unaffiliated Central Employers' Association, called by the *Népszava* a "League of Hounds." The *Népszava* praised the more "modern" character of the Association which, it claimed, need not resort to the provocative methods of the "League of Hounds," "whose aims are clearly to break up the unions."[148] The Association seems to have played only a peripheral part in the organization of employers' associations.

In general, the position taken by the Association on social policy issues tended to be progressive. The explanation for this lay partly in the fact that many Hungarian large industrialists, such as József Hatvany–Deutsch, the prime proponent of the original insurance reforms within the Association, and Manfréd Weisz, who was active on the housing issue, held progressive views. This was also true of the Managing Director, Lóránt Hegedüs, who helped spread the notion among industrialists that a progressive social policy was in their own best interest. However, the leadership of the Association was guided in this direction by political considerations as well.

The demands of the Association for economic policies such as the ones we have outlined met with only partial success. In several cases— most notably foreign trade, railroad policy, and social policy—the Association's goals were not fully realized. Even in the areas where its success was greater—as with industrial promotion—the treatment of Hungarian industry in government purchases and, most clearly, in cartel policy, the victories of the Association depended in large measure on its struggle with other interest groups.

We have presented in this section examples of some of the most prominent methods used by the Association to convince the authorities that it was a spokesman for industry and that it knew what the best interests of industry were. These methods included the compilation of statistical data, conducting opinion polls of the membership and holding inquiries on various subjects. Recommendations were made to the proper authorities through detailed memoranda often containing draft law proposals. Through such methods a relationship was built between the authorities concerned with specific areas of administration and the Association whereby administrators viewed it as a factor helpful in the proper fulfillment of their administrative tasks. This type of relationship has been called by political scientists a "clientela" relationship, which is one factor determining the degree of influence an organized interest group can have on policy.

Another factor on which such influence depends is political. This second type is a "parentela" relationship defined as the perception of politicians that the given interest group belongs to their political camp or party.[149] The Association sought to maximize its influence through the political dimension as well as the professional one. Parentela relationships, or the alliance of interest groups with political parties, however, are not based simply on opportunism—though this may enter into the picture—but also on a certain degree of congruence of interests. In the next part of the study we shall follow the efforts of the Association to form political alliances that would help it to promote the interests of industry. As we shall see, these efforts were directed not only towards the established holders of power but, because of a dissatisfaction with the policies of the latter, also toward such other forces as the working class and the opposition on the left.

Chapter 5
THE DECLINE OF THE LIBERAL PARTY
1902–1906

It stands to reason that an organization as important as the Association could not avoid involvement in the political arena. The era was marked by the crises of Dualism and of Liberalism. The political atmosphere was charged with the clash of the forces attempting to conserve both Dualism and Liberal–Party rule—often with little regard for the sacrifice of liberal principles that this involved—and those, both within and outside the traditional ruling establishment, on the left and on the right, who claimed to offer an alternative.[1] At a time of such fundamental change, business circles could not be indifferent as to which groups of men and ideas were to lead Hungary.

In a sense, every public policy position taken by the Association was a political one if it involved a struggle for influence in the acts of the government. Yet in this section we shall be concerned with a more limited sense of the term political, one more in line with the common usage. We are interested in the support or opposition, the degree of proximity or distance expressed in the statements or behavior of the Association with regard to the various major groups vying for power in Hungary, and to the programs by which these sought to determine the system within which power should be exercised. More specifically, we are interested in the relationship of the Association to the major political parties and its points of contact with ideological movements which explicitly challenged the existing distribution of power and influence. In this way we can form a picture of the political order which the members of the Association saw as most in line with their needs and interests.

Although in its official publications, the Association generally made its position known on issues related to economic policy, it rarely did so on questions of party politics. Unfortunately, few unofficial sources are extant in which we might have found more candid statements of sympathy or opposition. The connections of the Association

to the major political parties or groups is, therefore, difficult to re-
construct. Its attitude to the various parties and governments was in
part determined by the economic policies proposed or implemented by
these. Yet, the reaction of the Association to the economic policies of
a government are not a wholly reliable basis for inference concerning
its political allegiances since the two "variables" are to some extent
independent of each other. The Coalition Government, for example,
passed a number of laws that the Association had demanded and welcomed. And yet, as we shall see, it could not be counted among the
supporters of the Coalition.

A further problem concerns the degree to which we can speak
of the views of the Association as a corporate entity. Even where
its official position is known, we are faced with the problem that
the official position need not have had the support of a majority of
the leadership—as in the case of the independent customs issue—and
in such cases the actions of the organization bore little relation to its
declared principles. On most political issues, however, the Association
did not take an official position at all and all the evidence we have
are the views of certain members or leaders. Without wishing to
suggest that the views of the leaders were always representative of
the organization, such cases have been included in the discussion on
the grounds that these are probably the views that counted most. We
have tried, wherever possible (though here we are limited again by
the problem of sources), to indicate the existence of conflicts within
the Association.

Traditions of Political Allegiance Among the Association's Membership

It is impossible to understand the political alignments of the Association after the turn of the century without taking into consideration the traditional allegiances that large and medium industry had
evolved in the preceding decades of Dualism on the most important
division within Hungarian politics, the conflict between the parties
of 1867 and those of 1848. As we have already seen, the Hungarian bourgeoisie had flourished under the benevolent rule of the pro–
1867 parties. Committed to the maintenance of Dualism, these ruling
parties were convinced that a powerful Hungary required the development of industry and trade, and they sought to give a hospitable
environment to those involved in such activities. Ethnic considerations bound much of the bourgeoisie to the rule of the Liberal party

which had resisted the rise of political anti–Semitism. The Party's struggle against the privileges of the Catholic Church, culminating in the mid–1890s, resulted in the attainment of equal rights in all civil and religious matters for Hungary's Jewish citizens.[2] While the new wealth and political power were largely distinct under Dualism, a close cooperation evolved between the two. Liberal governments, uninterruptedly in power since the formation of the Party in 1875, relied on their ties to the large private bankers, who possessed close ties to the Austrian and foreign financial markets, to secure the capital necessary for the projects of the state as well as for the lavish electoral campaigns which insured Liberal rule. In exchange, the bourgeoisie enjoyed the patronage of the government not only in the case of individuals but collectively as well. Government contracts, favorable railroad rates, laws for the promotion of industry and low taxes were only the major aspects of the so–called "mercantilist" economic policy which the Hungarian bourgeoisie associated with the golden age of Liberal rule.

The primary commitment of the Liberal Party was to the maintenance of the *status quo* in Hungary's ties to Austria. Generally, the upper bourgeoisie favored this policy which guaranteed a stable international climate, provided the benefits of a large market for Hungary's industrial exports and most importantly, facilitated the access of Hungarian industry to foreign (mostly Austrian) capital.

While it is relatively easy to demonstrate the fact that Hungarian large industrialists moved within the orbit of the Liberal Party, it is more difficult to judge the amount of support that the 1848 opposition had among the membership of the Association. This difficulty itself tends to show that strong political conflicts around the 1848/1867 axis did not exist within the Association. There was, however, one issue on which the position of the Association was often closer to that represented by the Independent Party than by the Liberals. This issue was that of the independent customs area. Throughout the period of Dualism, the Association was committed in principle to the achievement of customs independence.

Generally, the smaller a firm, the more likely was it to demand customs independence.[3] Yet middle–sized industries formed the bulk of the Association's membership, and a considerable share of them also supported the demand for independence. They even found allies within the leadership in the person of no lesser a figure than Ferenc Chorin, the organization's president.

If such sentiments provided points of contact between some industrialists and the Independence Party, it should not be concluded that the issue was a determining factor in the party allegiances many of the Association's members. Almost without exception, the Parliamentary representatives who counted as spokesmen of industry sat in the benches of the 1867 parties, even when they were such outspoken critics of the common customs area as Chorin. True, on occasion, Chorin left the Government Party but he wandered only as far as the moderately 1867 oriented group around Gyula Andrássy. Chorin never made the transition into the 1848 camp.[4] A number of factors may account for this. First of all, it was clearly disadvantageous for an industrialist to associate himself with a party which seemingly had no chance of being in power. Second, the Independence Party had a populist tinge, which was closer in spirit to the small–holder Magyar peasantry and the lower nobility than to the newly arrived, ethnically–mixed upper bourgeoisie. Finally, this party, committed to the ideal of national independence, throve more on the emotional than on the economic instincts of its voters. In its struggle for power, the Independence Party was forced to manipulate its demands in a way that could not be meshed with the delicate balance between the various economic interests of industrialists. On the whole, industrialists, especially those representing larger enterprises, tended not to be moved by the causes embraced by the Independent Party. However, even on their single major point of agreement, the question of the independent customs area, the conception of the Association differed from that of the Independence Party on the means by which independence should be achieved. Industrialists were concerned that the separation of the customs area should happen without any sudden disruptions, that it should be preceded by sufficient preparation and should go only so far and so fast as economic interests demanded. For the party, however, the issue of the independent customs area was a slogan like any other, to be used when politically, though not necessarily economically, expedient.

Towards the turn of the century, the agrarian and anti–Semitic elements began to occupy a more significant place in the Independence party than among the "Liberals," making the alliance of the bourgeoisie with the former even less likely than it had been in the past.[5]

* * * * *

The political history of the years 1902–1914 may be divided into four subperiods on the basis of the political regimes in power. After its foundation in 1875, the Liberal Party ruled uninterruptedly for thirty years. Its fall brought about a fundamental crisis of the Dualist system, the institutions of which were the main target of attack—at least rhetorically—of the victorious opposition. The crisis was bridged unconstitutionally by the Monarch through the appointment of an extraparliamentary government under General Baron Géza Fejérváry which did not enjoy the support of any of the major parties in Parliament. This second period, lasting until April 8, 1906, was followed by the accession to power of the former opposition parties, the "Coalition." The final period was that of the resurrection of the old Liberal guard on January 17, 1910, under the aegis of the new Party of National Work which was to rule until the final crisis of the Monarchy in 1918.

As long as the Liberal Party remained in existence—that is, until the end of the Fejérváry era—the Association showed little independence from the policies of the Party. The crisis of Dualism took precedence over whatever reformist plans concerned the Association's leaders. During the rule of the Coalition, the Association became more of an opponent than a supporter of the Government and evolved a pattern of cooperation with other "urban" opponents of the regime. With the return of Tisza's political leadership in 1910, the two tendencies—support for the forces of 1867 and identification or cooperation with the "urban," reformist interests—merged in the actions of the Association, making it a sort of internal opposition within the party of National Work.

The Crisis of Liberal Rule

We have already described the internal weakening of the Liberal party under the impact of neo–conservative movements in the 1890s. The rise of neo–conservatism was paralleled by the growing strength of the Independence party, which had been instrumental in the overthrow of Kálmán Tisza in 1890 after fifteen years of rule. In Hungary, as in most of Europe and the United States, the latter part of the nineteenth century was characterized by the rise of a jingoistic nationalism. Only the most general outlines of the social changes, which account for the ascending fortune of the Independence Party, have been studied. It is clear, however, that the support for the Party came mostly from the classes for which the economic development of the preceding decades had brought a decline in status, or which were at least excluded from the consortium of influence enjoyed by the large estates and the upper bourgeoisie: that is, in the first place, the gentricized middle and lower nobility, but also the urban petite bourgeoisie and the landed peasantry of the Hungarian plains.[6] It was one of the misfortunes of the Dualist system that centuries of struggle between Crown and Nation had left so strong an imprint on the popular mentality that social discontent, even when its origins were independent of Hungary's situation within the Monarchy, was channeled into demands for national independence.

As a result of the government–manipulated elections of 1901, the Opposition had only 137 representatives in the Lower House compared to 267 for the Liberals. Still, the Independence Party was able to exercise greater influence than its numbers would suggest by the use of filibuster.[7] The House Rules permitting obstruction were a chronic disease of the Hungarian parliamentary system, one that could bring all legislation to a halt until the government and the opposition were prepared to compromise. Such compromise was, however, made very difficult by the fact that it had to be acceptable not only to the government but also to the Monarch, to whom the government was responsible; and, the issues raised by the Independence party, involving the constitutional aspects of Dualism, were matters on which the Monarch was inflexible to the extreme.

It was characteristic of the period of crisis starting in the 1880s that the opposition made increasing use of its ability to filibuster. Ironically, the last great period of filibustering, whose incessant waves were to sweep away the rule of the Liberal Party, begun under the Széll Government, the Government which went farthest among the Liberal successors of Kálmán Tisza in trying to appease neo–conservative demands. Through persistent and hard bargaining, Széll secured an agreement of the decennial economic compromise from the Austrian Prime Minister, Koerber, on December 31, 1902, which met many of the demands of the Hungarian agrarians. In addition, the duty on wheat was to be raised considerably in the autonomous tariff. Széll did not submit the proposal on the hard–won economic compromise to Parliament immediately. He hoped to wave it before the eyes of the Parliamentary representatives as an incentive to be awarded only after the passage of a new army bill.[8]

The military development bill had long been urged by the leadership of the Common Army which felt that the Monarchy was falling dangerously behind the other Great Powers. Essentially, the bill would have raised the number of recruits sent from each half of the Monarchy to the Common Army. The hopes of Széll for a swift passage of this bill along with the economic compromise were to be dashed by the filibustering of the Independence Party.

In principle, the Independence Party was not opposed to the foreign policy of the Monarchy or to the strengthening of the Common Army. The form of the army, however, was one of the most sensitive points of Hungarian nationalist sentiment. It was the area in which absolutism and Austro–German dominance maintained themselves most conspicuously after the Compromise of 1867. The unity of "his" army was the area where Francis Joseph was least willing to make concessions to the nationalism. The structure of the army pointed to the limits of the sovereignty of the Hungarian Parliament and thus, according to nationalist thinking, to the limits of the sovereignty of the Hungarian nation. The nation was, after all, vulnerable to an army over which it had little control. Other considerations also made the army a matter of contention. Magyarizers hoped to use it as a means of imparting to those who passed through it a loyalty towards the Hungarian colors and a better knowledge of the Hungarian language. The middle and lower nobility also saw in the officer corps opportunities for employment in which Hungarians were, in fact, badly underrepresented. The Independence Party, therefore, demanded what amounted to the splitting of the army into a Hungarian and an Austrian half. The Hungarian half was to be part of the Common Army but was to take its oath to the Hungarian constitution. Its official language was to be Hungarian, all its officers were to be required to know Hungarian, and its emblem was to be Hungarian as opposed to the double–headed eagle. Furthermore, Hungarian military academies were to be set up.

These demands were unacceptable to the King, and found a resounding echo in public opinion. Bolstered by the public reaction and by dissention within the Liberal Party, the speakers of the Opposition dug in their heels and unleashed what promised to be an unending filibuster. By May 1903, the Government was in a state of *Ex Lex*, the approval of its budget having been made impossible by the obstructionist tactics of the Opposition. In may 1903, the Széll Government was dismissed by the Monarch and after a short–lived experiment at compromise under Baron Khuen–Héderváry, Count István Tisza, the foremost advocate of a strong–hand policy, was appointed on November 3, 1903, to break the filibuster.[9]

While most of Hungary's political leaders were still dazzled after the turn of the century by the splendors of the Millennial Exposition of 1896, István Tisza was a doomsayer, almost alone in his premonition of the threats facing the maintenance of the sovereignty of the thousand–year–old Kingdom and of the dominant position of the Magyar ruling classes. Tisza noted with alarm the political activism of the minority nationalities, the influence exercised upon them by their Balkan neighbors, and mistrusted the expansionist policies of Russia. His fears made him most impatient with the "irresponsible games" of the Party of Independence.[10]

Although Tisza may be credited with greater perspicacity than most of Hungary's establishment politicians, in his approach to the solution of the problems he was no more imaginative than the majority of his class. This shortcoming was to become most evident later in face of the growing demands for an extension of the suffrage of which Tisza was to be a fierce opponent. On this, and on a number of other matters, the thinking of Tisza and of the Association's leadership were to diverge. Still, throughout the period under discussion, Tisza remained the favorite politician of Hungarian large industry. He was seen as a link to a receding age of Liberal rule in which his father had played so important a part. Close personal ties also existed between Tisza and many of the major figures of Hungary's business world. In the 1890s, Tisza himself had vacillated between a business and political career. He became the president of the Hungarian Bank for Industry and Commerce, one of Hungary's most dynamic investment banks at the turn of the century. In fact, the bank proved somewhat too dynamic under Tisza's leadership. Having overextended it in a bid for control of Romanian oil, Tisza was politely removed from his post by the same men who in a few years were to be his most ardent backers as prime minister.[11]

Tisza's commitment to a reversal of the pro–agrarian economic policies of the later years of the Széll regime and his close ties to the Association were demonstrated by his choice of ministers. As Minister of Commerce he chose Károly Hieronymi, one of the "mercantilist" staff members of the Ministry and an honorary member of the Association. Another honorary member, Béla Serényi was appointed State Secretary in the Ministry of Commerce.[12] On the other hand, Ignác Darányi, the pro–agrarian Minister of Agriculture was removed from his post after an eight–year tenure of office.[13] Tisza's main concern, however, was not the redressing of the balance of agrarian–mercantilist forces in the government or with economic policy making. Though he lost the support of the conservative Apponyi group, this was not so much because of an open attack against agrarianism as because of Apponyi's personal ambitions. Sándor Károlyi's group of radical agrarians remained in the Liberal party, despite their dislike of Tisza. Tisza's main aim was to reform the House Rules so that the obstruction of the Opposition could be permanently brought to an end. Economic policy was put on the back burner until the vital functioning of the system of Dualism could be restored.

After his own experiment at compromise had failed, Tisza prepared for the attack. He sought the support of public opinion "for securing the permanent guarantee of Hungary's constitutional life" through a reform of the House Rules.[14] On November 15, 1904, he submitted to Parliament a bill whereby the "necessities of state," the budget and the voting of the recruits, would have to be debated within a limited time. The bill naturally met with the obstruction of the Opposition, to which Tisza responded with a sort of *coup* by ignoring the House Rules. According to a previously arranged maneuver, Tisza interrupted the filibuster with a speech violently attacking the Opposition. At the end of his speech, members of his party shouted for a vote. The House President gave the signal by raising a handkerchief whereupon the majority voted Tisza's bill. Before the Opposition had a chance to fully come to its senses, Tisza handed the President of the House a rescript from the King prorogueing the Parliament until December 13. In response, the Opposition vented its fury on the furniture of the House. On January 3, the King dissolved Parliament hoping that the voters could be induced to vindicate the actions of his Government. Exactly the opposite was to take place. In the elections of January 1905, the Liberal Party was to lose an election for the first time since its creation in 1875, thus precipitating the most serious constitutional crisis in the system of Dualism.

The Association did not openly take sides in the debate over the reorganization of the army. Unlike the nationalistic press and politicians, it saw the question of Hungary's relationship to Austria from the standpoint of economics rather than from a concern with the army's national character. Yet the Association was quite concerned over the fact that the army debate had plunged the Parliament into a state of incapacity. There was a considerable backlog of legislation in Parliament that was of interest to the Association. The most important such bill was the decennial economic agreement, already initialled by Széll and Koerber for their respective Governments on December 31, 1902. Until the passage of this bill, one could not be sure whether the common customs area of the Monarchy would be maintained or whether Hungary would become an independent customs area. The bill also contained the autonomous tariff which was essential to the conclusion of trade treaties with other lands. There were aspects of this bill to which the Association objected, especially with regard to the disposition on the railroad tariffs and the taxation of goods traded between Austria and Hungary. In fact, the Association was officially opposed to a common customs area. The worst was that the debate of the bill was indefinitely postponed by the filibustering that had broken out over the army issue. In its first annual report, the Association complained that the uncertainty resulting from this state of affairs had increased the severity of the economic recession and that the Parliamentary crisis had led to a decline in government contracts, adding further to the depressive factors in the economy. In the same report the central office of the Association as well as a number of its regional branches complained that despite low interest rates, the uncertainty of the political situation discouraged investments.[15] Similar complaints were voiced in the second annual report in which the Association claimed that not only did Parliament ignore industry's struggle for existence, but even hindered this struggle by producing a chaotic political environment. In its brief moments of relative peace, the legislature only passed one law relating to industry, the regulation of government purchases, and this in a manner that left many industrialists disappointed.[16] Ede Vest, a leading economic writer and president of the Temesvár branch of the Association pointed out in the annual report of 1906 that the political crisis had prevented the legislature from dealing with such important issues as the trade treaties, workers' accident insurance, the legalization of limited liability, a law on patents and the regulation of cartels.[17]

Though the Association refused to become publicly involved in the struggle between the Liberal Party and the Opposition beyond condemning the struggle itself, its later political orientation was no doubt influenced by the events of this period. It seemed evident to the Association's leaders that the political system, or more precisely, that Parliament was less interested in the economic problems of the country than in the constitutional question and, therefore, this Parliament was unlikely to create laws for the industrialization of the country. As in the above quotations, the complaint against the government's apathy to the needs of industry runs through nearly most of the Association's publications. The frustration with Parliament as it was presently constructed was one of the main factors which induced the Association to support a revision of the suffrage laws.

This issue had been much discussed around the turn of the century. Quite naturally, it was a standing demand of the Social Democratic Party and of the representatives of the nationalities. In a more moderate form, it was even demanded by the Party of Independence for whom the issue was not only a largely ingenuous means of creating a popular image but a policy based on the belief that a moderate reform would improve the Party's chances at the polls. In the customary hypocritical style of the Independence party, Ferenc Kossuth, the Party's president (and son of Lajos Kossuth), criticized Tisza's program speech for not containing a proposal for the introduction of universal suffrage.[18] Tisza himself was a staunch opponent of anything approaching universal suffrage which he feared would lead to "mob rule," the advance of socialism, the decline of Parliament's intellectual level, growing internationalism and the sharpening of chauvinistic conflicts.[19]

Still, his Government was forced to study the matter, if only to gauge the extent to which the demand was genuine among the upper classes. It was probably with this in mind that Tisza addressed a questionnaire to the Association regarding the possible effects on industry of the extension of the suffrage to some members of the industrial working class. Although the full reply is lost, an excerpt from the 1904 memorandum was quoted in the *Magyar Gyáripar:*

> As industrialists, not only are we not opposed to the extension of the suffrage to certain strata of the workers, but on the contrary, we believe that the parameters of the suffrage set by the laws of 1848 must be adjusted in line with the changed circumstances. The broadening of the suffrage would not lead to the loosening of discipline in the factories. Indeed, the representation of the working class in Parliament would be an appropriate means of decreasing the severity of social conflict.[20]

Thus, already in 1904, the Association supported an extension of the suffrage by a concern with social peace as well as by frustration with a Parliament primarily interested in the problems of national independence rather than in industrialization. No doubt the Association hoped that changes in the structure of the electorate would result in changes in the topics of political debate, and it even preferred Parliamentary conflicts with the Social Democrats to the crippling debates of the existing parties in the House.

When asked, the Association declared itself in favor of suffrage reform but when possibilities for action involving opposition to Hungary's political establishment presented themselves, during the period discussed in this chapter, the Association largely maintained silence and held itself aloof. The limits of its political activism in the early years of existence were revealed in the hectic months between the elections of January 1905 and the coming to power of the Coalition.

The Fejérváry Era

The elections of 1905 were a watershed in the history of Dualism. For the first time in its thirty years of existence the Liberal party failed to win a majority of the seats in Parliament. Only 159 candidates of the Liberal Party were returned to the House of Representatives against 235 candidates of the Coalition of opposition parties that had been formed prior to the elections. Nine independents and ten representatives of the parties of the nationalities were also returned. The largest party of the Coalition was the Independence Party with 166 representatives. The rest of the Coalition was composed mostly of groups that had broken off from the disintegrating Liberal Party.[21] By the unwritten norms of Hungarian parliamentarism, the government should have been chosen by the King from the ranks of the majority, in this case, the Coalition. Tisza drew the consequences of the elections and handed in his resignation. A suitable successor was, however, not found, for the program of the Coalition—though more moderate than the demands of the Independence Party had been in 1904— proved still unacceptable to the King. The military circles of the Court firmly backed the King's obdurate opposition to the slightest diminution in the supranational character of the Common Army as did all the parties in the Austrian *Reichsrat*. These parties, famous for their rivalries, could unite effectively only in their opposition to Hungarian nationalism or what they perceived—with good reason— as an attempt to shift the center of gravity of the Monarchy towards Hungary. The Monarch did not accept Tisza's resignation. He was forced to stay on until May 25, when the King sought to apply a solution to Hungary's Parliamentary crisis that had already become standard procedure among the anarchic parliamentary conditions of Austria: the appointment of an extra–parliamentary government. The man chosen for the job was the aged Baron Géza Fejérváry, the commander of the regiment of Royal Hungarian Body Guards. Fejérváry, aware that he would be seen as the representative of Austrian absolutism, accepted the appointment only reluctantly and out of a soldier's sense of duty. As he explained to Parliament at the presentation of his Government on June 21, he saw his job as temporary, its purpose being to arbitrate between the Crown and the Coalition in the working out of a program acceptable to both sides. The Coalition, however, was not to be brought so easily to heel on the military question, where Fejérváry only reiterated the Crown's past position. The Parliament refused to accept the new Government's credentials and refused to vacate the House when Fejérváry submitted a Royal rescript proroguing Parliament. Even Tisza declared himself against the Government so that Fejérváry was left without any following in Parliament, besides the half–hearted and cautious support of some representatives of the nationality parties. The Coalition declared a "national resistance," a phrase reminiscent of centuries of anti–Habsburg struggle. Under the circumstances, this meant the passive resistance of the state and county public administration. Taxes were not collected and the Government's orders were not carried out. The Coalition's stance had broad support among the population. To the magical attraction of the slogans of nationalism the Coalition added hints of its commitment to a broadening of the suffrage. Even the Social Democratic Party offered its support in exchange for an open declaration of the Coalition's commitment to universal secret suffrage, a commitment which the Coalition was, however, not prepared to make.

The stalemate which developed between the King and the Coalition was moved off dead center by a threat from the Government to reach over the heads of the ruling classes and to forge an alliance with the masses by decreeing the introduction of universal suffrage. At a meeting with representatives of the Social Democratic Party on July 27, József Kristóffy, the Minister of the Interior, voiced his personal support for such a step. Everyone knew that he had permission of the King to make such a declaration. For the time being, Kristóffy's declaration was intended by the King only to serve as a warning to the Coalition and to divide the ranks of the Opposition. It did indeed achieve the separation of the Social Democrats and a part of the radical intelligentsia from the Coalition. As an important side effect, it also brought to fruition a movement which had been building for some time in Austria for the granting of universal suffrage in that half of the Monarchy. Mass movements reached such a pitch that the Conservative Gautsch Government, which had opposed even the mention of universal suffrage by the government in Hungary, was forced to promise to work out a bill in favor of the reform in the Austrian half in the Monarchy in November 1905. This bill was finally approved by the *Reichsrat* on December 2 of the following year. In Hungary, however, the hopes of the partisans of universal suffrage were to be sadly disappointed. Although Fejérváry took up the cause publicly on October 22 when he included it in a far–reaching program of reforms around which he hoped to recruit a Progressive Party, his call had hardly an echo in Parliament. Only those outside the political establishment, the Social Democrats, (with no political representation,) some of the radical intellectuals and only some representatives of the nationalities openly gave their support to Fejérváry.

The decreeing of universal suffrage was only one of three alternative plans which the King was considering during Fejérváry's tenure as a means of overcoming the crisis. The most drastic of the three would have been the military occupation of Hungary, plans for which had been drawn up in the Common Ministry of War. Francis Joseph was, understandably enough, reluctant to return to such open absolutism. He much preferred to come to an understanding with the leaders of the Coalition—who were themselves looking for a way out of a situation that threatened to get out of hand. Not only the example of the revolution raging in Russia but also the increasing violence in Hungary gave them pause. On September 15, about 100,000 workers demonstrated under red flags demanding universal suffrage. Worse still for the more conservative members of the Coalition's leadership as well as for the Crown was the fact that the nationally most radical wing of the Independence Party, the faction led by Gyula Justh, was inclined towards the granting of universal suffrage in an independent Hungary. The Coalition was in a dilemma. To continue the struggle meant to risk revolution from below as well as from above. To accept the conditions of the King, however, would have been an open admission of opportunism before those who had voted for the Coalition, for the King stood firm in his opposition to the reform of the army.[22]

Only in April 1906 was the crisis resolved deceitfully by masking the complete capitulation of the Coalition. A secret pact was concluded between the King and two leaders of the Coalition, Ferenc Kossuth and Gyula Andrássy. For its appointment to the government, the Coalition vowed to set aside its military demands, to secure passage of the budget, of the military draft proposals, and of the foreign treaties that were concluded under the Fejérváry Government. It promised the absolution of the members of the Tisza and Fejérváry Governments of all financial and legal responsibility for their official acts and, finally, a reform of the suffrage on at least as broad a basis as that proposed by Kristóffy. The prime ministership was to be entrusted to someone outside the leadership of the Coalition, Sándor Wekerle, though he was to choose his Government mostly from the Coalition Parties.[23]

The coming to power of the Coalition put the finishing touches to the decline of the Liberal Party, which was officially dissolved on April 10, 1906. The Party did not participate in the elections of that month and Tisza temporarily withdrew from politics. His strong-handed methods had backfired. Rather than achieving the reform of Parliament, they led to the anarchic times of the Fejérváry Government in which the pressures from above and below threatened to break apart the archaic framework of Hungary's political system.

The third annual meeting of the Association's General Assembly was held on April 1, 1906, only days before the resignation of the Fejérváry Government, when the coming to power of the Coalition seemed already assured. In his speech to the Assembly, Chorin claimed that the Association had had nothing to do with the unconstitutional Fejérváry Government.[24] While Chorin may indeed have opposed cooperation with that Government, his absolute denial of cooperation was an overstatement.

The Fejérváry Government had attempted to enlist the support of industry and of the Association through the granting of government contracts. Chorin sought to restrain the membership which, needless to say, was tempted to accept the bait. Yet, the Association did not boycott the Government altogether. Indeed, it submitted a legislative proposal to the Minister of Commerce, László Vörös, for a law on public contracts which would have given Hungarian firms absolute preference over foreign competition. The Minister answered encouragingly on January 3, 1906.[25] Perhaps the point best illustrated by these facts is the distinction made by the Association between politically supporting a government and doing business with it. Regardless of the government in power, it persisted in its efforts to secure favorable economic legislation. It did so under Fejérváry, it was to do so under the Coalition and, after the period covered by this study, under a variety of governments from Michael Károly's Social Democratic regime to that of Admiral Nicholas Horthy and eventually, to that dominated by the Communist Party in 1948 when the Association was finally dissolved.[26]

One might also surmise, however, that the Association would not have involved itself with the Fejérváry Government had its leadership not considered it possible that Fejérváry's attempt at forming a Progressive party might succeed. We have already seen the Association's discontent with the established political order. Let us now consider the extent to which some of its leaders would have welcomed the forging of an alliance aimed at opening up that order to its extraparliamentary challengers.

The Association and Bourgeois Radicalism

Since the turn of the century a variety of new forces on the left had made themselves felt in Hungarian political life. For a short time, with the breakdown of the old political order under Fejérváry's rule, it seemed as if these new forces might be able to break out of their isolation and participate in the shaping of a new order. Contact between these movements and the Association were few in this early period. Still, it is worth surveying the connections between those active in the Association, and the challengers of the "Establishment," if only to outline their limited involvement at the time and thereby gauge the progress that the Association was to make towards the programs of the left subsequently.

The most radical challenge to the prevailing order came from the Social Democratic Party. Though the problems of the nationalities and of the peasantry were potentially just as threatening to the existence of the social and political *status quo* as the demands of the workers, the movements of the nationalities and peasantry were much less organized than those of the working class. Hence, their movements tended to be sporadic and spontaneous or, as in the case of the nationalities, channeled into reformist, weak parliamentary parties. By contrast, the Social Democratic Party had a powerful organization which was always ready to mobilize its members. In its analyses and policies the Social Democrats, closely linked with the semi–legal labor unions, functioned more as an interest group representing industrial labor than a party seeking to organize all those groups, especially agricultural labor, which in the particular conditions of Hungary, might have formed an alliance in the struggle against the existing order.[27] Still the Socialists were the main force struggling for an extension of the suffrage. In practice, this was its main political demand.

For the Association, the Social Democrats were, of course, primarily an adversary, because they not only supported the demands of workers for higher wages and better working conditions, but posed an ideological challenge to capitalism. Yet, possibilities for cooperation were present in the struggle to both the bourgeoisie and the workers against the "feudal" remnants of Hungarian political life. Prior to the passage of the workers' health and accident insurance law in 1907, however, there was no significant area of cooperation between the Association and the Socialists or its associated labor unions. Even on suffrage reform, where the Association had shown a willingness to accept change at the time of the first István Tisza Government, the Association did not officially raise its voice in support of the common efforts of Kristóffy and the Social Democrats.

Though at a slower tempo than the working class, the urban middle classes also started to go their own way politically around the turn of the century, or at least to search for independent paths. The cooperation between Hungary's ruling classes after the Compromise of 1867 was predicated on a division of labor between the Hungarian nobility and the largely "foreign" bourgeoisie. Until the turn of the century, the bourgeoisie had been content to leave politics to the "historic" classes, whose ruling members professed a liberal political philosophy and had shaped laws conducive to the social integration and economic progress of the bourgeoisie. By the turn of the century this formula no longer worked. As we have seen, the commitment of the historic classes to liberalism had been considerably eroded by neo–conservative and intransigent nationalist currents. Even Tisza, who stood closest to the bourgeoisie among major leaders of the Liberal Party, saw the task of the Party as basically a conservative one. At the same time, the middle classes—including the upper bourgeoisie—tended to be no longer content with a passive role in the political process, a fact to which the historic classes reacted by forcing a number of industrialists out of the House of Representatives through the law of incompatibility.

The tendencies towards the emancipation of the bourgeoisie should not be overstated. Conflicts between Magyar–speaking and non–

Magyar, upper and lower middle class, the "rising" middle classes of the economic elite and the "descending" genteel middle class of birth prevented the development of a unified political movement of the bourgeoisie. The weakness of the movements also reflected the retarded development of Hungarian society; in 1910, 80 percent of the population still lived in the countryside.[28]

Despite their political alliances in the early period of Dualism, the bourgeoisie and the nobility were socially separated groups. The bourgeoisie had never been accepted into the social clubs of the nobility, such as the National Casino of the aristocracy or the Countrywide (*Országos*) Casino of the untitled, (or more recently titled), nobility. The bourgeoisie had to content itself with forming similar groups of its own. The prestigious and oldest bourgeois Casino of Lipótváros tended generally to imitate the customs of its noble counterparts. After the turn of the century, however, a change may be discerned in the life of the bourgeois casinos, which points to the growing independence of the bourgeoisie. Such clubs multiplied in number in the bourgeois districts of Budapest and tended to become less exclusive, their membership ranging from the lower middle class to the elite of the industrial, banking and intellectual professions. More significantly still, their proposed aims and programs bore distinct signs of the emancipation of the bourgeoisie. The Casino of Erzsébetváros, founded in 1905, declared its aim as

> the concentration of the bourgeoisie of Budapest's largest district into a prestigious club dedicated to supporting the spirit of good companionship, developing the conscious cooperation of the bourgeoisie and increasing its weight as a factor in society.

The Casino strove for the solution of certain "social, cultural and economic questions in the spirit of the Enlightenment, progress and civil equality." The Casino had 1,000 members by 1915. Its first officers included Zsolt Beöthy, a university professor, the retired General József Debiecky and an executive member of the Association, Dr. Adolf Kohner.[29]

A similar, or even more radical spirit was to be found in the renascent Masonic movement of the turn of the century. The roots of Hungarian Freemasonry reach back to the end of the eighteenth century when the lodges served as important transmitters of the Enlightenment for the Hungarian nobility and early bourgeoisie.[30] A second, even more abundant flowering came with the economic development and introduction of a liberal order following the Compromise of 1867. The Hungarian Symbolic Grand Lodge was founded in 1886 and the movement developed rapidly thereafter. By the end of World War I, there were 126 lodges with over 13,000 members. The Hungarian Symbolic Grand Lodge was the unofficial center of the entire Central and East–Central European movement.[31]

Although much contemporary opinion equated Freemasonry with a progressive bourgeois movement in opposition to the established political order, such opinion tended to overstate the case by generalizing from the example of the movement's radical wing. It is true, however, that membership in the movement did mean a certain degree of commitment to the furthering of social equality and the alleviation of the economic hardships of those in need. The interpretation of this commitment spanned a broad spectrum. Some Socialists and many leading radical intellectuals were Masons, but most members saw their public commitments fulfilled by acts of charity and the struggle against the remnants of clericalism in public life.[32]

Members of the Association, especially its leaders, played important roles in Hungarian Freemasonry. Twenty of the 104 industrialists who were members of the Association's leadership in 1903 were also Masons. Among the 48 elected regular members of the Executive Committee there were 12 Masons but only 8 among the 56 regular members of the Steering Committee, suggesting that the concentration of Masons was higher among the top leaders.[33] The Grand Master of Hungarian Masonry, Marcell Neuschloss was a member of the Association. His brother, Ödön, who reportedly shared the older brothers' views, was a founding member of the Association. The Grand Master, who died in 1905, was remembered as a man of advanced social views who had worked for the legal recognition of the right to strike (though he himself was the employer of several thousand workers), initiated the setting up of daycare centers for the children of workers and helped to establish a large number of important charities.[34] His relative, Lajos Neuschloss, sometime Vice–Grand Master, gave expression to his own progressive views when he warned that "we either set to work on solving the problems besieging mankind or we shall cease to exist."[35] A number of Association members belonged to lodges which had an especially progressive or anti–clerical reputation as advertised in some of their names: "*Demokrácia*," "*Haladás*" [Progress], "Neuschloss," "Eötvös," "Galilei," and "Comenius." According to Marcell Benedek, the last Grand Master of Hungarian Masonry (which was dissolved under the Communist regimes in 1919 and 1947) the upper bourgeois members, however uncomfortable they may have felt with the radical connections of Masonry, "always had their pocketbooks open" for the cultural, social and even for some of the political actions that were inspired by the radicals.[36]

The casinos and Masonic lodges were not political movements *per se.*, but they served as forums for the exchange of ideas and of social contacts among the bourgeoisie. They helped to integrate this class, and their mere existence promoted the political cooperation between the various layers of the bourgeoisie. They were an important element in the formation of an urban interest—and culture—which was to play an important role in the development of the political behavior of the Association.

The only truly urban middle class movement which developed into a political party before 1914 was the Vilmos Vázsonyi–led Bourgeois Democratic Party [Szabad Polgári Párt]. Backed primarily by the Jewish lower–middle class of the capital, the party's program was aimed at a broader constituency. First published at its founding meeting held at Kolozsvár in 1900, this program demanded the banishment of the "spirit of estates" from Hungarian public life and society, the reform of the suffrage, the abolition of virilism,[37] a progressive taxation, effective government support of small industry and peasant farmers, and an independent customs area. The program attacked the privileges of the nobility, including the *main morte*, the monopolies and cartels of the upper bourgeoisie but also rejected the "utopianism" of the Social Democrats. Vázsonyi's party gained some say in the politics of the capital. Vázsonyi himself was elected to Parliament in 1901 and his party gained two seats in 1905.[38]

Despite his attacks against the finance oligarchy, Vázsonyi did have supporters in the Association, especially among the middle industrialists. The machine–industry owner, István Rock, for example, who was on the Executive Committee of the Association in 1903, was also a member of the Independent Bourgeois Party of Budapest's 1st district.[39]

The turn of the century in Hungary also witnessed the flowering of an intellectual reform movement which for a short time succeeded in bringing together in its institutions representatives of many of the movements we have mentioned so far, including some members of the Association. The intellectual ferment of the period was to some extent a facet of the emancipation of the bourgeoisie. A considerable contingent of the young writers, musicians, social scientists and publicists associated with the modernizing movement, which is best subsumed under the broad heading of the "second reform generation," were descendants of noble families, though generally of the impoverished gentry. The other and largest contingent, however, did come from the middle classes—more specifically, from the Jewish upper and lower bourgeoisie. To a considerable extent the political views of the second reform generation were critical not only of the "feudal" remnants in Hungarian public life and institutions, but also criticized its capitalist aspects from a socialist point of view. Even those who were not socialists but adherents of the ideology which after 1906 was known as bourgeois radicalism, sympathized with the lesser bourgeoisie's attacks on the cartels of the "finance oligarchy."[40]

At its broadest, the birth of the new cultural trend was a reaction on the part of the more sensitive student generation of the 1890s to the wave of chauvinism and "epigonism" which took hold of Hungarian intellectual life in its established forums: the university, the literary societies, the theater and the press. The chauvinism of the period, proud to call itself by that very name, was in large measure the intellectual expression of the social and national crisis of the Hungarian ruling class and ideology.[41] The nobility, which at the beginning of the nineteenth century had championed the liberal transformation of Hungary, could not accept the demands which the end of the century placed on the philosophy of liberalism. The nobility faced an economic crisis at every level. The gentry, as that segment of the common nobility that could no longer live from revenues of its land had come to be known in the 1880s, sought to maintain its privileged status through government service. It provided the creators and consumers of a culture steeped in national self–idolatry, given its most spectacular expression at the time of the Exposition of the Hungarian Millenium in 1896. At this time, though with increasing reservations, the official Hungarian intellectual elite was still open. The price of admission, however, was conversion to the ethos of Magyar national supremacy.

Many young intellectuals rejected this cult of conservative nationalism which was unable to face the realities of the twentieth century or to integrate the artistic and intellectual achievements of the period into its system. The reform generation was intent on creating a different culture complete with its own institutions. In place of the university, they formed their "free schools" where some of the greatest intellectuals of the period, including such figures as George Lukács, Ervin Szabó, Oscar Jászi, Karl Mannheim and Béla Bartók taught courses to an audience consisting largely of workers and intellectuals. Young sociologists who had little chance of teaching at the university or publishing their work in the official scientific journals created the *Huszadik Század* [Twentieth Century], appropriately on January 1, 1900, to provide a forum for the free exchange of ideas, regardless of ideological outlook. They founded the *Társadalomtudományi Társaság* [Society for Social Science] in 1901 on an even broader basis to debate and propagate the teachings of modern sociology.[42] As the titles of the two journals most closely associated with this movement, the *Nyugat* [West], founded in 1908, and the *Huszadik Század* indicate, the reformers of the turn of the century sought to raise Hungarian social science and artistic taste to the highest levels prevailing in the West, hoping thereby to transform society as well.

The *Huszadik Század* was not founded by the movement known as bourgeois radicalism. On the contrary, the movement itself grew out of the journal and its closely associated Society for Social Sciences after 1906. At the birth of both the journal and of the Society there were present young intellectuals with political views ranging from a mild liberalism to a doctrinaire anarchism and included most of the intermediate shades of the political ideologies current in Europe at the time. Besides the previously named intellectuals, one finds among those active in the circle of the *Huszadik Század* two men who became executive directors of the Association, Lóránt Hegedüs and Gusztáv Gratz. Among the original members of the Society for Social Science, there were also such important Association members as Marcell Benedek and Sándor Hatvany–Deutsch. The common denominator of such men was their interest in modern sociology and their aim of promoting the modernization of Hungary through the sociological analysis of its problems.

Though the writings of Hegedüs and Gratz in the *Huszadik Század* cannot be treated as the official expression of the philosophic and political views of the Association, they nonetheless reveal the opinions current among some of the leaders of the Association on such important matters as the decline of the Liberal Party and the reforms proposed by the Fejérváry Government. The significance of their writings, as we shall see, is enhanced by the fact that both Hegedüs and Gratz were for a long time in a position, as managing directors of the Association, to translate their personal views into organizational policy. Both recognized the deep-seated social problems in Hungary and were dissatisfied with the way in which established opinion and the government were treating these problems. But, contrary to the majority of the co-workers of the *Huszadik Század*, who tended to analyze Hungary's problems from a perspective quite close to Marxism, Hegedüs and Gratz were enthusiastic spokesmen for capitalism and liberalism. Gratz objected to identifying liberalism with the programs of the actual "Liberal" parties in Hungary or elsewhere which, he claimed, had not tried to fulfill the program of a true liberalism. The latter he defined as the guarantee of complete political equality; the right of every group to compete for its interests within the limits of permitting the same right to other groups. Gratz pointed out that the ameliorative demands of the Social Democrats were ones which liberals dedicated to the maintenance of the capitalist order could also support, and he advocated the recognition of the right of the Socialists to work for such aims. He even admitted that the tendency of the times was towards socialism and predicted the emergence of socialist regimes in Europe, though these were tendencies which he, of course, did not favor nor hold to be inevitable. He deplored the ideology of socialism on the grounds that if all the means of production belonged to the state, human freedom would be even more limited than it was under the rule of existing Liberal parties.[43]

Gratz placed the blame for the political crisis of 1905 squarely on the shoulders of the Liberal Party. On the pages of *Huszadik Század*, he proposed a solution to the crisis that was rather close to what the Fejérváry Government and Francis Joseph hoped to bring about in the fall of the same year. It is quite clear that Gratz sympathized with Fejérváry's plans to institute universal suffrage and gain the support of a progressive block in Parliament. Gratz rejected the possibility of the revival of the old Liberal Party on the grounds that "thirty-eight politically nearly-stagnant years have convinced the population that the Liberal Party rarely translates its promises into deeds." At the same time he strongly attacked the program of the Party of Independence whose popularity he saw as resting on totally false beliefs concerning Hungary's relationship with Austria. He pointed out that the admitted inequality with regard to the Common Army hardly affected the population, while the economic advantages of the common customs area were of great importance, especially for the large agricultural producers, though many of these were its strongest opponents. As the most favorable way out of the political crisis, he favored the formation of a "new majority" dedicated to the principles of 1867 but much more progressive than the Liberal Party had been. Such a new majority could only be achieved in a Parliament elected on the basis of universal suffrage. Gratz laid stress on the importance of a radical broadening of the suffrage.

> A careful, limited extension of the suffrage would not help the situation, since the classes closest to the categories enfranchised today would give their support to the Party of Independence. . . . New ideals, new formations can only be expected from the institution of universal suffrage.[44]

In another article Gratz made clear that under universal suffrage he understood the proposal of Kristóffy which would have enfranchised all men above twenty-four years of age who could read and write—not an uncommon definition of the term at that time.[45]

During the 1905/1906 crisis Hegedüs, then Managing Director of the Association, does not seem to have distanced himself so clearly from Tisza's camp. He proved more careful and more realistic than Gratz and probably better represented prevailing opinion within the Association. In theory, if not in practice, however, the political philosophy of Hegedüs was quite similar to that of Gratz. He too declared himself a liberal.[46] He saw the aim of liberalism as the creation of conditions which would enable greater and greater numbers to rise by their own efforts socially and politically. He pointed out that, to this end, liberals in Europe had struggled for the removal of constitutional, electoral and even economic barriers to advancement. Hegedüs was less harsh in his judgment of actual Liberal parties than was Gratz, though he admitted that "on occasion they may have erred" against their universalist principles by too narrow a defense of the interests of the middle classes. Hegedüs was more optimistic than Gratz on the international fate of liberalism and on the passing of socialism, pointing to the example of the United States, "where all the conditions for socialism are present, only socialism is nowhere in sight." He, therefore, rejected the view held by many participants in the debate that liberalism had served its purpose and ought to yield to socialism. In the case of Hungary, Hegedüs pointed out the many tasks still awaiting the work of a liberal movement. He saw obstacles at all levels to those who wished to improve their lot. The "feudal" spirit, he claimed, tolerated and respected old wealth regardless of its size, but it envied and looked down on the newly rich or on those who wished to advance. This prejudice was applied not only to industrialists but also to the peasants who wished to acquire more land or the small shopkeepers who wished to become larger merchants. The institution of *main morte*, the tax system, public administration and social values all obstructed the advance of the talented and had still to be reformed by liberalism.

In 1905 Hegedüs published a path–breaking study on the causes of emigration. The result of seven years of meticulous field work, it drew the praise even of its socialist critics.[47] According to his analysis, the primary push factor for emigration was not poverty, even though there was plenty of that, but barriers to social mobility. Hegedüs blamed the "feudal" mentality and privileges of the Church and nobility for a problem that was widely held to be a national disgrace.

While they agreed on many points, Hegedüs did not follow Gratz's activism during the Fejérváry period. The latter was an executive member of the League for Universal Suffrage, formed on August 26, 1905, in response to Kristóffy's indication of the possibility of electoral reform. The initiative for the founding of the League came from the *Huszadik Század* and its associated organizations as well as the somewhat distinct Society of Free–Thinkers. The League issued a summons calling on all those "who hold as their ideal a free, wealthy, cultivated West–European Hungary" to join the movement for suffrage reform.[48] The League declared itself "independent from every party, all the more so from the unparliamentary government." Nevertheless, its agitation for a proposal which came from the Government, as well as the League's close cooperation with the Social Democrats, who explicitly supported the Fejérváry Government, labeled the League in the eyes of the political classes as supporters of Vienna's plans. Among the fifty–seven signators, the name of Hegedüs or, for that matter, of any prominent Association member is conspicuously absent.

Considering the previous and subsequent support given by the Association as a body and its members—especially Hegedüs—to the movement in favor of reforming the suffrage, their absence from the League requires explanation. Tactical considerations undoubtedly played a role. The Association and other spokesmen of industry feared the consequences of identifying themselves too closely with the "unnational" Fejérváry Government. While, as we have seen, the Association was willing to negotiate with that Government on matters of economic policy, it was not prepared to participate in the attempts to lay the foundation of a new political order in Hungary.

The absence of the Association from the League is an indication of the fragmentation of the bourgeoisie, especially during the Fejérváry administration. The early cooperation between liberals like Gratz and Hegedüs on the one hand and the more radical members of the *Huszadik Század*, gave way to open conflict within the editorial staff of the journal and within the Social Science Society. The cause of the conflict was not the question of suffrage reform, on which there was more or less general agreement, but the increasingly socialist orientation of the *Huszadik Század*. During the Fejérváry era, the *Huszadik Század* and its associated institutions became radicalized. They agitated against not only the political but also the economic interests of the "finance oligarchy" and leaned towards a socialist vision of the future. This new orientation alienated even such liberals as Hegedüs and Gratz.[49] Though the Association was to return to its support of suffrage reform, it was to do so under circumstances in which the supporters of capitalism had greater control than in the hectic days of the Fejérváry regime.

Chapter 6

THE BURDEN OF AGRARIAN DOMINANCE

The ascension to power of the Coalition on April 7, 1906, raised great hopes in most Hungarian political circles. The supporters of the Party of Independence, largely unaware of the compromise that their leaders had made in connection with the reform of the military and other vital aspects of their program, thought themselves the victors of the struggle between King and Nation. To their Party went the greatest number of Cabinet portfolios in the new Government. The devotees of 1867, on the other hand, could take comfort in the appointment of Sándor Wekerle as Prime Minister. Wekerle had served in that post as a Liberal from 1893 to 1895. He participated in the Coalition as a member of the newly formed Constitutional Party which concentrated the 1867 forces that had not been too severely compromised by their connections with Tisza's attempted parliamentary *putsch*. The leader of the new Party was Andrássy, the Coalition Minister of the Interior, who, from a basically 1867 standpoint, sought through his career to mediate between the supporters and opponents of Dualism. His stated goal was summed up by the characteristically high sounding but empty formula of "the further development of the Compromise of 1867 by means of constitutional guarantees." Thus the forces of 1867 had little cause for fear. Tisza himself felt satisfied that he could leave the guardianship of the arrangements of 1867 to the Constitution Party and helped it to increase its membership and prestige by formally dissolving the Liberal Party on April 11, 1906.

The advocates of universal suffrage also saw reason for optimism. The Coalition Government made broad promises before the elections of 1906. Even the Socialists, who had firmly supported Fejérváry, declared: "We also are the victors."[1] As events were to show they were to be as mistaken in expecting a radical reform of the suffrage from the Wekerle Government as they had been in placing their hopes in Fejérváry.

The group with the greatest influence in the Coalition Government, however, were the agrarians. The Minister of Agriculture, Ignác Darányi was, despite his Liberal Party origins, one of the recognized leaders of the moderate branch of the agrarian movement. This branch was less concerned with the anti–urban, cultural and ideological agrarian programs that had come to life at the turn of the century than with the forceful representation of the economic interests of the large landholders. Although its conditions were somewhat different from those prevailing around 1900, the agrarian mercantilist conflict remained quite intense under the Coalition. In the 1890s, the agrarians had been the outsiders and, befitting their position, had turned to ideological or demagogic weapons with which to storm the "mercantilist" political establishment. Under the Coalition, the agrarians felt themselves to have "arrived" and could dispense with some of their more radical views. In the making of economic policy, however, the struggle was even more intense under the Coalition than it had been at the turn of the century and generally the agrarians were at an advantage because of their connections with the Government. It was now the turn of the urban interests to lead the ideological attack.

The strength of the agrarians did not reside merely in the person of the Minister of Agriculture or his staff. In the era of Liberal rule, the "mercantilists" had had their greatest supporters in the group of politicians around István Tisza. Having been compromised by Tisza's parliamentary policies, this group was largely absent from the leadership of the Coalition. Most of the new leading politicians had agrarian leanings. The elections which followed soon after the appointment of the Coalition were to confirm and reinforce the agrarian color of the Coalition's rule. A contest between the parties of the Coalition—the Party of Independence, the Constitution Party and the neo–conservative Catholic People's party—and an extremely weak opposition consisting of the independent parties of the nationalities, the Independent Socialist Peasant Association of András Achim, the Bourgeois Democratic Party of Vázsonyi and the Social Democrats, the elections of 1906 gave an absolute majority to the Independence Party. The Constitution Party and People's party picked up most of the remaining seats vacated by the defunct Liberal Party. Among the opposition parties, the nationalities did the best, picking up a record twenty–five seats. No Social Democrat won election to the new Parliament, but András Achim, leader of the Independent Socialist Peasant Union regained his seat. The new Parliament was more agrarian than its predecessors had been, and the new representatives had fewer ties to the bureaucracy and the boards of directors of the large firms than had their predecessors under Liberal Party rule.[2] There were more lawyers and fewer landholders in the new Parliament than in its predecessors but, nevertheless, the tone of the new Parliament was generally agrarian.[3] The lawyers probably reflected the strength of the gentry in the Independence Party, the dominant wing of which was agrarian by 1906. Such well known "mercantilist" deputies as Berthold Weisz, Mór Révai and Ármin Neumann were not reelected.[4]

If the agrarians occupied a secure and recognized position within the Government and Parliament, the bourgeoisie also had reason to hope that its needs would be taken into consideration. Wekerle enjoyed great respect in liberal reformer circles and among the great bourgeoisie. He had been the first non–noble Prime Minister of Hungary, having risen on his merits through the channels of the Ministry of Finance. He had been a close associate of the *spiritus rector* of the economic modernizers of the 1880s and 1890s, Gábor Baross, and had himself performed a most important economic task: the stabilization of the Hungarian monetary system. During his first prime ministry (1893–95) Wekerle had led the struggle against the remaining privileges of the Catholic Church. Francis Joseph committed a great injustice towards Wekerle in 1895 when he dismissed him out of a personal distaste for his secularizing reforms though these had been inspired by a desire to strengthen Dualism. Until his second prime ministry, for which Francis Joseph had chosen him "because there was no one else at my disposal,"[5] Wekerle had been in political retirement. The personal injury done him had changed Wekerle, though this was hardly known to his contemporaries. His convictions had given way to his ambition. He was inclined towards the appeasement of conservatism, agrarianism and the Independence movement to the extent that this would help him maintain his position.

Industrial and commercial circles could also look to the Ministry of Commerce with optimism. Although the nominal Minister of Commerce was Francis Kossuth, the leader of the Independence Party, it was clear that the ministry's economic policies would be in the hands of József Szterényi, whom Kossuth had chosen as his advisor and state secretary. Szterényi shared many of Werkerle's qualities, faults and much of his political background. Wekerle, who was of German origin, and Szterényi, a Jew, symbolize the precarious position of non–Magyars and Commoners among the Magyar noble politicians.

Weaned under Baross, Szterényi was an expert in industrialization policy and was the architect of the 1899 law for the support of industry. Like Wekerle, Szterényi was slightly unprincipled in his ambition. He served equally under a Liberal Government, under Fejérváry and under the nationalist and somewhat anti–Semitic Minister of Commerce, Ferenc Kossuth. But despite his political peregrinations, he retained his commitment to the industrialization of Hungary.[6]

The history of the Coalition is riddled with contradictions. From the standpoint of its origins and electoral mandate, it ought to have been committed to increasing Hungary's economic, military, and constitutional independence from Austria. Yet, it was tied in these respects by the pact it had made with the King. The coalition began its rule with no significant parliamentary opposition. Rather than concentrate on the constitutional question, the Coalition sought to maintain its broad but heterogeneous following through an activist economic and social policy including concessions to agriculture, large and small industry and, as far as could be compatible with these, concessions to the urban and agricultural labor force. It proposed, therefore, a new and expanded law for the promotion of industry, a new tax law, a workers' health and accident insurance law and the regulation of the contract and social conditions of agricultural labor.[7] Though these laws had many shortcomings, leaving the lower classes greatly dissatisfied and in the case of the tax law, bringing about an intensification of the conflict between the rural and the urban population, they did contain many modernizing aspects.

Besides the need to reconcile the conflicting demands of the various economic interest groups, the economic policies of the Coalition were designed to document its commitment to furthering the independence of Hungary from Austria. However much some of the members of the new Government may have wished to forget the slogans and promises that had brought them to power, the Coalition as a whole was incapable—for both political and personal reasons—of a complete break with its past. On the other hand, the pact that the Coalition had made with the King limited the freedom of movement of the Government with regard to its nationalist goals. The issue of the reform of the army could not be raised for a long time, and then only in a very watered–down version; the Coalition was forced to seek an outlet for its national goals in the field of Hungary's economic relations with Austria. The "national viewpoint" is definitely discernible in the 1907 law for the promotion of industry, in the Coalition's renegotiation of the economic agreement with Austria and in the attempt to separate the Austro-Hungarian Bank, the issue which was to catalize the final crisis of the Coalition.

The attitude of the Association towards the Coalition was largely determined by the two major principles on which the economic policies of the Government were based. Though the Coalition tried to meet major demands of both large landholders and industry, it could not halt the process of polarization that was taking place between these two groups; for all its efforts the Coalition only ended in eliciting the dissatisfaction of both. The tendency of the Coalition to support the demands of Hungarian nationalism in issues dealing with Hungary's economic relations with Austria also alienated a large part of the Hungarian upper bourgeoisie and of the Association. Despite the Association's official support of the program of an independent customs area many of its leaders were opposed to a loosening of the ties between the two halves of the Monarchy and an even larger group of industrialists opposed the continuation of the uncertainty that had prevailed for the last decade.

Having failed to win ratification of the agreements that had been reached between the Széll and Koerber Governments in 1902, the economic relations of Austria and Hungary had been conducted on an *ad hoc* basis ever since 1897. In 1906, the Fejérváry Government decreed the institution of the Széll-Koerber Pact so that the Monarchy could negotiate its trade treaties with third countries. By the terms of its agreement with the King, the Coalition Government ought to have secured ratification of this decree, the provisions of which had the support of both industry and agriculture. To have done so, however, would have been to contradict one of the perennial demands of the Independence Party, the demand for a separate customs area. To overcome this difficulty, Szterényi proposed a change in the wording, though not the essence of the agreement. The separate customs area would be declared to have come into existence and Hungary would conclude a "treaty" for a common customs area with Austria. The autonomous tariff should no longer be called the tariff of the Austro-Hungarian customs union but "autonomous tariff treaty"; a wording which allegedly better expressed Hungary's right to an independent customs area, though "for the moment" Hungary preferred "not to exercise its right" to its independence. This proposal renewed the debate with Austria and played a part in the resignation of the Hohenlohe Government. The new Prime Minister, Max Wladimir Beck,

was willing to consider the Hungarian proposal on condition that substantial parts of the agreement be renegotiated. The new negotiations
dragged on until October 8, 1907. The final agreement was economically far less advantageous to Hungary than the Széll–Koerber pact
had been. Hungary's share of the quota was raised from 34.6 percent to 36.4 percent. Though such a rise in Hungary's contribution
to the common expenses was not out of line with the economic advance that Hungary had achieved vis-à-vis Austria since 1867, it was
a great price to pay for the changes demanded by Hungary: the alteration of the name of the autonomous tariff and the dissociation of
the decennial Bank agreement from the economic agreement.[8]

On the whole, the Association was unenthusiastic about the handling of the economic agreement by the Coalition. Leaders such as
Hegedüs considered the manipulation of economic issues for political ends a dangerous exercise. Sándor Hatvany–Deutsch and Vilmos
Herz, two strong opponents of economic independence openly challenged the hallowed article of faith and official policy of the Association that an independent customs area would benefit Hungary's
industrialization. Even Chorin admitted that the time was not right
to push for the breakup of the common customs area since the continuation of the conflict with Austria would disrupt Hungary's economic
relations with the rest of the world, especially Germany with which
Austria–Hungary was due to conclude a new trade treaty. He urged
a speedy settlement with Austria which meant the acceptance of the
common customs area for another ten or twelve years.[9]

The issue that contributed most to the sharpening of the
agrarian–industrialist conflict was tax reform. Wekerle had advocated
tax reform already in the 1890s. He saw the modernization of the tax
structure as a necessary correlate of the currency reforms for which he
had been responsible in 1892. At that time Wekerle had worked the
near–miracle of balancing a budget that had been chronically in deficit
and he sought to take advantage of the golden opportunity presented
by this feat for reforming the tax structure. He claimed that with a
balanced budget the tax structure could be reformed without having
to increase the revenue from taxation and hence, without having to
increase substantially the taxes of any group. This was also to be his
declared aim in 1907.[10]

To understand the proposed reforms and the ensuing debate, it is
necessary to consider the essential aspects of Hungary's tax structure.
The principles of a "modern" tax system were laid down by the April

Laws of 1848 which abolished the exemption of the nobility from taxation. The tax laws actually in existence at the turn of the century, were the descendants of laws transplanted from Austria by the neo-absolutist regime in the 1850s. The greatest proportion of the tax revenue of the state, about 60 percent in 1900, derived from indirect (sales) taxes. Naturally, these weighed most heavily on the poorer segments of the population. Yet the share of indirect taxes was still higher in Great Britain (72.5 percent), France (75.8 percent), Prussia (64.3 percent) and Russia (83 percent).[11] Wekerle, for the time being, made no effort to reform the system of indirect taxes or to alter the proportion between direct and indirect taxes. He confined his efforts to the "modernization" of the system of direct taxes.

This system consisted of sixteen taxes, the most important of which were: the land tax, the house tax, four classes of occupational income tax, the tax on interests and dividends and the general sur-tax on incomes. The majority of these taxes were levied on the assessed yield of income-bearing property rather than on the incomes themselves.[12] Such property taxes were essentially pre-industrial in origin, reflecting an age when slow technological change permitted the easy classification of property and the assumption of a more or less fixed yield on fixed capital. Such a system was undermined by two factors during the course of the nineteenth century. Technological change meant that even such forms of property as cultivated land could give vastly different yields per unit— and this was all the more so for the newer branches of the economy. In the second place, a progressive taxation, the need for which came to be accepted by the European states towards the end of the century, could more easily be implemented when the object of taxation was individual income rather than property. Prussia had reformed its tax system in 1891 and 1893 along these lines, transferring taxes from property to income and taxing the latter on a scale which ranged from 0.6 to 5.0 percent. A minimum taxable personal income was also defined making the Prussian system one of the most progressive at the time. Austria introduced a similar, though more moderate reform in 1896.[13] There was growing consensus among Hungarian economic administrators on the need to follow these examples.

One does not have to make complex calculations to demonstrate that Hungary's tax structure favored agriculture over other sectors of the economy and that it favored the rich over the poor in both city and countryside. The yield of the land tax formed 36.1 percent of the total of direct taxes in 1902 while the yield from taxes paid almost exclusively by other classes (the four classes of occupational income tax and the tax on corporations) provided 29.8 percent—that is, in the proportion of about 55 to 45.[14] In fact, the disparity was probably greater than these rough figures would suggest since the other major direct taxes—the house tax (13.8 percent), mines tax (0.2 percent), the tax on interests and dividends and the general income surtax were by their nature also skewed to favor agriculture.

The regressivensss of the tax system with respect to income was hardly a matter of debate even for contemporaries. Hegedüs, in a study written at the request of the Association and published by it in 1906, admitted this openly, and gave many illustrations. He pointed out that according to the existing laws, the tax on 5 percent interest from a loan of 400 K would be 37 percent of the principal while that on a loan of 40,000 K would be 13.5 percent. Land assessed to yield an income of ten K would have to pay 97 percent (if it could be collected) while land assessed at 10,000 K would pay 33 percent on the same basis. The smallest apartments were taxed at nearly 50 percent of their rent, while the largest paid around 17 percent.[16] The unrealistically high rates of taxation at the lower end of the scale meant that much of the levied tax could not be collected, one of the reasons given by Wekerle himself (he was also Minister of Finance) for his proposed reform in the preamble to his bill.[17]

During his first Prime Ministry, (1893–95), Wekerle had advocated a scheme, which broadly speaking, would have shifted some of the burdens of the lower classes to the shoulders of the wealthier landholders and bourgeoisie.[18] It would also have given greater scope to the taxation of income as opposed to property. Wekerle's "mercantilism," seen by conservatives also in his secularizing reforms, had nearly cost him his political career. When he returned to power in 1906, Wekerle made allowances for what he saw as the immovables of the Hungarian political landscape. His newly proposed tax reforms reflected his wish to lay the foundations of a "modern" tax structure without incurring the danger of a new collision with agrarianism.

The agrarian character of the proposed reforms is best seen in the case of the land tax bill. The land tax had been based on an outdated cadastral register compiled in 1875. The net incomes given in this register were low estimates already at the time and had become unrealistically low as prices and methods of cultivation changed. Wekerle's bill proposed to maintain this cadaster with only minor corrections in the registered net incomes and an updating of the register where changes in land use had taken place. The revisions would have been implemented by committees elected by the landlords themselves. To compensate for the theoretical increase that would result from the new surveys, the rate of the tax was reduced from 25.5 percent to 20 percent of the registered net income. It was one of the principles of the entire tax reform that an increase in the taxes of the individual payers should be avoided as far as possible. In the case of landowners, the reform succeeded in this respect. According to the official calculations presented with the proposals, the direct taxes paid by landowners would have decreased regardless of the size of holdings. For the smallest holders the decrease would have been around 70 percent but even the largest estate owners would have received a reduction of about 1 percent in their combined direct taxes.[19]

The situation was more complex in the case of city dwellers. The greatest innovation proposed by Wekerle was the introduction of a progressive personal income tax to replace some of the least egalitarian direct taxes, especially the income surtax. Incomes below an annual 600 K were to be tax-exempt while higher incomes were to be taxed at a rate ranging from 0.7 to 5.0 percent (at 200,000 K). The new tax, which was to be paid on personal incomes by all heads of families was "fixed" at 46 million K so that if the revenue from the tax remained below this figure a surtax could be charged to make up the difference. On the other hand, if the revenue exceeded 46 million K the minimum taxable income could be raised in the next fiscal year, thus building in a further concession to the lower classes. Though this tax would not have increased the total direct taxes paid by landlords, it would probably have increased that paid by the wealthier bourgeoisie who, unlike the landlords, were not compensated elsewhere in the reforms.[20]

The other major tax to which city dwellers would have been subject was the occupational income tax. Besides renters of land for profit—many of whom belonged to the bourgeoisie—the subjects of this tax before the reform were all urban professions and profit-yielding activities—that is, it was paid by both persons and corporations. Unlike the new personal income tax, the old as well as the new occupational income tax was levied on the assessed income value of property and income-yielding activities rather than on actual income. If the introduction of the progressive personal income tax showed the modern intent of Wekerle's reforms, the maintenance of the occupational income tax demonstrated the limitations of his efforts. It would have been more logical to reclassify the objects of this tax into either the personal income tax or the tax on corporations and perhaps to create a small–business tax for unincorporated business. Wekerle and other experts were aware of these possibilities which had largely been implemented in Prussia.[21] Wekerle rejected these costs probably on the ground that a thorough reform would have required the creation of an entirely new mechanism for the collection of taxes and the investigation of the taxed. Such a system was unthinkable in Hungary where tax morality, by common admission, was at an extremely low level: the close supervision posited by a thorough reform would have been unacceptable to most taxpayers. Even the moderate steps taken in this direction were to lead to the general uproar of the urban population. The reformed occupational income tax, like the new personal income tax, would have established a minimum taxable income of 600 K. The rate of the tax would have been reduced from its previous 10 percent to 4 percent for the intellectual professions and 5 percent for all others. The reduction was intended not so much to serve as a tax cut as to encourage the honesty of the taxpayers. This goal would have been further served by the increased efficiency of the levying and supervising committees and the increased severity of the penalties for fraud. Contrary to the case of the land tax, the principle of self taxation would have been given diminished scope in the case of the occupational income tax, though it was not abolished altogether.[22]

Of particular interest to large industry were the corporate tax and the tax on interests and dividends. Wekerle proposed to leave the rates of the corporate tax unchanged though he made the methods of detection stricter than they had been. If called upon, corporations would have had to open their books to the assessing authorities. The "penalization of usury," one of the perennial demands of agrarianism, was to be realized in the tax on interests and dividends which would have levied a tax of 15 percent on receipts from interests above 8 percent.

The urban population would also have been adversely effected by the reform of the house tax, which would have raised the tax on rented housing in the inner–city districts of cities with a population over 15,000.

The proposed reforms displeased most sectors of the urban middle classes. The proposals evoked a protest movement that united the large and small bourgeoisie and even enjoyed the support of the Social Democrats. The movement was seen by many, including the leadership of the Association, as a step towards the development of a self-consciously urban interest united by its opposition to an agrarian-dominated political system.

The focal points and leading organizations of the movement were the city governments and the economic interest organizations such as the National Association of Hungarian Merchants, the Chambers of Commerce and Industry, the Industrial Federation, and the Association. But one also finds such generally subservient groups as the National Association of Government White-Collar Employees turning to the Ministry of Finance with a list of grievances concerning the proposals and objecting to being treated less advantageously than those in agriculture.[23]

The economic-interest groups organized protest meetings in Budapest and through their affiliates in most other cities as well.[24] For the time being, the various groups put aside their organizational rivalries and met in 1908 to draft a joint list of grievances. Their protest was backed by the Budapest City Council which also declared its objection to Wekerle's proposals and called for a national conference of cities to discuss the reforms.[25] This conference met at the end of February 1908. Delegations were sent by nearly all of Hungary's city governments as well as the central and branch organizations of the economic interest groups. Although all members of Parliament from urban districts were invited, only eight or ten actually attended. Whatever the reason for this may be, it certainly points out the shortcomings of Hungarian parliamentarism and the underrepresentation of the urban middle classes. The conference approved a declaration according to which "the proposals in their present form are unacceptable both from the point of view of the finances of the local authorities and from the situation of the taxpaying population." The conference also approved the text of a memorandum submitted to the Government and to Parliament containing a detailed list of grievances.[26]

The Association as well as other lobbies also submitted separate memoranda which predicted that, contrary to the claims of the proposals, the taxes of both large and small commerce and industry would rise considerably. They all found the fixed sum of 46 million K for the personal income tax to be excessive and unachievable even at the "high" and "steeply progressive" rates proposed by Wekerle. All demanded the establishment of a higher minimum taxable income

than the proposed 600 K. For this figure the Association proposed 800
K, the Industrial Federation and the Merchants' Organization, many
of whose members were directly effected by this proposal, demanded
a higher figure of 1,200 K. The latter organizations also protested the
too steep progressivity of the rates at the middle levels while the Association complained that the maximum rate of 5 percent would put
Hungarian industry at a disadvantage vis-à-vis Austria, where the
maximum was only 3 percent. A common complaint was also lodged
against the failure of the proposed personal and occupational income
taxes to take into account consistently the incentives promised to industrial enterprise by the recently approved law for the promotion of
industry and by its 1899 predecessor. With regard to the occupational income tax the Industrial Federation observed that though the
old official rate on the assessed incomes of large and small industry
and on commerce was 10 percent, most taxpayers in these categories
paid only 2.5 to 3 percent of their actual income. Hence, the proposed
lowering of the rate to 4 or 5 percent and the simultaneous tighten-
ing of the methods of assessment and collection would in fact mean
a rise in the rates. In the case of the land tax, such "irregularities"
were taken into account by the proposals themselves; the cities and
industry asked only to be accorded equal treatment.

Indeed, it was in their methods of enforcement that the proposals (and the eventual laws) discriminated most against the urban
populations. The reform of the tax administration would have left
intact the influence and autonomy of the large landlords, but would
have diminished the autonomy and influence of urban groups in the
formation of assessing, collecting and appellate bodies.[27] The interest groups of commerce and industry protested against granting the
administrative bodies the authority to inspect the books of business
establishments. General dissatisfaction was also voiced with respect
to the new proposed house and rent taxes. The Association demanded
special exemptions for the dwellings built for industrial labor and argued that in no case should the tax on rents of houses be above 8
percent. Most groups also protested against the punitive taxation of
interest rates over 8 percent.[28]

The unexpected vehemence of the urban protests forced Wekerle
to withdraw his proposals from Parliamentary debate. He met with
the representatives of the urban interest groups in early March of 1908
to discuss their grievances. As a result of the inquiry, he promised to
revise the proposals before resubmitting them to the House.[29] With

this the wave of protest meetings came to a temporary halt, though the Association did demand that as an immediate "emergency" measure, the lower classes in both industry and agriculture should be exempted from the payment of the occupational income tax in consideration of the severe difficulties experienced by these classes from the rapidly increasing cost of living.[30]

Only in November 1908 were the proposals resubmitted to Parliament and placed before its Finance Committee for modifications. The debates in the Finance Committee once again created a great stir. While Wekerle tried to satisfy most of the grievances of the cities, the agrarian members of the Finance Committee opposed such concessions and sought to effect a number of changes which were even more discriminatory towards commerce and industry than the original proposals had been.[31] The result was a set of proposals which made some important concessions to the lower and middle layers of the urban taxpayers at the expense of large industry and commerce. The contingent for the occupational income tax was lowered, the minimum taxable income was raised to 800 K and the scale was made to rise steeply at the lower end and reached the maximum of 5 percent at 120,000 K rather than the original 200,000 K. Furthermore, the proposed rate of taxation on interest was raised from 5 percent to 10 percent.[32]

The debates of the Finance Committee brought the protest movement once again to life. The Association organized twenty–seven public protest meetings between December 27, 1908 and January 31, 1909, which called upon the members of Parliament to support the demands of the urban population. On January 17, 1909, when the debates began in Parliament, a mass meeting of protest was held in Budapest in which forty–six industrial and commercial interest groups and the organizations of private commercial employees and officials participated. Within the Parliament, the attack was led by Pál Sándor, President of the National Merchant's Association. Sándor's speech was emblematic of the newly militant tone of urban anti–agrarianism. He directed his attack squarely against the "politics of agrarianism" which, he claimed, was not only disadvantageous for the cities but also for the lower and lower–middle layers of agricultural employees. He supported his claim by showing, (with not always reliable illustrations), that the proposed tax reforms would maintain the gaping disparities between the burdens of the large estates and those of the small holders. In an unusually militant maneuver, he called for the alliance of the cities, the small–holders and the peasantry against agrarianism.[33]

For all the efforts of the representatives of the bourgeoisie, the laws passed in March 1909 differed only slightly from the proposals that had come out of the Finance Committee. The Parliament made a concession to the owners of stocks by raising the rate of taxation on interests and dividends to only 5 percent. Otherwise, the land and house taxes became effective on January 1, 1901, the others were due to come into effect on January 1, 1911—though, as we shall see, this was not to come about.[34]

Since it was only during the War and in rather altered form that the most important reforms came into effect, it is extremely difficult to assess the redistributive effects that the reforms might have had. According to one evaluation, the reforms would have lessened considerably the burden of the poorer peasantry, small industrialists and shopkeepers and low–salaried employees. The tax burden of the great estate owners would have remained largely unchanged or decrease slightly and the taxation of the "finance bourgeoisie" would have increased significantly. The burden of the poorest classes would have been reduced by 70–80 percent and that of the middle layers by about 30–40 percent. These estimates are based on figures cited in the premable of the law proposal itself. While they should be treated with a certain amount of care, they are probably correct in the main. It appears then that, while their taxes were to be lowered, the lower classes nonetheless took an active part in the urban protest movements against the reforms.[35] Indeed, the possibility of manipulating the lower classes, or at least of leading them in movements which joined their interests to those of the upper bourgeoisie against the interests of the large landholders, was the most important lesson drawn by the leaders of the Association from the tax–law movement. The experience of the tax–reform movement was an important milestone along the road which led the Association to lend its support to the efforts of the lower classes to reform the franchise.

The social debate concerning the reform of the taxes was not the only issue around which one can note a rallying of diverse urban forces and the growing dissatisfaction of these with what they perceived to be the agrarian economic policies of the Coalition. The rise in the cost of living had a similar political impact. In this case, too, the Association followed a strategy of allying itself with a broad range of urban groups.

As in most of the industrialized world, prices, which had been falling since 1873, began to rise in Austria–Hungary in the mid–1890s. Computed on the basis of an index comprising forty–five goods, the turning point in the Monarchy came in 1896. Rising gradually around 1900, prices began to climb steeply in 1903. Between 1896 and 1908, prices had risen by 32 percent (three–year moving averages).[36] The price rise that was of most concern to the urban population was that of rent and foodstuffs, especially meat. Between 1901–09 the price of vegetable and animal foodstuffs alone had risen 27 percent in Hungary and 34 percent in Austria. The increase was considerably lower in England, Germany and France (though it was higher for meat in the United States).[37] Contemporaries attributed the inflation to a number of factors: the growth in the quantity of gold in circulation; the push of increasing wages; the drift of populations towards the cities and the resulting changes in lifestyle and diet; the restriction of free trade through cartels and high tariffs; and the "usury" of the commercial classes.[38] Although the inflation had general causes, no doubt the trade policies of the Monarchy had an important impact on increasing the price of foodstuffs. In the late 1890s, the Monarchy had become a net importer of foodstuffs, including grains and meats. The agricultural interests in Hungary and Austria took advantage of this fact by raising agricultural tariffs. The duty on wheat jumped from 3.75 K per 100 kg to 6.30 K in 1906 and to 7.50 K in 1907.[39] The effect of these high tariffs was further increased by the promotion of agricultural exports through premiums. More important still was the fact that since the beginning of 1906 Hungary had been conducting a customs war with Serbia, an important source of pork. Political rather than economic causes were responsible for the outbreak of the customs crisis. The Serbian regime wished to decrease its political dependence on Austria–Hungary and, as a sign of its approach to the Allied Powers, announced that it would switch its orders for military equipment from the Austrian Skoda firm to the French Creusot. It was Goluchowski, the Monarchy's Foreign Minister, who urged the Hungarian government to close its borders to Serbian goods, but Hungarian agrarians and some Austrian industrialists backed the continuation of the customs war under the Coalition. A new trade treaty with Serbia was signed only in July 1910, after the fall of the Coalition. The Coalition also closed Hungary's borders to the importation of livestock from Romania, allegedly for reasons of health.[40] While it is true that Romanian livestock did on occasion infect Hungarian animals, the drastic methods by which the Hungarian government chose to deal with this problem was no doubt motivated by the interests of domestic livestock producers.

The concern over the rise in the cost of living was expressed in the press, in the statements, resolutions and petitions of the urban economic or professional interest organizations and political parties as well as at the inquiries sponsored by the national and Budapest governments. The Association was an active participant in these inquiries. The rise in the cost of living was of concern to industry for several reasons. Most importantly, it was the cause of much labor unrest and it forced up wages. Industrialists were also dissatisfied with the customs wars with the Balkan states since in retaliation, those states had closed their borders to Hungarian industrial products. Germany and other great powers were establishing themselves in markets which Hungarian (and Austrian) industrialists saw as the Monarchy's "natural" trading partners.[41] Thus, the Association found allies in protesting the restrictive trade policies of the Monarchy. At an inquiry held by the government at the beginning of March 1908, the Association demanded an end to the customs war with the Balkan states, the easing of agrarian protectionism, the withdrawal of export premiums from agricultural products and the restoration of the milling transit trade.[42] In response to the complaints of the socialist press that the working class was not represented at an inquiry which concerned it the most, the Association suggested that a permanent committee, composed of representatives of all major interest organizations, including those of the workers, be set up to advise the government. As a further remedy for the problem, it demanded that at least within the vicinity of the capital the institution of *main morte* should be immediately abolished so that better use could be made of the land for the provisioning of the city.

The protest over the rise in the cost of the living naturally did not end all conflict between workers and capitalists or even between various layers of the bourgeoisie. In fact, it intensified the sensitivity of the public to the operation of cartels. Yet, even the Social Democrats agreed with the Economic Committee of the Budapest city government in attributing the prime cause of the problem to the concessions made by the national government to the "1,000–acre men."[43] And the Association was increasingly willing to exploit all such areas of cooperation between the "urban classes."

The clearest manifestation that the Association was in search of

political allies among the urban classes was its call for the formation
of a League of Industrial and Merchant Voters (Magyar Iparosok és
Kereskedők Választó Lígája). On January 26, 1909, the Association
organized a conference of the urban interest groups to discuss the possibility of forming the League, the aim of which as Chorin explained,
was to improve the representation of the urban productive classes and
intelligentsia in the legislative process by organizing support for those
Parliamentary representatives, irrespective of party, who are judged
reliable supporters of the urban interests. In his introductory speech
Chorin spoke of the ground lost by the urban interests to an emergent
agrarianism in the last ten years. Allegedly, the latter had come to
"dominate the legislature, influence the government and direct the
structure and thinking of society." As illustration, he mentioned not
only the tax laws, but a list of other economic policy matters, ranging
from the decrease in the quota of industrial distilleries to the prohibition of the exportation of dried hog feed. He declared that

> we can no longer stand idly by while the cities, the reposi-
> tories of the great cultural and economic interests, are rel-
> egated to the role of a Cinderella in our legislative process.
> We want [the League] to document the strength that exists
> in the cities, on which the present Hungarian culture is built;
> we want to make that strength felt and respected in all its
> manifestations.[44]

It is interesting to note, that while most of the representatives of
large industry at the conference supported the formation of a League,
the representatives of small business were more in favor of forming a
political party. Small business had in fact a political party, Vázsonyi's
Bourgeois Democratic Party, and in essence its spokesmen at the
conference were calling on large industry to support it. The Social
Democratic newspaper *Népszava*, which had expressed a willingness
to support the struggles of the bourgeoisie against agrarianism in the
course of the tax reform and anti–inflation movements, also welcomed
the "awakening of the bourgeoisie" represented by the call of the Association for political action, but commented that it was difficult to
understand why a "league" and not a party was being formed.[45] The
Association rejected such criticism on the grounds that a purely bourgeois party could not hope to win a strong position in the next elections while "a handful of brave, determined men" within the existing
parties could have a decisive influence on the policies of the latter.[46]

At the same time, the highly respected economic–policy expert, Sándor Matlekovits, found even the formation of a league to be too bold a political move. The ageing Matlekovits reflected perhaps the thinking of a passing era, in which the large bourgeoisie had tried to secure its interests not through opposition to the prevailing powers but by demonstrations of loyalty coupled with presentations of expert memoranda. The attitude of Matlekovits illuminates by contrast the trend towards greater activism and independence in the political style of the Association.

The League proposed by the Association was never formed. In the spring of 1909, the Coalition entered a crisis which made the survival of its constituent parties highly questionable. The rebirth of the Liberal Party seemed a distinct possibility for which its old guard was busily organizing. As the year 1910 approached, the efforts of the Association's leadership were aimed at reorganizing the Liberal party and with securing a strong position within it.

The alienation of the urban groups from the Coalition was only one of the factors leading to its downfall. In the words of József Szterényi, "the Coalition drowned in its own fat."[47] Trying to be universally popular—that is, with the groups that counted—the Coalition ended by losing the support of most of its original followers. Large and small business were both alienated by the seemingly pro–agrarian economic policies of the Coalition, but a large group of agrarians also turned away from the Wekerle Government in disappointment with what seemed to them its pampering of large industry and the peasantry.

The most serious problems of the Coalition involved its handling of the constitutional question. The Coalition's secret pact with the King had been published by a member of Parliament, Géza Polónyi, revealing the duplicity of the Coalition's program. Nor could the Coalition point to any significant national victories that it might have gained from the King. Even its watered–down demands for the reform of the army were definitely rejected by the King in April 1909.[48]

The most damaging blow in this respect involved the demand for the reform of the Austro–Hungarian Bank. This problem was itself largely of the Coalition's making. In 1907, the Coalition gained a nominal victory over the Austrian Government in divorcing the renewal of the charter of the Common Bank from the decennial economic agreement. In 1909, the Austrians, through the person of the King, started to push for a settlement on the basis of the status quo.

It is generally held that from an economic point of view Hungary was a beneficiary of the arrangements of the Common Bank.[49] This opinion was shared by Hungarian banking and big business circles as well. Nevertheless, the spell of the word "independence" was irresistible to a certain sector of the politically active population and the Coalition could not pass up the opportunity to demand a nominal if practically meaningless bifurcation of the Bank. The Coalition's proposal was too moderate for the more radical wing of the Independence Party, whose dissatisfied members rallied around the House President, Gyula Justh, in support of an independent National Bank. This issue catalyzed the dissatisfaction within the Coalition's largest party. At the same time, the stance of the Government helped to further alienate the upper bourgeoisie.

The critical blow to the Coalition came on April 24, 1909 when the Monarch rejected the Coalition's proposal for a nominal alteration of the Bank's status. Having lost the confidence of the Monarch and of its own former supporters, the Coalition resigned the next day.

It was easier for the Monarch to bring down the Coalition than to find an alternative. The King was forced to recall Wekerle to the prime ministry in July. At the same time, he secretly instructed László Lukács, one of the prominent figures of the old Liberal Party, to start the search for a 1867 government. The internal rivalries within the Independence Party prevented a strong response to the obvious attempts of the Monarch to restore the rule of the partisans of 1867.[50] The Association, which had always kept itself at a distance from the Coalition, welcomed and supported this restoration.

Chapter 7

IN THE PARTY OF NATIONAL WORK, 1910–1914: THE ASSOCIATION IN INTERNAL OPPOSITION

With the appointment of Count Károly Khuen–Héderváry on January 17, 1910, Hungary returned to the rule of the forces of 1867. The Party of National Work, formed soon after Khuen–Hédervárty's appointment, provided Hungary's governments until the final crisis of the Monarchy at the end of the War. The leader of the Party was István Tisza whose forceful determination to restore stability to Hungary's relations with Austria, and to Hungarian political life in general, united within the Party various contradictory factions: agrarians and "mercantilists," political conservatives and reformist liberals. Consequently, the actions of the Party showed contradictory tendencies towards the reform of the political system; some actions suggested democratization and a revitalization of Hungarian liberalism, while others, in fact the majority, foreshadowed the authoritarian system instituted during the War and that which characterized the post–war Horthy regime.[1]

Although Tisza did not become prime minister until June 10, 1913 (the post was filled by Khuen–Héderváry until April 22, 1912, then by László Lukács until Tisza's appointment), he was nevertheless the recognized leader of the Party and the most influential person throughout the period. Among Hungarian politicians Tisza showed the greatest concern about the threat posed to the Hungarian state by the conjunction of the nationality problems of the Monarchy and the deterioration of its position in the Balkans. The annexation of Bosnia–Herzegovina in 1908 had not only added more dissatisfied nationalities to the multinational empire and increased the enmity of Serbia, but also upset Austria–Hungary's relations with its nominal ally Italy, and brought the Monarchy dangerously close to war with

Russia. To decrease tensions, Tisza was willing to negotiate with some Romanian nationalists in Hungary and to make concilliatory gestures towards Croatia. But the gap between the demands of the nationalities and what the Hungarians—not only Tiza but also the majority of his Party—were willing to grant was so great that Tisza's efforts brought no agreement with the Romanians and only an unstable truce with Croatia. More central to Tisza's efforts to safeguard the national and, as we shall see, also social status quo in Hungary was his determination to strengthen the Monarchy militarily, to bring legislation that would increase the repressive capabilities of the government and to stabilize the system of Dualism by making Hungary a firm pillar in its structure.

The growing crises of the Monarchy served as powerful arguments for Tisza in his old struggle against the 1848 Opposition. When the Opposition returned to its filibuster over a military bill requested by the Common Army, Tisza resorted again to the methods that had failed him in 1904. He was determined to end once and for all the technical (and physical) obstruction of Parliament. On June 4, 1912, as President of the Lower House, Tisza called for a vote on a bill without regard to the order of debate prescribed by the House Rules. With his party firmly behind him, the bill was passed and the session closed. For the next session, Tisza ordered the gendarmerie into the House and forcefully removed the disorderly members of the Opposition.[2] With much of the Opposition excluded or boycotting Parliament, Tisza obtained passage of a revision of the House Rules which included the setting up of a police guard within the House. Tisza's actions did not lead to a muzzling of the Opposition in Parliament. Their results might even be seen as an improvement of parliament's ability to legislate according to the will of its majority. However, Tisza's disregard of the Constitution was symptomatic of his determination to strengthen unconstitutionally, if necessary, the grip of his party on political life. His success in achieving the revision of the House Rules showed that unlike in 1904, public opinion among the politically influential groups was on his side. Tisza's coup in 1912 did not cause a split between the various factions of his party.[3]

The Party of National Work had the overwhelming support of the Association when it entered into office. The Association expected from Tisza a return to the pro–industrial policies of the Liberal Party. It also expected to be able to exercise greater influence on policy than had been possible under the Coalition. These hopes seemed justified by the appointment of three men close to the Association to key ministerial posts. Károly Hieronymi, one of the old guard of Liberal Party administrators from the circle of Gábor Baross and an honorary member of the Association since its founding, became Minister of Commerce.[3] An even greater victory was the appointment of Count Béla Serényi, a landowner but also a member of the Association's Steering Committee, to the Ministry of Agriculture. László Lukács, who was also associated with the former Liberal Party and enjoyed close connections to the Hitel Bank and a number of other large firms became Minister of Finance.

Lóránt Hegedüs writes that he joined the Party of National Work "along with my industrial friends" in 1910 before the Parliamentary elections held in June. Hegedüs campaigned for Tisza in the city of Arad, the city from which many of the Hungarian bourgeoisie hailed.[4] No doubt, the industrialists of the Association contributed financially also to the electoral campaign from which the new Party returned overwhelmingly victorious with 258 seats out of a total of 412. Twenty–one other delegates, followers of Gyula Andrássy, Jr., also supported the Party. The 1848 opposition was split into three warring factions led by Ferenc Kossuth (fifty–five delegates), Gyula Justh (forty–one delegates) and Michael Károlyi (ten delegates). The People's Party (Catholic, neo–conservative) had thirteen representatives, the nationality parties, eight; the Smallholders Party, three; the Democratic Party, two; and the Christian Socialists, one.[5] Among the candidates elected, there were seven members of the Association, including Hegedüs. All of them were allowed to serve despite the law of incompatibility. Two other prominent members, József Hatvany–Deutsch and Péter Herzog were appointed by the King to the Upper House.[6] In 1912, another Deputy of the Party of National Work, Gusztáv Gratz joined the Association, replacing Hegedüs as Executive Director. (Hegedüs became a vice president of the organization so that he could devote more of his time to his new job as a vice president of the Kereskedelmi Bank.) In Parliament Hegedüs was appointed to two posts of considerable importance to industry. He was the Reporter of the Financial Committee of the House of Representatives as well as Military Reporter of the Hungarian Delegation. The reporter was in charge of drawing up and presenting legislative proposals to the committees, Hegedüs was in a good position to make the Association's opinions heard.

The close relationship of the Association to the ruling party was evident in certain, though not all, economic policy measures of the period. The greatest victory of the Association and the bourgeoisie in general was the postponement and minor revisions of the tax laws passed under the Coalition. The effective date of the laws were pushed back in 1910 from January 1, 1911 until January 1, 1913. Before that second deadline, however, the laws underwent some modifications in favor of industry (Law LIII of 1912) and were further postponed, first until January 1, 1914 and then indefinitely in response to the credit crisis and the downturn that began in some branches at the end of 1912. The long-term postponement of tax reform was not the permanent aim of the Association. Hegedüs claimed that it was inconceivable that Wekerle's entire reform,

> which stood under the sign of European progress and contained several social-political ideas, should be entirely abandoned and the laws of today, imported by Napoleon into Austria and by Austria into Hungary, should remain in effect.[7]

Nevertheless, whenever a deadline arrived, the Association sought further postponements and revisions.[8]

Some revisions were made in favor of industry. The progressivity of the income tax was decreased from a maximum of 5 percent to 3 percent and the tax on reserve funds was lowered.[9] But it is evident that the governments of the Party of National Work preferred to postpone the introduction of the laws to undertaking their basic revision and thereby risking a new eruption of the agrarian–mercantilist conflict.

On the whole, the economic policies of the National Work Governments, as those of the Liberal Party under Széll and of the Coalition, represented an attempt to mediate between agrarians and mercantilists. Although urban groups, including the Association, continued to protest the rising cost of living, the Khuen–Héderváry Government refused to increase the import quota on meats from the Balkans. On the other hand, it also protected the commercial establishments dealing with foodstuffs from the limitations that agrarians proposed placing on their profits.[10]

Despite its close connections to the Party of National Work, the Association showed considerable dissatisfaction with the policies of the government and tended to criticize its actions more openly than it had ever done in the past. No doubt the economic policies of the Government were a factor in the Association's restiveness. It

complained in connection with the railroad policies of the Khuen–
Héderváry administration that even the Coalition Government had
treated industry with more consideration.

> How glad we were when the Coalition era was over. And in-
> dividually we are still glad, for as industrialists, we could not
> sympathize with the politics of the Coalition which, with its
> unpredictable contingencies kept us in constant anxiety. But
> as a body of industrialists we are aggrieved that the present
> Government, *our* Government, the foundation of which, the
> Party of National Work, we helped to build with all our
> might, puts us aside, while even the Coalition—which in
> sentiment stood hundreds of miles from us—listened to our
> pleadings.[11]

The differences between the Association's leadership and the
Tisza–dominated Party were not confined simply to economic issues.
They emerged already at the Party's founding in 1910 and centered
essentially around the issue of suffrage reform. Hegedüs recalled after
the War that

> during the preparatory stages of the organization, I often
> argued with Tisza because I wished to place the new Party
> on a broader basis by having it support the introduction
> of universal suffrage. Thus . . . I joined the "League for
> the Right to Vote" while at the same time campaigning for
> Tisza.[12]

The introduction of universal suffrage had been one of the key issues of Hungarian politics since 1905, when the Fejérváry Government
threatened to institute it as a way out of the constitutional crisis. The
Coalition Government itself had promised suffrage reform but delayed
the presentation of its plans until 1908. The so–called "plural suffrage
plan" presented then by Gyula Andrássy, was deemed inadequate not
only by the Social Democrats but by the wing of the 1848 opposition
led by Gyula Justh. To increase its popularity at the time of its doubt-
fully constitutional appointment, the Khuen–Héderváry Government
also promised an extension of the suffrage. Like the Coalition, the
Party of National Work dragged out the preparation of a proposal for
years.

Most members of the Hungarian nobility (except for the Justh
Party) opposed any but the mildest extension of the right to vote.
They feared that the institution of universal suffrage would expose

Hungary to the twin threat of nationality clashes and social upheaval. One of the most outspoken critics of suffrage reform was István Tisza. In his arguments, one finds an elitism and snobbery that seems to have been much more characteristic of the nobility than of the bourgeoisie. Given the conditions prevailing in the Hungarian Parliament, where Tisza himself was nearly shot by an Opposition deputy in 1912, one can only attribute to social prejudice Tisza's insistence that a broadening of the suffrage would remove Parliamentary rule from the hands of "those individuals who are most suitable to participate in it."[13] At the bottom of such arguments lay the fears of the nobility not only for its landed economic interests but also for its privileged position as a political and administrative class. Moreover, as the guarantors of Magyar domination in Hungary, the nobility had to consider the effects that a broadening of the suffrage would have had on the Hungarian character of the state. The introduction of universal suffrage would certainly have increased the representation of the nationalities in Parliament and raised demands that would have been unacceptable to most Hungarian nationalists. Finally, in addition to the social and nationality considerations, Tisza was concerned with the effects that even a moderate extension of the suffrage would have on the relative strength of the 1848 and 1867 parties.

These views were not shared in their entirety by the Association. While the organization did not advocate the introduction of universal suffrage, it did work out a well defined position with regard to the enfranchisement of the industrial working class in response to a request by Khuen–Héderváry. In 1910, the Association submitted a resolution to the Government declaring:

> Economic and social reasons make it absolutely necessary
> that the right to vote be extended to the industrial classes
> and the industrial labor force. . . . In respect to the suffrage
> of these classes the Association does not consider the setting
> up of special restrictions as justifiable. . . [14]

The restrictions the Association considered as generally necessary were that voters be male, at lease twenty–four years of age, and show evidence of a certain "permanence" by possessing an independent "hearth," or residing in one place for two years or being a permanent member of the National Workers' Health or Accident Insurance Fund for a certain time. The Association rejected the notions advocated by the Government that suffrage be based on a minimum tax payment, plural voting, or that the worker be employed for a given period of time by the same firm.[15] The proposals of the Association would have enfranchised about 500,000 workers, or about half of the total males in industry.

No doubt this position represented a compromise within the Association, most likely in favor of the leadership of Ferenc Chorin, Lóránt Hegedüs and the Hatvany–Deutsches. A member organization of the Association, the National Association of Hungarian Iron Workers and Machine Factories openly dissented from the resolution. Its dissent stated that the Association's resolution "takes a position following fashionable radical slogans and advocates an extension of the suffrage so broad that neither the interests of the country nor those of industry would be well served by it."[16] The organization of the iron and machine manufacturers, whose members paid the highest wages and faced the country's strongest unions, would have set up financial, "moral" and educational conditions. Finally, the Székler branch of the Association (in Transylvania) would have restricted the suffrage to those able to read and write Hungarian.[17]

Although, as we have seen, the Association had favored suffrage reform already in 1904, its support of the movement was much more intense after 1910 than it had been previously. Its support had grown along with the movement itself and was no doubt influenced by the fact that the reform would be instituted by the political party to which it belonged. The situation may have seemed considerably more propitious to the Association for a reform from above than it had under Fejérváry's rule or even that of the Coalition. In considering the liberal stance of the Association, it should be remembered that in most branches of industry, labor unions were not very militant and Hungarian Social Democracy was more inclined towards compromise than towards conflict. As one bourgeois radical wrote: "The simple worker knows that he will have to continue his life full of deprivation. But he wants to have a say in the lawmaking process."[18] The Association believed that timely political concessions would promote the reformist tendencies of the working–class movement. When, on May 22 and 23, 1912, bloody clashes took place before parliament between the police and a mass of perhaps 100,000 demonstrators demanding universal suffrage, the Association defended the right of workers to organize and rejected the proposal attributed by rumor to certain industrial groups that the unions of the workers be broken up.[19] It wrote:

Having no representation in Parliament, all the passion that would otherwise have been spent there flooded the streets—let us add, in all its awesomeness. . . . [Observing these events] we have become all the more convinced that just as the productive working of a turbine transforms the destructive energy of water so must we transform through intelligent and benevolent laws that harmful and destructive awesomeness into national energy placed in the service of national production.[20]

The Association hoped that the entry of the working class into Parliament would help to change the nature of that body in two respects: making it more attuned to economic issues than to the constitutional question and strengthening the forces in favor of industrialization and in opposition to the agrarians. In response to the criticism of Prime Minister Lukács that the Association's suffrage proposals might serve the cause of industrial peace but would not be in the national interest, the *Magyar Gyáripar* wrote:

> It is not a "calm" through a law against strikes that we want—we have rejected such experiments on numerous occasions in the past. We want a parliament and a public opinion filled with a sense for the economy, with a capacity to recognize its future great interests which depend, in the first place, on the development of factory industry. It would be useless for us to expect this "calm"—in the higher sense of the word—from today's Parliament. This is why we strive—in honorable conviction—for a different Parliament. The interests of industry are here identical with the interests of the country and, as with the interests of the country, the interests of industry cannot be secured by "special" measures.[21]

Finally, the Association tied to its support for the representation of labor in Parliament a demand for the revision of the law of incompatibility, claiming that it is absolutely essential for the maintenance of social balance. If the working class gains admittance to Parliament, the employers should also not be excluded.

The suffrage legislation submitted by the Lukács Government to Parliament in December 1912 was considerably stricter than that envisioned by the Association. Commenting on the proposals that had been worked out by the Ministry of the Interior under the secret supervision of István Tisza, the *Magyar Gyáripar* wrote:

> All the barriers of which the Association did not even dare
> to dream, which it rejected as impossible, are in the pro-
> posal: educational qualification, tax census, employment by
> the same employer for a certain time, everything![22]

Indeed, the Government's proposal included a rather complex educational and tax requirement: the payment of any direct tax for workers
who completed sixth grade schooling, or the payment of at least 40 K
income fax for those who did not. It raised the voting age from twenty
to thirty (twenty-four for those with twelve years of education) and
required that workers be employed by the same firm for two, three,
or five years for the various categories of workers.[23]

The Association protested that the present proposal would not
bring the desired peace that the interests of the country and industry
required. It complained that the qualifications of "stable employment" would be a great source of conflict in industrial relations, and
argued against the high educational and tax requirement as well as
the raising of the voting age to thirty. These protests had two effects, only one of which related to the direct interests of the workers.
The requirement of stable employment was modified to the condition that workers were engaged three out of the last five years in the
same trade. To win the support of the industrialist deputies, the
Government committed itself in the House to reform the law of incompatibility, though it did not make good on its promise before the
outbreak of the War.[24]

Although the reform of the suffrage, accepted by the House on
March 8, 1913, fell far short of the wishes of the Social Democrats
and even of the Association, it was nevertheless an improvement over
the existing law in effect since 1874. The law raised the number of enfranchised citizens from one million to about 1,800,000. The number
of enfranchised industrial workers rose from 44,000 to 120,000 (approximately one quarter of all male industrial workers). In addition,
it provided for the secret ballot in Budapest and twenty-five other
cities.[25] The new law would most likely have led to the election of
some Social-Democratic representatives, but with the coming of the
War, elections in Hungary were suspended. The law was never put
to the test.

A broad extension of the suffrage had the support of a definite
block within the Party of national Work. The so-called suffrage group
consisted of about eighty deputies of the Party, including those close
to the Association. Their leader was the Minister of the Interior,

Ferenc Székely. The bill placed before the House by Tisza split this group into two. A number of deputies, including Székely, as well as Pál Sándor, President of the Merchants Association, quit the Government Party in protest. Hegedüs and Gratz, however, remained within the Party, despite their grievances against the proposals. It would seem that among the key leaders of the Association, only Ference Chorin quit the Party because of dissatisfaction with its policies. Chorin joined the National Constitution Party, formed in September 1913, by Gyula Andrássy who criticized Tisza's parliamentary methods and the authoritarian tendencies of his Government, while agreeing with Tisza on the vital issue of Hungary's relations to Austria.[26]

That most leaders of the Association did not break with the Party despite their differences with Tisza is not surprising. In the first decade of its existence, the Association had evolved a political program calling for the promotion of industrialization, the restraint of the advance of agrarianism and the institution of liberal reforms to relieve some of the social pressures building up against the political and economic systems. Without advocating revolution, the struggle for this program could not be waged except in alliance with a significant part of those already in power. The Social Democrats themselves had relied on the support of the Justh faction of the Independence Party in their campaign for universal suffrage. When the Opposition backed out of its promise to support the planned general strike and street demonstrations of the Social Democratic Party through Parliamentary obstruction at the time of the debate of the suffrage law in January 1913, the Socialists called off the strike.[27]

If the Association had to choose a partner among the ruling classes through whom it could try to reform the political system, it could only meaningfully choose between the incumbent 1867 forces and those of the 1848 Opposition. The Association was committed to stability of the political (though not necessarily economic) structure of Dualism. While it may have favored a revision of the terms of the common customs area, its leaders wished to do this gradually, if at all, and without the disruption of capital flows or changes in the monetary and banking system. The stability they desired could only be guaranteed by the rule of the Party of National Work. Andrássy's party was formed too late and, despite its criticism of Tisza's anti-democratic actions, had too many agrarian members to be sufficiently attractive to the Association's leaders. Nor did it have much chance of coming to power. On the question of suffrage reform, the Association stood

closer to the faction of the Opposition led by Gyula Justh than it did
to its own party. However, the radicalism of the Justh faction on the
constitutional question precluded a political alliance between it and
the Association.[28] Moreover, as leaders of an economic interest group,
men like Gratz and Hegedüs were more eager to maintain their ability
to exercise influence on economic policy through their ties with the
Government Party than they were with the struggle to create a new
political order.

Although the Association was forced to share the Party with the
agrarians and complained of the unresponsiveness of the Party to the
wishes of industry, its influence was, nevertheless, greater than it had
been under the Coalition. As we have seen, the tax laws of the Coalition had not been put into effect after 1910. In this period the military
spending of the government had greatly increased. Although the Association does not seem to have favored the high degree of military
spending of the Monarchy, fearing that it would lead to tax increases
at the expense of industry and higher interest rates, industrialists
nevertheless welcomed the government orders they received.[29] As a
further sign of its willingness to help large industry, the Tisza Government undertook plans for the revision of the ban on the milling
transit trade. The invitation to the Association to become a member
of the Foreign Trade Council created in the Ministry of Agriculture
in 1913 also helped to bind it to the Party of National Work.

It would hardly be fair to accuse the Association of opportunism
for its failure to take part in an independent progressive movement.
Forming a part of the internal opposition of the Government Party,
it was able to moderate the authoritarian tendencies of the more
conservative faction of that Party and of its leader, István Tisza. In
fact, with the reform of the suffrage law in 1913, the strengthening of
the liberal forces at the polls seemed a distinct possibility. At worst,
the Association might be accused of naivete. The outbreak of war and
its unexpected consequences dashed all hopes for the amelioration
of social and national conflict through economic development and
gradual political reform.

CONCLUSION

Prior to the mid–1890s, the governments of Dualist Hungary provided a benevolent political atmosphere for the development of capitalist large industry. In the 1880s and 1890s, the state itself took an active role in promoting industrialization through such measures as tax incentives, direct subsidies, preferential railroad rates and government purchases. Under the impact of agrarianism, a movement to protect the interests of large landowners, liberal governments after the mid–1890s backed away from their former policies and permitted the exclusion of industrialists from the House of Representatives.

The Association of Industrialists was formed in the first place to reverse this trend and in this it was generally successful. Having the support of a significant portion of large industry from the start and arguing forcefully that the interests of large industry coincided with the best interests of the nation, the Association was able to halt all further major agrarian incursions against industry. In the area of cartel policy, for example, industry continued to enjoy the protection of the state, despite the attempts of agrarians to make political capital out of this issue. Even on the question of tax reform, though unable to prevent the acceptance by Parliament of a system that it considered pro–agrarian, it was instrumental in ultimately preventing its implementation.

Furthermore, the Association brought pressure on the government for an expansion of programs in support of industry. The passage of the industrial promotions law of 1907, which included a regulation of government contracts that went far towards meeting the wishes of the Association, showed that it had been effective in its positive demands as well.

Still, the government did not comply with every major demand of the Association. In the case of the railroads, the Association believed that the post–1902 governments had retreated for fiscal reasons from the policies of the 1890s in which an efficient low–fare railroad system had been a key element of industrial promotion. In its trade policies with the Balkans, the government seemed to favor the agrarian interests with respect to imports and failed to support Hungarian exports with sufficient energy. Throughout the period, the Association remained dissatisfied with what it felt to be an insufficient commitment of both government and public opinion to industrialization.

In its demands for a pro–industrial economic policy the Association equated the interests of the country with the interests of industry. During the twelve years under review here, the validity of this equation was sometimes questionable. The most prominent examples are provided by the vigorous defense by the Association of cartelization and in the fears it expressed concerning the competition to existing industries that might result from the industrial promotion activities of the state. On the whole, however, the identification of the country's interest with that of industry was justified. By securing the protection of the state against anti–industrial currents and the support of the state for positive actions to help Hungarian industry, the Association contributed to the impressive economic modernization that took place in Hungary before World War I.

The Association attempted to increase its influence not only through pressure upon, and information provided to, the administration but also through its political ties to those in power. Its traditions and interest in preserving the political and financial unity of the Monarchy bound the Association to the pro–1867 parties. Upon the demise of the Liberal Party in 1905, it made tentative approaches to the Fejérváry Government by negotiating with it for the passage of a law regulating government contracts in favor of Hungarian industry. Yet, following István Tisza's lead and in fear of being unpatriotic, the Association did not support the efforts of that Government to form a Progressive Party based on an alliance uniting the bourgeoisie, the Social Democrats and Vienna. The Association also avoided forming close ties with Wekerle's Coalition Government which aimed at loosening Hungary's ties to the Monarchy, despite seeming attempts on the part of the Coalition to enlist the support of the Association. We might surmise that the Association felt the domination of the agrarians to be too overwhelming in the Coalition, disagreed with its politics on the constitutional question and did not expect it to remain in power very long. When the 1867 forces returned to power under the banner of the Party of National Work, the Association once again lent them its full support and succeeded in gaining a greater representation in Parliament, as well as in the ministries, than it had ever enjoyed before.

The Party of National Work was committed in the first place to a stance on the constitutional question rather than on issues of economic policy. Thus, the Association was forced to share its insider position in that party with the representatives of agrarianism. It also sought to increase the weight of the anti-agrarian forces in Parliament by advocating the reform of the suffrage laws. It had been encouraged in this direction by its involvement with the development of an urban movement against the Coalition's tax reform proposals and against inflation. The Association had supported suffrage reform also as a means of decreasing the tension between labor and capital. Yet, it did not pursue the struggle for suffrage reform to the point of breaking with the Party of National Work. Rather it acquiesced in the moderate reform brought about by that Party in 1913.

The conservatism of the Hungarian ruling class derived from the social conflict between the ruling land-holding nobility and the land-hungry peasantry, from the nobility's jealous protection of its political functions and social preeminence and from the Magyar hegemony over the nationalities. In this important respect the leaders of the Association represented a novel element in the Hungarian ruling class. Although its leaders went far towards assuming the values of the noble ruling elite, they also brought new values into the camp of those in power. Liberals such as Hegedüs and Gratz transmitted a sense of classical liberalism even when that creed was on the wane in most of Europe. By siding with popular forces on such issues as suffrage reform, the Association's leaders formed a sort of internal opposition to Tisza's Party of National Work and helped to moderate the conservatism of that Party.

In comparing the political role of the Association to that played by its counterparts in other European countries it appears that the Hungarian Association of Industrialists was perhaps the more liberal. This generalization certainly holds true for the interwar history of industrial interest organization. In that period, the Jewish origins of the majority of the Association's leaders prevented the organization from taking a course similar to German or Austrian groups many of which supported Hitler. For the years preceding the War, however, such a generalization becomes more perilous. Recent scholarship has revealed previously unsuspected progressive tendencies—along with already known conservative ones—in the industrial interest movements of early twentieth century Germany. According to Hartmut Kaelble, after 1896, the *Centralverband deutscher Industrieller* moved away from the protectionism and alliance with the *Junkertum* that had characterized the first twenty years of its history. The middle–sized industrialists tended towards a pluralistic ideology which influenced the *Centralverband* and, in 1909, led to the formation of the distinctly liberal *Hansa-Bund für Gewerbe, Handel und Industrie*.[1] An examination of the records of Austrian industrial interest groups also shows a surprising degree of support for the suffrage reform of 1906.[2] Thus, if there were differences between the political roles of the Hungarian Association and its German and Austrian counterparts, they were differences in degree.

Several factors might be adduced to explain these differences. In the first place, the Hungarian working class was weaker and less developed and was therefore less of a threat to Hungarian industrialists than was the case in the industrially more advanced countries. We have already noted that the most conservative industrial interest group was that representing the metallurgical industries, where the working class was also most powerful. Fear of the lower classes was perhaps the most important bond between conservative German industrialists and landowners. Secondly, while Bismarck had built his conservative system of rule and his economic policies on the alliance of these two classes, Hungarian industry had evolved in a liberal era. When the Hungarian ruling class turned towards a conservative ideology, it was an ideology heavily laden with agrarian anti–industrial sentiment which militated against an alliance between landlords and industrialists and, as we have seen, impelled industrialists to seek allies on the left. Finally, the ethnic background of Hungarian industrialists was another factor. Most of them were Jews and a significant minority were non–Magyars, especially Germans. The precarious position of these groups predisposed them towards a more pluralistic ideology than that which prevailed among industrialists who were not subjected to ethnic discrimination.

The seeds of political liberalism that the leaders of the Association helped to plant in Hungary never grew to full maturity. Intransigent nationalism, of which the men of the Association were as guilty as most inhabitants of the Monarchy, the War and its aftermath, strengthened the conservative tendencies in Hungarian society. Hungary was subjected to authoritarian rule in the interwar period and, for a short but fatally tragic time, fascist rule during World War II. Still, the influence of liberalism and moderation was present in the regime of Admiral Horthy in the interwar years and even under the difficult circumstances of World War II. Building on the pattern of internal opposition that it had evolved under the Party of National Work the Association was a main factor in the maintenance of what moderation there was in the Horthy era.

EPILOGUE

By the end of the period covered in this study, the key elements that were to mark the entire history of the Association had become apparent. During World War I, it enhanced its lead over other contenders as the chief spokesman of large industry. It greatly increased its role in both the official economic councils which flourished during the War and in the self-regulating industrial organizations created at the promptings of the government. During the Horthy era, too, despite the anti-Semitic climate of that regime, the leaders of the Association enjoyed a close relationship to the Regent, Horthy, as well as to the influential politician and long-time Prime Minister István Bethlen and his circle. Again, in the Horthy era, the Association played a moderating influence on the new style of conservatism that prevailed in the interwar period. It was only during World War II with the advance of fascism that anti-Semitism found its way into the Association. The Jewish leaders of the organization were forced to resign and most fled the country, with Horthy's aid, after the German occupation of March 1944. After 1945, the Association was once again to play a prominent role in the reconstruction of Hungary's economy, until the nationalization of industry in early 1948 brought about its dissolution.

Today, at the end of the 1980s, the history of the Association may have a renewed relevance. Hungarian society is again in ferment. A series of economic reforms since 1982 have permitted the growth of a considerable number of small private firms. Voluntary economic interest groups are beginning to reappear. In 1988 an organization which, *mutatis mutandis*, would in some ways be justified to consider itself a descendant of the Association of Industrialists, called the National Association of Entrepreneurs [Vállalkozók Országos Szövetsége, V.O.Sz.] was formed, boasting approximately 3,000 members.[1] One hopes that the flourishing of private enterprise and of voluntary interest groups is allowed to continue and that these organizations, having absorbed the lessons of the past, will contribute to the open dialogue and compromise of interests that is the mark of a successful pluralistic society.

BIBLIOGRAPHY

A Note on Archival Sources

There are few archival sources for the history of the Association. Its archives have been "lost" except for a few documents relating to the post–1945 period, kept in the Hungarian National Archives. I was unable to see these documents. Rumor has it that the present Minsitry of Foreign Affairs might possess the remnants of the Association archives that were not destroyed during or after World War II. The archive of the Ministry of Commerce for the period of this study is also not extant. The archive was destroyed by a fire in the National Archives at the end of the same war.

Archival Sources

Budapest Fővárosi Bíróság, Cégbírósági Levéltár, Cg 628, Nyugat Irodalmi és Nyomda R. T.

OL.K 150, 3772. cs. Belügyminisztérium.

———. K 255, 1198, cs. Pénzügyminisztérium (Elnöki).

———. K 255, 1908, 600. cs. Pénzügyminisztérium (Elnöki).

———. Z 193, 41. cs. Kamarai Választások.

———. Z 213, Magyar Üveggyárosok Országos Egyesülete.

———. Z 248. Salgótarjáni Kőszénbánya Vállalat.

———. Z 425, 3. cs. Ganz Vállalat.

Publications of the Association

Magyar Gyáriparosok Országos Szövetsége. *A Magyar Gyáriparosok Országos Szövetségének Alapszabályai.* Budapest: Pesti Lloyd Társulat, 1903.

Magyar Gyáriparosok Országos Szövetsége. *Évi jelentések.* Budapest: Magyar Gyáriparosok Országos Szövetsége, 1903–1947.

Magyar Gyáriparosok Országos Szövetsége. *Közlemények.* Budapest: Magyar Gyáriparsok Országos Szövetsége, 1903–1910.

Magyar Gyáripar. Budapest: 1911–1919.

Pre–1914 Sources

Aradi Kereskedelmi és Iparkamara. *1904. évi jelentés.* Arad: 1905.

Bálint, Béla, and Zachár, Gyula. *A drágaság okai Budapesten és elhárításának módjai.* Budapest: Országos Iparegyesület, 1910.

Bernát, István. "Mi az igazság. Válasz Pap Dávidnak," *Magyar Gazdák Szemléje,* January 1897.

Budapesti Kereskedelmi és Iparkamara. *Kereskedelmünk és Iparunk.* Budapest: Budapesti Kereskedelmi és Iparkamara, 1898–1906.

Bund Österreichischer Industrieller. *Festchrift herausgegeben aus Anlass seines 10 jahrigen Bestandes.* Vienna: Bund Österreichischer Industrieller, 1907.

———. *Protokoll der ordentlichen General Versammlung.* Vienna: Bund Österreichischer Industrieller, 1897–1914.

Edvi–Illés, Aladár, and Méhely, Kálmán. *A vasút és az ipar.* Budapest: 1910.

Egyenlőség. June 1, 1902.

Galántai Nagy, Sándor, (ed.) *Mihók-féle Magyar Compasz.* Budapest: Magyar Compasz, 1903–1905.

Géber, Antal. "Az utolsó évek munkásmozgalmai Magyarországon," *Magyar munkásszociográfiak, 1881–1945,* György Litván (ed.). Budapest: Kossuth, 1974.

Gelléri, Mór. *Hetven év a magyar ipar történetéből, 1842–1912.* Budapest: Országos Iparegyesület, 1913.

———. *Ipartörténeti vázlatok.* Budapest: Wolfner és Singer, 1906.

———. "Tömörülés a gyáripar érdekei körül," *Magyar Ipar,* Vol XXIII, No. 6 (February 9, 1902), 1–3.

———. *Újabb napi kérdések a Magyar Ipar köréből.* Budapest: Wolfner és Singer, 1914.

Handelsministerium. *Verhandlungen der von k. k. Handelsministerium veranstalteten Kartellanquete.* 2 vols; Vienna: k. k. Hof- und Staatsdruckerei, 1912.

Hegedüs, Lóránt. *Adórendszerünk betegségei.* Budapest: Magyar Gyárparosok Országos Szövetsége, 1906.

———. "A dunantúli kivándorlás," Budapesti Szemle, 1905.

Hertz, Friedrich. "Les organization des industriels en Autriche," *Revue économique internationale.* (Brussels) 1908, No. III, 569–80.

Huszadik Század. 1900–1914.

Köztelek. 1899–1906.

Kutas, Bálint. *Uzsorairtás.* Budapest: 1902.

Lánczy, Leó. *Huszonöt év a magyar közgazdaság terén, Lánczy Leó munkássága, beszédei és dolgozatai,* Ernő Makai (ed.). Budapest: Grafikai Intézet, 1907.

Láng, Lajos. *A vámpolitika az utolsó 100 évben.* Budapest: Grill Károly, 1904.

Magyar Gazdák Szemléje. 1896–1914.

Magyar Királyi Kereskedelemügyi Minisztérium. *A Kereskedelemügyi Minisztérium 1889. évi működéséről a törvényhozás elé terjesztett jelentése.* Budapest: 1890.

Magyar Királyi Központi Statisztikai Hivatal. *Árstatisztika. Magyar Statisztikai Közlemények, Uj Sorozat,* Vol. 44. Budapest: Magyar Királyi Központi Statisztikai Hivatal, 1913.

———. *A Magyar Korona Országainak 1900. évi népszámlálása.* Budapest: Központi Statisztikai Hivatal, 1923.

———. *A Magyar Szent Korona Országainak 1882–1913. évi külkereskedelmi forgalma. Magyar Statisztikai közlemények, Új Sorozat,* Vol. 63. Budapest: Központi Statisztikai Hivatal, 1923.

Magyar Közgazdasági Társaság. *A drágaság.* Budapest: 1912.

Magyar Országgyűlés. *Országgyűlés Nyomtatványai.* Budapest: 1896–1914.

Magyar Pénzügy. July 19. 1902.

Magyar Törvénytár. Budapest: 1896–1914.

Magyar Vas- és Gépgyárak Országos Egyesülete. *1911. évi jelentés.* Budapest: Patria, 1911.

Matlekovits, Sándor. *Az ipar alakulása a capitalizmus korszakában.* Budapest: Országos Iparegyesület, 1911.

———, (ed.) *Magyarország közgazdasági és közművelődési állapota ezeréves fennállásakor.* Vol. II. Budapest: Pesti Kónyvnyomda, 1898.

Mezei, Ferenc. *A közalap aktái.* Budapest: 1900.

Népszava. 1900–1914.

Offergeld, Wilhelm. *Die Grundlagen und Ursachen der industrieller Entwicklung Ungarns.* Jena: Gustav Fischer, 1914.

Országos Iparegyesület. *Évi jelentések.* Budapest: Országos Iparegyesület, 1900–1914.

Papp, Dávid. *Magyar vámterület.* Budapest: Grill Károly, 1904.

Pesti Hírlap. 1900–1914.

Pesti Napló. 1910, No. 133.

Petrassevich, Géza. *Zsidó földbirtokosok és bérlők Magyarországon.*

Budapest: Stephaneum, 1904.

Rácz, Gyula. "A választójogi törvényjavaslat és a városi polgárság," Városi Szemle, 1913.

Rubinek, Gyula. *Parasztszocializmus.* Budapest: Patria, 1895.

Scheiber, Endre. *Magyar közgazdasági politika: közös vámterület, önálló vámterület, magyar vámterület.* Budapest: Kilián Frigyes, 1905.

Szende, Pál, (ed.) *A magyar közgazdaság és az Országos Magyar Kereskedők Egyesülete, 1904-1914.* Budapest: Országos Magyar Kereskedők Egyesülete, 1914.

Szterényi, József. *Emlékirat a hazai kis- és gyáripar fejlesztéséről.* Budapest: Állami nyomda, 1909.

——. *Iparfejlesztés.* Budapest: Franklin Társulat, 1902.

——. "Iparfejlesztés Magyarországon," *Közgazdasági Enciklopédia,* Halász and Mandello (eds.). Budapest: Atheneum, 1900.

T. E. (Thék Endre.) "Glosszák Wekerle felolvasásáról," *Magyar Ipar,* Vol. XXIII, No. 6 (February 9, 1902), 164–66.

Varga, Jenő. "A magyar kartellek," *A proletárdiktatúra gazdaságpolitikája, Válogatott írások (1912-1922),* Ferenc Böröczfy (ed.). Budapest: Kossuth, 1976.

Zemaljski Savez Hrvatsko–Slavonskih Industrijalaca. *Godisnji izvestaj saveznog vijeca.* Zagreb: 1904–1914 (contents in Croatian and German).

Post–1914 Sources

Balázs H., Éva. *Berzeviczy Gergely, a reformpolitikus, 1763-1795.* Budapest: 1967.

Balla, Antal (ed.). *A Magyar Országgyűlés története, 1867-1927.* Budapest: Légrády, n. d.

Bárány, George. "The Széchenyi Problem," *Journal of Central European Affairs* XXII, No. 2 (1962), 153–60.

Berend, Iván, and Ránki, György. "A kisipar szerepe a kapitalista fejlődésben," *Gazdaság és társadalom. Tanulmányok hazánk és Kelet-Európa XIX-XX. századi történtéből.* Budapest: Magvető, 1974.

——. *Economic Development in East–Central Europe in the 19th and 20th Centuries.* New York: Columbia University Press, 1974.

——. *A Century of Economic Development.* Budapest: Szikra, 1955.

——. *Magyarország gyáripara, 1900-1914.* Budapest: Szikra, 1955.

Södy, Paul. *József Eötvös and the Modernization of Hungary, 1840–1870. A Study of Ideas of Individuality and Social Pluralism in Modern Politics.* Philadelphia: American Philosophical Society, 1972.

Brusatti, Alois. *Österreichische Wirtschaftspolitik von Josephinismus zum Ständestaat.* Vienna: Jupiterverlag, 1965.

Dolmányos, István. *A magyar parlamenti ellenzék történetéből, 1901–1904.* Budapest: 1963.

———. "Lehet–e rehabilitálni a koalóició adótörvényeit?," *Történelmi Szemle,* 1976, No. 3, p. 496–98.

Eddie, Scott M. "Cui Bono? Magyarország és a dualista Monarchia védővámpolitikája," *Történelmi Szemle, 1976,* No. 1–2, 156–66.

Erényi Gusztáv. *Graf Stefan Tisza.* Vienna, Leipzig: 1935.

Fenyő, Miksa. *Emlékbeszéd Chorin Ferencről.* Budapest: Magyar Gyáriparosok Országos Szövetsége, 1925.

———. *Feljegyzések és levelek a Nyugatról,* Erzsébet Vezér, (ed.). Budapest: Akadémiai Kiadó, 1975.

Futó Mihály. *A magyar gyáripar története.* Vol. I. *A gyáripar kialakulása az első állami iparfejlesztési törvényig (1881).* Budapest: Magyar Gazdaságkutató Intézet, 1944.

Gluck, Mary. *Georg Lukács and His Generation, 1900–1918.* Cambridge: Harvard University Press, 1985.

Gratz, Gusztáv. *A Dualizmus kora, Magyarország története, 1867–1918.* 2 vols. Budapest: Magyar Szemle Társaság, 1934.

Hajdu, Tibor. *Károlyi Mihály, Politikai életrajz.* Budapest: Kossuth, 1978.

Hanák, Péter. "Economics, Society and Sociopolitical Thought in Hungary during the Age of Capitalism," *Austrian History Yearbook,* XI, 1977, 123–35.

———, (ed.) *Magyarország története, 1849–1918, Az Abszolutizmus és a Dualaizmus kora.* Budapest: Tankönyvkiadó, 1975.

———, (ed.) *Magyarország története, 1890–1918. Magyarország története tíz kötetben.* Vol. VII. Budapest: Akadémai Kiadó, 1978.

Hass, Ludwig. "The Socioprofessional Composition of Hungarian Freemasonry (1868–1920)," *Acta Poloniae Historica,* 1974, No. 30, 71.

Hegedüs, Lóránt. *Ady és Tisza.* Budapest: Nyugat, n. d.

Horváth, Zoltán. *Magyar századforduló, A második reformnemzedék története (1896–1914),* 2nd ed. Budapest: Gondolat, 1974.

Janos, Andrew C. "The Decline of Oligarchy: Bureaucratic and Mass

Politics in the Age of Dualism (1867–1918)," in *Revolution in Perspective, Essays on the Hungarian Soviet Republic of 1919,* Andrew C. Janos and William B. Slottman, (eds.). Berkeley: University of California, 1971.

Jenei, Károly. "A Magyar Gyáriparosok Országos Szövtségének iratai a Központi Gazdasági Levéltárban," in *Levéltári Hírek,* X, No. 1, 1960.

Kabos, Ernő, (ed.) *A magyarországi Szociáldemokrata Párt és a szakszervezetek kapcsolatai 1890 és 1918 között. Tanulmányok a magyarharországi szakszervezeti mozgalom történetéből.* Budapest: Táncsics, 1969.

Kaelble, Hartmut. *Industrielle Interessen politik in der Wilhelminischen Gesellschaft.* Berlin: Walter de Gruyter, 1967.

Katus, László. "Economic Growth in Hungary during the Age of Dualism (1867–1913), A Quantitative Analaysis." *Studia Historica Academiae Scientiarum Hungaricae,* No. 62. Budapest: Akadémiai Kiadó, 1970.

Kempelen, Béla. *Magyarországi zsidó és zsidóeredetű családok.* 3 vols. Budapest: Viktória Nyomda, 1937–1939.

Komlos, John. *The Habsburg Monarchy as a Customs Union, Economic Development in Austria–Hungary in the Nineteenth Century.* Princeton: Princeton University Press, 1983.

Kovács, Endre, (ed.) *Magyarország története, 1848–1890. Magyarország története tíz kötetben.* Vol. VI. Budapest: Akadémiai Kiadó, 1979.

Lackó, István. *A magyar munkás- és társadalombiztosítás története.* Budapest: Táncsics, 1968.

Laky, Dezső. "Az iparosok szociális és gazdasági viszonyai Budapesten." *Statisztikai Közlemények,* Lajos Ilyfalvi, (ed.) Budapest: Budapest Székesfőváros Statisztikai Hivatala, 1930, Vol. 60, No. 3.

LaPalombara, Joseph. *Interest Groups in Italian Politics.* Princeton: Princeton University Press, 1964.

Lengyel, Ernő. "A koalíció," in *Magyar Országgyűlés története, 1867–1927,* Antal Balla, (ed.) Budapest: Légrády, n. d.

Litván, György. "Magyar gondolat—szabad gondolat," *Nacionalizmus és progresszió a század eleji Magyarországon.* Budapest: Magvető, 1978.

——, and Szűcs, László. *A szociológia első magyar műhelye.* Budapest: Gondolat, 1973.

Macartney, C. A. *The Habsburg Empire, 1790–1918.* New York: Macmillan, 1969.

Matis, Herbert. "Wirtschaftspolitik." *Die Habsburgmonarchie, 1848–1918.* Band I. *Die wirtschaftliche Entwicklung.* Vienna: Österreichische Akademie der Wissenschaften, 1973.

May, Arthur J. *The Habsburg Monarchy, 1867–1914.* New York: Harper and Row, 1965.

McCagg, William O., Jr. *Jewish Nobles and Geniuses in Modern Hungary.* New York: Columbia, 1972.

Mérei, Gyula. *A magyar polgári pártok programja (1867–1918).* Budapest: Akadémiai Kiadó, 1971.

Michel, Bernard. *Banques et banquiers en Autriche au début du 20ᵉ siècle.* Paris: Fondation Nationale des Sciences Politiques, 1976.

Nagy L., Zsuzsa. *Szabadkőművesség a XX. században.* Budapest: Kossuth, 1977.

Palatinusz, József. *A szabadkőművesség bűnei.* 3 vols. Budapest: 1920–1939.

Paulinyi, Ákos. "Die sogenannte Gemeinsame Wirtschaftspolitik Österreich–Ungarns," in Vol. I. *Die Wirtschaftliche Entwicklung.* Alois Brussati, (ed.) *Die Habsburgmonarchie, 1848–1918.* Vienna: Österreichischer Akademie der Widdenschaften, 1973.

Pölöskei, Ferenc. *Kormányzati politika és parlamenti ellenzék, 1910–1914.* Budapest: Akedémiai Kiadó, 1970.

Radnóti, József. *Kornfeld Zsigmong.* Budapest: n.d.

Ránki, György, (ed.) *Magyarország története, 1918–1919, 1919–1945. Magyarország története tíz kötetben.* Vol. VIII. Budapest: Akadémiai Kiadó, 1976.

Rudolph, Richard. *Banking and Industrialization in Austria–Hungary, The Role of Banks in the Industrialization of the Czech Crownlands, 1873–1919.* Cambridge: Cambridge University Press, 1976.

Salgó, István. *Kisipari vállalkozások a tőkés Magyarországon.* Unpublished Diploma Essay, Karl Marx University of Economics, Budapest, 1976.

Sándor, Vilmos. *Nagyipari fejlődés Magyarországon, 1867–1900.* Budapest: Szikra, 1954.

Sárközy, Zoltán. "A Budapesti Kereskedelmi és Iparkamara hivataltörténete," *Levéltári Szemle, 1976.* No. 1.

Sarlós, Béla. *Közigazgatás és hatalompolitika a Dualizmus rendszerében.* Budapest: Akadémiai Kiadó, 1976.

———. "Válasz Dolmányos István kritikai megjegyzéseire," *Történelmi*

Szemle, 1976. No. 3, 499–503.

Szabó, Miklós. "Új vonások a századfordulói magyar konzervatív politikai gondolkodásban," *Századok,* Vol. 108 (1974), No. 1, 3–65.

Szávay, Gyula. *A mayar kamarai intézmény és a Budapesti Kamara története.* Budapest: Budapesti Kereskedelmi és Iparkamara, 1927.

Szterényi, József. *Régmúlt idők emléke.* Budapest: Pesti Könyvnyomda, 1925.

————, and Ladányi, Jenő. *A magnar ipar a világháborúban.* Budapest: Franklin, 1933.

NOTES

Notes to Chapter 1

[1] C. A. Macartney, *The Habsburg Empire, 1790–1918*, (New York: Macmillan, 1969), 43, 17.

[2] John Komlos, *The Habsburg Monarchy as a Customs Union, Economic Development in Austria–Hungary in the Nineteenth Century* (Princeton: Princeton University Press, 1983).

[3] Vilmos Sándor, *Nagyiparifejlödés Magyarországon, 1867–1900* (Large–Industrial Development in Hungary, 1867–1900), (Budapest: Szikra, 1954), 26–27.

[4] Péter Hanák, (ed.), *Magyarország, 1849–1918, Az Abszolutizmus és a Dualizmus kora* [The History of Hungary, 1849–1918, The Age of Absolutism and Dualism], (Budapest: Tankönyvkiadó, 1975), 176–177. Hereinafter, Hanák, *1849–1918*.

[5] Iván Berend and György Ránki, *Economic Development in East–Central Europe in the 19th and 20th Centuries*, (New York: Columbia University Press, 1974), pp. 63–65.

[6] Károly Vörös, *Budapest története a márciusi forradalomtól az öszirózsás forradalomig* [The History of Budapest from the March Revolution of 1848 to the Chrysanthemum Revolution of 1918], (Budapest: Akadémiai Kiadó, 1978), 161–162.

[7] For the general history of the Compromise, see Macartney, Ch. II; Arthur J. May, *The Hapsburg Monarchy, 1867–1914*, (Cambridge: Harvard University Press, 1965); A. J. P. Taylor, *The Habsburg Monarchy, 1808–1918*, (New York: Harper and Row, 1965), Ch. 11.

[8] Hanák, *1949–1918*, 129–130, 135.

[9] Andrew C. Janos, *The Politics of Backwardness*.

[10] Hanák, 1849–1918, 624.

[11] *Ibid.*, 149.

[12] George Bárány, "The Széchenyi Problem," *Journal of Central European Affairs* XXII, No. 2 (July 1962), 153–160.

13 Mihály Futó, *A magyar gyáripar története* [The History of Hungarian Factory Industry], Vol. I: *A gyáripar kialakulása az elsö állami iparfejlesztési törvényig* (1881) [The Development of Factory Industry until the First Industrial Promotion Law, 1881] (Budapest: Magyar Gazdaságkutató Intézet, 1944), 361–375.

14 Paul Bödy, *József Eötvös and the Modernization of Hungary, 1840–1870: A Study of the Ideas of Individuality and Social Pluralism in Modern Politics* (Philadelphia: American Philosophical Society, 1972), 87.

15 Janos, *The Politics of Backwardness.*

16 Károly Vörös, *Budapest története*, 181.

17 William O. McCagg, Jr., *Jewish Nobles and Geniuses in Modern Hungary* (New York: Columbia University Press, 1972), 28–44.

18 Hanák, *1849–1914*, 238.

19 McCagg, 120.

20 Kovács, *Magyarország története, 1849–1890*, Vol. II, 919.

21 Sándor, 26, 306.

22 Hanák, *1849–1914*, 198.

23 Iván Berend and György Ránki, *Magyarország gyáripara, 1900–1914* (Budapest: Szikra, 1955), 48.

24 Hanák, *1849–1914*, 183. Contemporary politicians agreed on this point: Lóránt Hegedüs, *Adórendszerünk betegségei* [Illnesses of Our Tax System] (Budapest: Magyar Gyáriparosok Országos Szövetsége, 1906).

25 Antal Vörös, "A magyar mezőgazdaság a kapitalista átalakulás útján (1949–1890)," [Hungarian Agriculture on the Path of Capitalist Transformation, 1849–1890], in *A magyar mezőgazdaság a XIX–XX században (1849–1949)* [Hungarian Agriculture in the 19th and 20th Centuries, 1849–1949], Péter Gunszt and Tamás Hoffman (eds.) (Budapest: Akadémiai Kiado, 1976), 32–33.

26 Komlos, *The Habsburg Monarchy as a Customs Union.*

27 *Ibid.*, 57.

28 Sándor, 593.

29 Katus, 57.

30 Péter Hanák (ed.), *Magyarország története, 1890–1918* [History of Hungary, 1890–1918] (Budapest: Akadémiai Kiadó, 1978), Vol. I, 282. Hereafter, Hanák *1890–1918.*

31 Katus, 112–115.

32 Hanák, *1890–1918*, Vol. I, 284.

33 Futó, 361–375; Kovács, Vol. II, 934.

34   József Szterényi, "Iparfejlesztés Magyarországon," in *Közgazdasági Enciklopédia* Halász and Mandelló (eds.) (Budapest: Atheneum, 1900), Vol. II, 45–58.
35   Berend and Ránki, *Economic Growth in East–Central Europe*, 89.
36   Katus, 78.
37   Quoted in Sándor Matlekovits (ed.), *Magyarország közgazdasági és közművelődési állapota ezeréves fennállásakor* (Budapest: Pesti Könyvnyomda, 1898), Vol. II, 111.
38   Berend and Ránki, *Magyarország gyáripara, 1900–1914*, 38–39.
39   See biography of Péter Herzog and Pál Elek, in Mór Gelléri, *Ipartörténeti vázlatok* [Sketches in Industrial History] (Budapest: Wolfner és Singer, 1906), 568–569.
40   Sándor, 355.
41   Hanák, *1890–1918*, Vol. I, 274.
42   *Ibid.*, Vol. I, 365.
43   Hanák, *1949–1918*, 239.

Notes to Chapter 2

1   Magyar Gyáriparosok Országos Szövetsége, *25. évi jel.* [25th Annual Report], 21–23.
2   Iván Berend and György Ránki, *Magyarország gyáripara, 1900–1914* [Hungarian Industry, 1900–1914]. (Budapest: Szikra, 1955), 35.
3   *Ibid.*, 15–39.
4   See, for example, GyOSz, *1903. évi jel.*, 17.
5   Berend and Ránki, *Magyarország gyáripara*, 15.
6   GyOSz, *1903. évi jel.*, 17.
7   *Ibid.*, 16.
8   Péter Hanák, (ed.), *Magyarország története, 1890–1918*, [History of Hungary, 1890–1918], (Budapest: Akadémiai Kiadó, 1978), I, 396.
9   Jenő Varga, "A magyar kartellek," in *A proletárdiktatúra gazdaságpolitikája, Válogatott írások, 1912, 1922* [The Economic Policies of the Dictatorship of the Proletariat, Selected Works, 1912–1922], Ferenc Böröczfy, (ed.) (Budapest: Kossuth, 1976, 56.
10   GyOSz, *1903. évi jel.*, 38.
11   Péter Hanák, *Magyarország története, 1849–1918* [History of Hungary, 1849–1918], (2nd ed., Budapest: Tankönyvkiadó, 1975), 321–27.

[12] GyOSz, *1903. évi. jel.*

[13] Magyar Gyáriparosok Országos Szövetsége, *Közlemények* [Bulletins], No. 3 (October 1903), 10–11. Hereinafter: *Közlemények*.

[14] Budapesti Kereskedelmi és Iparkamara, *Kereskedelmünk és iparunk az 1901. évben* [Our Commerce and Industry in 1901], (Budapest: Budapesti Kereskedelmi és Iparkamara, 1902), 16.

[15] GyOSz, *1903. évi jel.*, 72–73.

[16] Friedrich Hertz, "Les organizations des industriels en Autrich," *Revue economique internationale*, (Brussels), 1908, No. III, 569–80.

[17] Bund österreichischer Industrieller, *Festschrift herausgegeben aus Anlass seines 10 jahrigen Bestandes* (Vienna: Bund Österreichischer Industrieller, 1907), 4–5.

[18] *Ibid.*, see also Bund Österreichischer Industrieller, *Protokoll der elften ordentlichen General-Versammlung, November 1908*, (Vienna: Bund Österreichischer Industrieller, 1908), 25.

[19] Miklós Szabó, "Új vonások a századfordulói magyar konzervatív politikai gondolkodásban" [New Features in the Political Thought of Hungarian Conservatism at the Turn of the Century], *Századok*, Vol. 108 (1974), No. 1, 8–11.

[20] Antal Vörös, "A magyar mezőgazdaság a kapitalista átalakulás útján (1849–1890)" [Hungarian Agriculture in the Course of the Capitalist Transformation], *A magyar mezőgazdaság a XIX–XX. században (1849–1949)* [Hungarian Agriculture in the 19th and 20th Centuries], (Budapest: Akadémiai Kiadó, 1976), 70.

[21] Hanák, *1849–1918*, 298.

[22] "Törekvéseink és a *Magyar Ipar*" [Our Goals and the *Magyar Ipar*), *Magyar Gazdák Szemléje*, January 1903, 23.

[23] Gyula Rubinek, "Van–e túltermelés?" [Is there overproduction?], *Magyar Gazdák Szeml éj*, February 1879, 104.

[24] "Paper wheat" is a reference to the futures market. Géza Petrassevich, *Zsidó földbirtokosok és bérlők Magyarországon* [Jewish Landlords and Renters in Hungary], (Budapest: Stephaneum, 1904), 3.

[25] Szabó, *Új vonások*, 20, 26.

[26] István Bernát, "Mi az igazság. Válasz Pap Dávidnak" [What is the Truth. Answer to David Pap], *Magyar Gazdák Szemléje*, January 1897, 38.

[27] Gyula Rubinek, *Parasztszocializmus* [Peasant Socialism], (Budapest: Patria, 1895), 32–37.

28 János Asbóth, quoted in Szabó, "Új vonások," 21.

29 Bálint Kutas, *Uzsorairtás* [The Extirpation of Usury], (Budapest: 1902), 17.

30 Szabó, *Új vonások*, 18.

31 *Ibid.*, 17–18; for cooperative movements as cure against peasant socialism see also "III. Szövetségi nagygyűlés 1899. évi jelentése," [Report of the IIIrd General Meeting of Cooperatives], *Köztelek*, Vol. 9, No. 101, (1899), 1874.

32 Hanák, *1849–1918*, 239–40, 252.

33 *Ibid.*, 286–305.

34 *Ibid.*, 316–335. Because of the political crisis on both sides of the Leitha, the new tariff did not go into effect until 1907.

35 Szabó, "Új vonások," 17.

36 Hanák, *1849–1918*, 335. For text of "Agráriusok választási röpirata, 1901," see Gyula Mérei, *A magyar polgári pártok programja (1867–1918)* [Programs of the Hungarian Bourgeois Parties], (Budapest: Akadémiai Kiadó, 1971), 180–83.

37 Istvaán Dolmányos, *A magyar parlamenti ellenzék történetéből, 1901–1904* [From the History of the Hungarian Parliamentary Opposition, 1901–1904], (Budapest: 1963), 22–24.

38 Magyar Királyi Központi Statisztikai Hivatal, *Magyar Statisztikai közlemények* [Hungarian Statistical Publications], *Új sorozat*, (Budapest: Központi Statisztikai Hivatal, 1913), Vol. 44, p. 18.

39 Berend and Ránki, *Magyarország gyáripara*, 38–39.

40 Hanák, *1849–1918*, 335.

41 GyOSz, *1903. évi jel.*, 8.

42 Friedrich Hertz, "Les organizations des industriels," 569–580.

43 Hartmut Kaelble, *Industrielle Interessenpolitik in der Wilhelminischen Gesellschaft*, (Berlin: Walter de Gruyter, 1967), 54.

44 Hanák, *1890–1914*, I, 121–22.

45 *Ibid.*, I, 121–24; 534, II, 699–700.

46 Ernő Kabos, "A magyarországi Szociáldemokrata Párt és a szakszervezetek kapcsolatai 1890 és 1918 között," *Tanulmányok a magyarországi szakszervezeti mozgalom történetéből*, Ernő Kabos (ed.), (Budapest: Táncsics, 1969), 91–95; Hanák, *1890–1918*, I, 534–37.

47 Hanák, 1890–1918, I, 530–31.

48 Berend and Ránki, *Magyarország gyáripara*, 338, 347.

49 E. g., GyOSz, *1906. évi jel.*, 41.

Notes   183

50 István Lackó, *A magyar munkás- és társadalombiztosítás története* [History of Hungarian Workers' and Social Insurance], (Budapest: Tánsics, 1968), 43–85.

51 *Ibid.*, 66; GyOSz, *1903, évi jel.*, 58–60.

52 Sándor Matlekovits, *Az ipar alakulása a capitalizmus korszakában* [The Development of Industry in the Age of Capitalism], (Budapest: Országos Iparegyesület, 1911), 3.

53 Matlekovits, *Az ipar alakulása*, 37, 52, 76.

54 Berend and Ránki, "A kisipar szerepe a magyar kapitalista fejlőd-ésben" [The Role of Small Industry in Hungary's Capitalist Development], *Gazdaság és társadalom, Tanulmányok hazánk és Kelet-Európa XIX-XX. századi történetéről* [Economy and Society, Studies in the History of Our Homeland and of Eastern Europe in the 19th and 20th Centuries], (Budapest: Magvető, 1974), 181–86, 193.

55 Szterényi, *Emlékirat*, 68.

56 Aradi Kereskedelmi és Iparkamara, *1904. évi jelentés* [1904 Annual Report], (Arad: 1905), 62.

57 Dezső Laky, *Az iparosok szociális és gazdasági viszonyai Budapesten* [The Social and Economic Conditions of Small Industrialists in Budapest], *Statisztikai közlemények* (Budapest: Budapest Székesfőváros Statisztikai Hivatala, 1930), Vol. 60, No. 3, 80.

58 István Salgó, *Kisipari vállakozások a tőkés Magyarországon* [Small Industrial Enterprises in Capitalist Hungary], (Unpublished Diploma Essay, Karl Marx University of Economics, Budapest, 1976), 87–89, 194.

59 Zoltán Sárközy, *A Budapesti Kereskedelmi és Iparkamara hivataltörténete, Levéltári Szemle*, 1967, No. 1, 61–65.

60 In 1853 in Pest besides 587 master tailors, 40 "widows" and 98 "Israelite" tailors—all of whom were in some sense "recognized"—there were also 602 "bunglers" (kontárok). Besides 239 master carpenters, there were 353 "bunglers." In Buda there were 36 master carpenters and 140 "bunglers." *Ibid.*, 63.

61 Gyula Szávay, *A magyar kamarai intézmény és a Budapesti Kamara története* [The Institution of Chambers in Hungary and the History of the Budapest Chamber], (Budapest: Budapesti Kereskedelmi és Iparkamara, 1927), 1931.

62 *Ibid.*, 341, 342. The cameral electoral law was altered to the advantage of big business in 1934.

[63] Országos Levéltár, Budapest Kamarai Választások, Z 1931, 41. cs. 52. t., pp. 23–26, 306.

[64] Mór Gelléri, *Ipartörténeti vázlatok* [Sketches in Industrial History], (Budapest: Wolfner és Singer, 1906).

[65] GyOSz, *1903. èvi jel.*, 19.

[66] GyOSz, *1927. évi jel.*, 19.

[67] Gelléri, *Ipartörténeti Vázlatok*, 133–35.

[68] "A kartellügy," *Magyar Ipar*, January 23, 1898.

[69] Mór Gelléri, *Hetven év a magyar ipar történetéből, 1842–1912,* [Seventy Years in the History of Hungarian Industry], (Budapest: Országos Iparegyesület, 1913), 226.

[70] T. E. (Thék, Endre), "Glosszák Wekerle felolvasásáról" [Commentary on Wekerle's Lecture], *Magyar Ipar*, Vol. XXIII, No. 6 (February 9, 1902), 164–66.

[71] Mór Gelléri, "Tömörülés a gyáripar érdekei körül" [Organization around the Interests of Factory Industry], *Magyar Ipar*, Vol XXIII, No. 6 (February 9, 1902), 1–3.

[72] For iron works and machine factories, Hektor Van den Eynde, "A gépipar 25 esztendője" [The Twenty–five Years of the Machine Industry], GyOSz, *1927. évi jel.*, 159–211; for mines and forges, *Strum–féle Országgyűlési Almanach, 1905–1910* [Strum's Parliamentary Almanac, 1905–1910], (Budapest: Pester Lloyd, 1905), 148–150; for sugar and Hatvany–Deutsch, *Magyar Életrajzi Lexikon* [Hungarian Biographical Encyclopedia], (Budapest: Akadémiai Kiadó, 1967), I, 183.

[73] *Ibid.*, 7–12.

[74] The yearbook of the Hungarian National Association of Iron Works and Machine Manufacturers recalls: "With the active participation of our president, Nándor Förster and members, it was decided already in January 1902 that in the name of the more intensive representation of industrial interests a central organization of industrialists like those existing in Austria and Germany should be established." Magyar Vas- és Gépgyárak Országos Egyesülete, *1911. évi jelentés.*, (Budapest: Patria, 1911), 38.

[75] GyOSz, *1903. évi jel.*, 9.

[76] Leó Lánczy, *Huszonöt év a magyar közgazdaság terén, Lánczy Leó munkássága, beszédei és dolgozatai* [Twenty–five Years in the Service of the Hungarian Economy, The Deeds, Speeches and Articles of Leó Lánczy], Ernő Makai (ed.), (Budapest: Grafikai Intézet, 1907).

Notes to Chapter 3

1 GyOSz, *1903. évi jel.*, 11.

2 All information from formal structure based on: GyOSz, *A Magyar Gyáriparosok Országos Szövetségének Alapszabályai* [By-Laws of the National Association of Hungarian Industrialists], (Budapest: Pesti Lloyd Társulat, 1903). We have not considered it sufficiently important to outline various minor changes that took place in the by-laws during the period.

3 Közlemények, No. 4 (November 1902), 10. This was the first meeting of the Steering Committee.

4 GyOSz, *1907. évi jel.*, 65.

5 GyOSz, *1914. évi jel.*, 255–89.

6 Friedrich Hertz, "Les organisations des industriels en Autriche," *Révue économique internationale* 1908, No. III, 575.

7 Calculated from *Mihók-féle Magyar Compass*, 1902/1903, 1912/1913; and membership lists in GyOSz, *1903. évi jel.*, GyOSz, *1914. évi jel.*, 256–75.

8 For bank connections, see Iván Berend and György Ránki, *Magyarország gyáripara, 1900–1914* [Hungarian Industry, 1900–1914], 151–52.

9 GyOSz, *1912. évi jel.*, 309–28.

10 *Magyar Gyáripar*, Vol. II, No. 10, 22.

11 GyOSz, *1903. évi jel.*, 12.

12 *Ibid.*, 34.

13 GyOSz, *1914. évi jel.*, 246.

14 GyOSz, *1903. évi jel.*, 87; GyOSz, *1914. évi jel.*, 256–75.

15 Vilmos Sándor, *Nagyipari fejlődés Magyarországon, 1867–1900* [Large Industrial Development in Hungary, 1867–1900], (Budapest: Szikra, 1954), 509.

16 GyOSz, *1903. évi jel.*, 50; GyOSz, *1914. évi jel.*, 246, 250, 252.

17 Zemaljski Savez Hrvatsko–Slavonskih Industrijalaca, *Godisnji izvestaj saveznog vijeca, 1914* [1914 Annual Report], (Zagreb: 1914), 57, 58.

18 GyOSz, *1914. évi jel.*, 256–74.

19 The sketch of Chorin is based on: William O McCagg, Jr., *Jewish Nobles and Geniuses in Modern Hungary*, (Boulder: East European Quarterly Press, 1972), 37, 89–91, 95–98; Vilmos Sándor, *Nagyipari fejlődés Magyarországon*, 392, 411, 415, 428, 569; Mór

Gelléri, *Ipartörténeti vázlatok* [Sketches in the History of Indus-
try], (Budapest: Singer és Wofner, 1906), 555–58; Péter Ujvári,
(ed.), *Zsidó Lexikon* [Jewish Encyclopedia], (Buapest: Zsidó Lexikon
Kiadása, 1929), 170; Miksa Fenyő, *Emlékbeszéd Chorin Ferencről*,
(Budapest: GyOSz, 1925); see also necrologies in OL, Z248, 1.
cs.; for Jewish philantropic activities, Ferenc Mezei, *A Közalap
aktái* [Documents of the "Common Fund"), (Budapest, 1900),
found in OL, K150, 3772, cs.

20 McCagg, 95.

21 For the history of the family see: McCagg, 249, passim; Sándor,
694, passim; Ágnes Kenyeres, (ed.), *Új Magyar Életrajzi Lexikon*
[New Hungarian Encyclopedia of Biography], (Budapest: Akadémiai Kiadó, 1967), I, 683; Béla Kempelen, *Magyarországi zsidó és
eredetű családok* [Hungary's Jewish and Jewish–Origin Families]
(3 volumes, Budapest: Viktória Nyomda, 1937–1939); Újvári,
Zsidó Lexikon.

22 Sándor, 68, 89.

23 Lóránt, Hegedüs, *Ady és Tisza* [Ady and Tisza], (Budapest: Nyugat, n. d., 35.

24 *Egyenlőség* (June 1, 1902); for an estimate of the proportion of
GyOSz members who were Jews, McCagg, 28.

25 István Vida, "Some letters of Ferenc Chorin, Jr.," Három Chorin-
levél, in *Századok* 1977:2, 362–80.

26 Mór Gelléri, Ípartörténi vázlatok, 620; Mór Gelléri, *Újabb napi
kérdések a Magyar Ipar köréből* [Newer Current Problems from
the Magyar Ipar], (Budapest: Singer és Wolfner, 1914), 306ff.

27 Compiled from *Magyar Compass*, 1902/1903. "Officers of GyOSz"
was defined as members elected by General Assembly to Presidency, Managing Directorate or Executive Committee of GyOSz
in 1902: listed in GyOSz, *1903. évi jel.*.

28 Berend and Ránki, *Magyarország gyáripara*, 165.

29 McCagg, 28.

30 GyOSz, *1906. évi jel.*, 67; GyOSz, *1913. évi jel.*, Miksa Fenyő,
Feljegyzések és levelek a Nyugatról [Notes and Letters on the
Nyugat], Erzsébet Vezér, (ed.), (Budapest: Akadémiai Kiadó,
1975), 37; on Gratz see *Magyar Gyáripar*, Vol. VIII, No. 4,
(February 15, 1917) and Chapter 5 of present work.

31 GyOSz, *1905. évi jel.*

32 Hegedüs, *Ady és Tisza*, 51.

33 Erzsébet Vezér in Miksa Fenyő, *Feljegyzések*, 23.

34 Budapest Fővárosi Bíróság, Cégbírósági Levéltár, Cg628, Nyugat Irodalmi és Nyomda R. T. The author gratefully acknowledges his debt for this reference to Dr. Mario Fenyő.

Notes to Chapter 4

1 László Varga has made this point in his studies of the 1890 industrial promotion laws in *Történelmi Szemle*, 1980/2.

2 *Magyar Gyáripar*, I, No. 10 (1911), 1–2.

3 For the early history of the movement see: Mihály Futó, *A magyar gyáripar története* [The History of Hungarian Industry], (Budapest: Magyar Gazdaságkutató Intézet, 1944), Vol. I, 360–76; Dávid Papp, *Magyar vámterület* [Hungarian Customs Area], (Budapest: Grill Károly, 1904), 42–58.

4 Gyula Szávy, *A magyar kamarai intézmény és a Budapesti Kamara története* [The Institution of Chambers in Hungary and the History of the Budapest Chamber], (Budapest: Budapesti Kereskedelmi és Iparkamara, 1927), 394; Vilmos Sándor, *Nagyipari fejlődés Magyarországon, 1867–1900* [Large–Industrial Development in Hungary, 1867–1900], (Budapest: Szikra, 1954), 384.

5 GyOSz, *1903. évi jel.*, 19.

6 For views of a typical banker, see: Leó Lánczy, *Huszonöt év a magyar közgazdaság terén. Lánczy Leó munkássága, beszédei és dolgozatai* [Twenty–five Years in the Service of the Hungarian Economy. The Deeds, Speeches and Articles of Leó Lánczy], Ernő Makai (ed.), (Budapest: Grafikai Intézet, 1907), 47–48.

7 For Mauthner, see GyOSz, *Közlemények*, no. 16 (1905), 20; for Hertz, GyOSz, *Közlemények*, no. 23 (1906), 27–42; for Kohner, Iván Berend and György Ránki, *Magyarország gyáripara, 1900–1914* [Hungarian Industry, 1900–1914], (Budapest: Szikra, 1955), 232.

8 Berend and Ránki, *Magyarország gyáripara*, 103.

9 Jenő Varga, "A magyar kartellek," in *A proletardiktatúra gazdaságpolitikája. Válogatott írások, 1912–1922* [The Economic Policies of the Dictatorship of the Proletariat, Selected Works, 1912–1922], Ferenc Böröczfy (ed.), (Budapest: Kossuth, 1976), 71.

10 GyOSz, *Közlemények*, No. 33 (1906), 174.

11 *Ibid.*, No. 16 (1905), 8–9.

12 Endre Scheiber, *Magyar közgazdasági politika: közös vámterület, önálló vámterület, magyar vámterület* [Hungarian Economic Policy, Common Customs Area, Independent Customs Area, Hungarian Customs Area], (Budapest: Kilián Frigyes, 1905).

13 GyOSz, *1906. évi jel.*, 10.

14 GyOSz, *1909. évi jel.*, 16, 112–13.

15 *Magyar Gyáripar*, IV, No. 19 (1915), 3.

16 GyOSz. *1914. évi jel.*, 38–40.

17 *Magyar Gyáripar*, III, No. 14 (1914), 2.

18 OL PM (Elnöki), K255, 1198, külön csomó. Az 1906–1917 gazdasági kiegyezés okmányai. GyOSz, "Emlékirat a Magyarország és Ausztria közötti kiegyezésről" [Memorandum on the Agreement between Austria and Hungary].

19 OL PM (Elnöki), K255, 1198, külön csomó. *Észrevételek az Ausztriával való gazdasági kiegyezés tárgyalási anyagára vonatkozólag a Kereskedelmi Minisztériumban készült emlékiratra*, [Notes on the Memorandum of the Ministry of Commerce in Regard to the Material of the Negotiations of the Economic Agreement with Austria]; *ibid.*, *Kereskedelemügyi Minisztérium, Az Ausztriával, való gazdasági újabb megegyezés és a külföldi, államokkal újból kötendő kereskedelmi szerződések tárgyalása során döntést igénylő fontosabb kérdések* [Main Questions Requiring Decision in Connection with the Newer Economic Agreement with Austria and the Trade Treaties to be Tied Anew with Foreign States].

20 OL PM (Elnöki), K255, 1198, külön csomó. Földügyi Minisztériumnak a Kereskedelmügyi; Minisztériumi memorandumra vonatkozó megjegyzések [Comments of the Ministry of Agriculture on the Memorandum of the Ministry of Commerce].

21 GyOSz. *1915. évi jel.*, 5.

22 Lajos Láng, *A vámpolitika az utolsó 100 évben* [Tariff Policies in the Last 100 Years], (Budapest: Grill Károly, 1904), 471; see also Wilhelm Offergeld, *Die Grundlagen und Ursachen der industrieller Entwicklung Ungarns*, (Jena: Gustav Fischer, 1914), 187.

23 OL PM (Elnöki), K255, 1198, külön csomó. GyOSz, "Emlékirat . . .," 34–35.

24 *Ibid.*, 36–41.

25 GyOSz, *1910. évi jel.*, 7.

26 Péter Hanák, (ed.), *Magyarország története, 1890–1918*, [History of Hungary, 1890–1918], (Budapest: Akadémiai Kiadó, 1978), Vol. I, 37–38.

27 GyOSz, *1903. évi jel.*, 55.

28 *Magyar Gyáripar*, III, No. 9 (1913), 16–17.

29 GyOSz, *1909. évi jel.*, 149–51; *1913. évi jel.*, 30.

30 *Magyar Gyáripar*, II, No. 20 (1912), 1–2.

31 *Ibid.*, I, No. 19 (1911), 3–4.

32 *Ibid.*, I, No. 6 (1911), 1.

33 GyOSz, *1914. évi jel.*, 50–58.

34 *Magyar Gyárpiar*, II, No. 12 (1912), 3–4; *ibid.*, II, No. 20 (1912), 3–4.

35 Jószef Szterényi, *Iparfejlesztés* [The Promotion of Industry], (Budapest: Franklin társulat, 1902).

36 Varga, Manuscript . . . Ch. I, 38–66.

37 GyOSz, *1908. évi jel.*, 14.

38 GyOSz, *1907. évi jel.*, 17.

39 *Magyar Gyárpiar*, II, No. 2 (1912), 2.

40 GyOSz, *Közlemények*, December 1903, 5–6.

41 Magyar Királyi Keresdedelemügyi Minisztérium, *A kereskedelemügyi minisztérium 1889. évi működéséről a törvényhozás elé terjesztett jelentése* [Report of the Ministry of Commerce on Its Activities of the Year 1889 Presented to the Legislature], (Budapest: 1890), 205.

42 GyOSz, *1903. évi jel.*, 24–25.

43 GyOSz, *Közlemények*, No. 1 (1902), 4.

44 GyOSz, *1902. évi jel.*, 24–27.

45 GyOSz, *1905. évi jel.*, 8.

46 GyOSz, *1903. évi jel.*, 53.

47 Based on: Iván Berend and György Ránki, *Gazdaság és társadalom, Tanulmányok Hazánk és Kelet-Európa XIX–XX. századi törté- ntéről* [Economy and Society, Studies on the History of our Nation and Eastern Europe in the 19th and 20th Century], (Budapest: Magvető, 1974), 56. In an earlier book, the authors estimate the proportion to be 10–12 percent though it is not clear for what year: *Magyarország gyáripara, 1900–1914*, 287.

48 Berend and Ránki, *Magyaroszág gyáripara, 1900–1914*, 51.

49 GyOSz, *1905. évi jel.*, 34.

50   GyOSz, *1903. évi jel.*, 53–58; *1905. évi jel.*, 34–38; *1906. évi jel.*, 19; *Közlemények*, No. 21 (1905), 23–38.

51   GyOSz, *Közlemények*, No. 21 (1905), 24, 29.

52   GyOSz, *1905. évi jel.*, 26.

53   GyOSz, *Közlemények*, No. 31 (1907), 10–15.

54   Berend and Ránki, *Magyaroszág gyáripara, 1900–1914*, 29, 189, 201.

55   Sándor, 36, 201.

56   Hanák, *Magyarország története, 1890–1918*, Vol. I, 274.

57   GyOSz, *1905. évi jel.*, 26, 38; *1906. évi jel.*, 25–26.

58   GyOSz, *1903. évi jel.*, 52.

59   GyOSz, *1914. évi jel.*, 50–58.

60   GyOSz, *Közlemények*, No. 21 (1905), 23–38; *ibid.*, No. 31 (1907), 6–21.

61   Berend and Ránki, *Magyaroszág gyáripara, 1900–1914*, 51.

62   József Szterényi and Jenő Ladányi, *A magyar ipar a világháború-ban* [Hungarian Industry in the World War], (Budapest: Franklin, 1933), 16.

63   In Hungary, the "left" signified the forces of 1848, i.e., the critics of the Compromise of 1867.

64   GyOSz, *1907. évi jel.*, 25–26; *1912. évi jel.*, 97.

65   GyOSz, *Közlemények*, January 1907, 76.

66   *Ibid.*, May 1908, 75.

67   GyOSz, *1909. évi jel.*, 103.

68   *Ibid.*, 134.

69   Péter Hanák, (ed.), *Magyararoszág története, 1849–1918* [The History of Hungary, 1849–1918], (Budapest: Tankönyvkiadó, 1976), 176–77.

70   *Ibid.*, 177; Sándor, 368; Herbert Matis, "Wirtschaftspolitik," in *Die Habsburgermonarchie, 1848–1918*, Bd. I: *Die Wirtschaftliche Entwicklung*, (Vienna: Österreichische Akademie der Wissenschaften, 1973), 44.

71   Sándor, 368; Károly Vörös, (ed.), *Budapest története a márciusi forradalomtól az őszirózsás forradalomig* [The History of Budapest from the March Revolution [of 1848] to the Chrysanthemum Revolution [of 1918]], (Budapest: Akadémiai Kiadó, 1978), 529.

72   GyOSz, *Közlemények*, No. 4 (1902), 10–14.

73   *Ibid.*, 10–18.

74   GyOSz, *1903. évi jel.*, 29.

75 Károly Vörös, *Budapest története*, 529.

76 Jenő Vida, "A szénbányászat 25 esztendője," [The Twenty-five Years of the Coal Industry], in MGyOSz, *25. évi jel.*, (1927), 114.

77 *E.g.*, MGyOSz, *1906. évi jel.*, *1907. évi jel.*, 28; *1908. évi jel.*, 66–70.

78 GyOSz, *1908. évi jel.*, 28–29.

79 István Dolmányos, "Die Eisenbahnpragmatik vom Jahr 1907 und der Beginn der Kroatischen Obstruktion," *Annales Universitatis Scientarum Budapestiensis. Sectio Historica*, Vol. 14 (Budapest, 1973).

80 GyOSz, *1908. évi jel.*, 74.

81 GyOSz, *1909. évi jel.*, 170.

82 GyOSz, *1910. évi jel.*, 130–34.

83 GyOSz, *1912. évi jel.*, 148–59.

84 *Magyar Gyáripar*, II, No. 2 (1912), 3.

85 GyOSz, *1910. évi jel.*, 137–38.

86 *Magyar Gyáripar*, II, No. 10 (1912), 18–19.

87 GyOSz, *1905. évi jel.*, 51.

88 GyOSz, *1910. évi jel.*, 72–73; *1913. évi jel.*, 37.

89 GyOSz, *1910. évi jel.*, 110–11.

90 Quote from Dr. Ferenc Chorin, Jr., GyOSz, *Közlemények*, No. 23 (1904), 45.

91 GyOSz, *1910. évi jel.*, 18.

92 Berend and Ránki, *Magyarország gyáripara, 1900–1914*, 89.

93 For views of both agrarians and socialists, see articles in Magyar Közgazdasági Társaság, *A Drágaság* [The Inflation], (Budapest, 1912).

94 GyOSz, *Közlemények*, No. 33 (1906), 64–65.

95 Varga, *A magyar kartellek*, 70.

96 *Magyar Pénzügy*, July 19, 1902, 3–4.

97 See speech by Kálmán Szabó, president of the Debrecen branch of the GyOSz, *Közlemények*, No. 23 (1906), 47.

98 Berend and Ránki, *Magyarország gyáripara, 1900–1914*, 81.

99 Bernard Michel, *Banques et banquiers en Autriche au debut du 20ᵉ siècle* (Paris: Fondation Nationale des Sciences Politiques, 1976), 162–64; Richard Rudolph, *Banking and Industrialization in Austria-Hungary, The Role of Banks in the Industrialization of the Czech Crownlands, 1873–1914*, (Cambridge: Cambridge University Press, 1976), 102–121.

100 *E.g.*, Varga, *Magyar kartellek*, 91.

101 Berend and Ránki, *Magyaroszág gyáripara, 1900–1914*, 147–48.

102 Michel, *Banques et banquiers*, 147–48.

103 Berend and Ránki, *Magyarország gyáripara, 1900–1914*, 91.

104 *Ibid.*, 91–92; Michel, *Banques et banquiers*, 170.

105 Varga, *Magyar kartellek*, 89.

106 OL Z213. *Magyar Üveggyárosok Országos Egyesülete közgyűlési és igazgatósági ülési jegyzőkönyvek, 1908–1941* [Minutes of the General Assembly and Executive Council Meetings of the Hungarian National Association of Glass Manufacturers].

107 GyOSz, *1912. évi jel.*, 110.

108 GyOSz, *1906. évi jel.*, 59–60.

109 GyOSz, *1910. évi jel.*, 110.

110 GyOSz, *1908. évi jel.*, 37; *1910. évi jel.*, 110.

111 GyOSz, *1907. évi jel.*, 51; *1914. évi jel.*, 73.

112 GyOSz, *1914. évi jel.*, 255–89.

113 OL Z425, 3. csomag, 25. szám. Ganz titkárság (Gépgyári kartell), (Ganz Secretariat, Machine Cartel).

114 Berend and Ránki, *Magyaroraszág gyáripara, 1900–1914*, 95.

115 GyOSz, *1906. évi jel.*, 59.

116 GyOSz, *Közlemények*, No. 23 (1906), 49–50.

117 GyOSz, *1910. évi jel.*, 111–12.

118 *Magyar Gyáripar*, III, no. 13 (1913), 10.

119 GyOSz, *1912. évi jel.*, 85.

120 GyOSz, *1914. évi jel.* 63064; *Magyar Gyáripar*, III, No. 15 (1913), 3.

121 Varga, *Magyar kartellek*, 51, 62, 72, 77, 79, 82, 88.

122 Hanák, *Magyarország története, 1890–1918*, I, 348.

123 Berend and Ránki, *Magyarország gyáripara, 1900–1914*, 91–92, 224.

124 Hanák, *Magyararoszág története, 1890–1918*, I, 292; László Katus, "Economic Growth in Hungary during the Age of Dualism (1867–1913), A Quantitative Analysis," in *Studia Historica Academiae Scientiarum Hungaricae*, No. 62 (Budapest: Akadémiai Kiadó, 1970), 58.

125 Handelsministerium, *Verhandlungen der von k. k. Handelsministerium veranstalteten Kartellanquete.* 2 vols. (Vienna: k. k. Hof- und Staatsdruckerei, 1912).

126 *Magyar Gyáripar*, III, No. 23 (1913), 2.

127 Antal Géber, "Az utolsó évek munkásmozgalmai Magyarországon," [Working Class Movements in Hungary in Recent Years], in *Magyar munkasszociográfiák, 1881–1945* [Hungarian Worker Sociographies, 1881–1945], György Litván, (ed.), (Budapest: Kossuth, 1974), 129.

128 Calculated on the basis of figures in Berend and Ránki, *Magyarország gyáripara, 1900–1914,* 305, and Géber, 128.

129 Berend and Ránki, *Magyarország gyáripara, 1900–1914,* 314–15.

130 GyOSz, *Közlemények,* No. 33 (1907), 47–52.

131 Hanák, *Magyarország története, 1890–1918,* I, 412.

132 GyOSz, *Közlemények,* No. 33 (1907), 87; Géber, 130–131.

133 GyOSz, *Közlemények,* No. 33 (1907), 3, 228.

134 *Ibid.,* 182–83.

135 *Ibid.,* 409–14.

136 GyOSz, *1909. évi jel.,* 69–80.

137 István Lackó, *A magyar munkás- és társadalombiztosítás története* [History of Workers' and Social Insurance in Hungary], (Budapest: Táncsics, 1968), 66–85.

138 GyOSz, *1909, évi jel.,* 69–80.

139 *Magyar Gyáripar,* III, No. 13 (1913), 3–4; *ibid.,* III, No. 24, 5–6; *ibid.,* IV, No. 1 (1914), 2.

140 GyOSz, *1907. évi jel.* 62–63; *Pesti Napló* 1910, No. 133, 19.

141 GyOSz, *1912. évi jel.,* 180–88.

142 GyOSz, *1906. évi jel.,* 41.

143 GyOSz, *1905. évi jel.,* 48.

144 GyOSz, *1910. évi jel.,* 147.

145 GyOSz, *1906. évi jel.,* 63.

146 GyOSz, *1907. évi jel.,* 61.

147 GyOSz, *1909, évi jel.,* 181–83.

148 *Népszava,* June 6, 1908, p. 3; June 13, 1908, 1.

149 Joseph LaPalombara, *Interest Groups in Italian Politics,* (Princeton: Princeton University Press, 1964), 262, 300–307.

Notes to Chapter 5

1 For a synthesis, see Péter Hanák, (ed.), *Magyarország története, 1890–1918* [History of Hungary, 1890–1918], (2 vols., Budapest: Akadémiai Kiadó, 1978).

2 *Ibid.,* I, 105.

3   Vilmos Sándor, *Nagyipari fejlődés Magyarországon, 1867–1900*
    [The Development of Large Industry in Hungary, 1867–1900],
    (Budapest: Szikra, 1954), 382–85.

4   Miksa Fenyő, *Emlékbeszéd Chorin Ferencről* [Eulogy on Ferenc
    Chorin], (Budapest: GyOSz, 1925), 12; Ferenc Pölöskei, *Kormány-
    zati politika és parlamenti ellenzék, 1910–1914* [Government Poli-
    cies and Parliamentary Opposition, 1910–1914], (Budapest: Aka-
    démiai Kiadó, 1970), 241.

5   Tibor Hajdu, *Károlyi Mihály, Politikai életrajz* [Michael Károlyi,
    A Political Biography], (Budapest: Kossuth, 1978), 37, 45.

6   Hanák, *Magyarország története, 1890–1918*, I, 39, 383.

7   Péter Hanák, (ed.), *Magyarország története, 1849–1918. Az Ab-
    szolutizmus és a Dualizmus kora* [The History of Hungary, 1849–
    1918, The Age of Absolutism and Dualism], (Budapest: Tankönyv-
    kiadó, 1975), 335.

8   Hanák, *Magyarország története, 1890–1918*, I, 520.

9   *Ibid.*, 521–22, 526.

10 *Ibid.*, 526–30; Gusztáv Erényi, *Graf Stefan Tisza*, (Vienna, Leipzig:
    1935).

11 Hanák, *Magyarország története, 1890–1918*, I, 527.

12 GyOSz, *Közlemények*, No. 8 (1903).

13 Hajdu, *Mihály Károlyi*, 40.

14 Hanák, *Magyarország története, 1890–1918*, I, 553–55.

15 GyOSz, *1903. évi jel.*, 37, 24, 68–72, 77, 79.

16 GyOSz, *1905. évi jel.*, 8.

17 GyOSz, *1906. évi jel.*, 77–78.

18 Ernő Lengyel, "A koalíció" [The Coalition], in *A Magyar Ország-
    gyűlés története, 1867–1927* [History of the Hungarian Parlia-
    ment, 1867–1927], Antal Balla, (ed.), (Budapest: Légrády, n.d.),
    251.

19 Gusztáv Erényi, *Tisza*, 213.

20 *Magyar Gyáripar*, III, No. 2 (1913), 4. In a related article it
    continued: "Hungarian industry wants a Parliament and a public
    attitude which are imbued with a feeling for the problems of the
    economy and with the capacity to recognize the great challenges
    of our future, challenges which are in the first place related to
    the development of our industry. See also *Magyar Gyáripar*, I,
    No. 14 (1911), 1–2.

21 Hanák, *Magyarország története, 1890–1918*, I, 560.

22 *Ibid.*, 572–83, 587–90.

23 *Ibid.*, 599–606, 612.

24 GyOSz, *1907. évi jel.*, 8; Miksa Fenyő, *Emlékbeszéd* Chorin Ferencöl, 18.

25 GyOSz, *1906. évi jel.*, 19.

26 For the attitude of the GyOSz under the Károlyi regime, see Fenyő in *Magyar Gyáripar*, VIII, 24 (1918), 1–2; for the final years of GyOSz, see Károly Jenei, "A Magyar Gyáriparosok Országos Szövetségének iratai a Központi Gazdasági Levéltárban" [The Papers of the GyOSz in the Central Economic Archives], *Levéltári Hirek*, X, No. 1 (1960). 29–32.

27 Hanák, *Magyarország története, 1890–1918*, I, 186–88; György Litván, "*Magyar gondolat—szabad gondolat,*" *Nacionalizmus és progresszió század eleji Magyarországon* ["Hungarian Thought— Free Thought," Nationalism and Progressivism in Hungary at the Beginning of the Century], (Budapest: Magvető Kiadó, 1978), 70.

28 Hanák, *Magyarország története, 1890–1918*, I, 406, 447.

29 *Fővárosi Szemle*, 1915.

30 Éva H. Balázs, *Berzeviczy Gergely, a reformpolitikus, 1763–1795* [Gergely Berzeviczy, The Reformer, 1763–1795], (Budapest: Akadémiai Kiadó, 1967), Introduction.

31 Zsuzsa L. Nagy, *Szabadkömüvesség a XX. században* [Freemasonry in the Twentieth Century], (Budapest: Kossuth, 1977), 24–29; Ludwig Hass, "The Socioprofessional Composition of Hungarian Freemasonry (1868–1920)," *Acta Polinae Historica*, 1974, No. 30, 71.

32 Zsuzsa L. Nagy, 26–27; Hanák, *Magyarország története, 1890–1918*, 924–25.

33 József Palatinusz, *A szabadkőművesség bűnei* [The Sins of Freemasonry], Budapest, 1920–39.

34 Mór Gelléri, *Ipartörténeti vázlatok* [Sketches of Industrial History], (Budapest: Wolfner es Singer, 1906), 737–46.

35 Zsuzsa L. Nagy, 27.

36 Palatinusz, Vol. I; Hanák, *Magyarország története, 1890–1918*, 925; Zsuzsa L. Nagy, 28.

37 Local political privileges based on birth and property.

38 Hanák, *Magyarország története, 1890–1918*, I, 406, 518.

39 Mór Gelléri, *Ipartörténeti vázlatok.*

40 For the history of the movement see Litván, *Magyar gondolat*; Zoltán Horváth, *Magyar századforduló. A második reformnem-*

zedék története *(1896-1914)* [Hungarian Turn of the Century, The History of the Second Reform Generation (1896-1914)], (2nd edition: Budapest: Gondolat, 1974).

41 For the self–declared chauvinism of the *Fővárosi Lapok* [Journal of the Capital], see Horváth, *Magyar századforduló*, 37; on the social background of Hungarian conservatism, see Péter Hanák, "Economics, Society and Sociopolitical Thought in Hungary during the Age of Capitalism," *Austrian History Yearbook*, XI (1977), 123–35.

42 György Litván and László Szűcs, *A szociológia első magyar műhelye* [The First Hungarian Workshop of Sociology], (Budapest: Gondolat, 1973), 11–12; see also Mary Gluck, *George Lukács and His Generation, 1900–1918*, (Cambridge: Harvard University Press, 1985).

43 *Huszadik Század*, 1904, No. 2, 615–32.

44 "A magyar válság," [The Hungarian Crisis], *Huszadik Század*, 1906, No. 8, 130–49.

45 *Huszadik Század*, 1905.

46 *Huszadik Század*, 1904, No. 2.

47 Lóránt Hegedüs, "A dunántúli kivándorlás" [Emigration from Transdanubia], (Budapest: Budapesti Szemle, 1905); rviewed in *Huszadik Század*, 1905, No. 2, 436–40.

48 *Huszadik Század*, 1905.

49 Litván and Szűcs, *Magyar szociológia*, 16–19.

Notes to Chapter 6

1 Péter Hanák, (ed.), *Magyarország története, 1890–1918* [History of Hungary, 1890–1918], (2 vols.; Budapest: Akadémiai Kiadó, 1978), II, 610, 611.

2 Ernő Lengyel, "A koalíció" [The Coalition], in *A Magyar Országgyűles története, 1867–1927* [History of the Hungarian Parliament, 1867–1927], Antal Balla, (ed.), (Budapest: Légrády, n.d.), 284.

3 Hanák, *Magyarország története, 1890–1918*, II, 616.

4 Lengyel, 284.

5 Hanák, *Magyarország története,1890–1918*, II, 610.

6 William O. McCagg, Jr., *Jewish Nobles and Geniuses in Modern Hungary* (Boulder: East European Quarterly, 1972), 191–93.

7 Hanák, *Magyarország története, 1890–1918*, II, 623–53, 771–76.

8 József Szterényi, *Régmúlt idők emléke* [Memories of Times Long Past], (Budapest: Pesti Könyvnyomda, 1925), 39–44.

9 GyOSz, *Közlemények*, No. 23 (1906), 27–42.

10 "Az egyenes adók reformjának alapelvei" [Principles of the Reform of the Direct Taxes], in *Az 1906. évi május hó 19–ére hirdetett Országgyűlés Nyomtatványi: Képviselőház, Irományok* [The Publications of the May 19, 1906 Cycle of Parliament: House of Representatives, Documents], Vol. XVIII, 13–25.

11 Lóránt Hegedüs, *Adórendszerünk betegségei* [The Ills of Our Tax System], (Budapest: GyOSz, 1907), 49.

12 Károly Vörös, "Budapest legnagyobb adófizetői, 1903–1917" [Budapest's Greatest Tax Payers, 1903–1917], *Tanulmányok Budapest Múltjából*, XVIII (1966), 145; Pál Szende, (ed.), *A magyar közgazdaság és az Országos Magyar Kereskedők Egyesülete, 1904–1914* [The Hungarian Economy and the National Association of Hungarian Merchants, 1904–1914], (Budapest: OMKE, 1914), 244.

13 Hegedüs, *Adórendszerünk*, 40–48.

14 Szende, *OMKE*, 244.

15 Iván Gerend and György Ránki, *Gazdaság és társadalom. Tanulmányok hazánk és Kelet–Európa XIX–XX. századi történetéből* [Economy and Society. Studies in the History of Our Nation and Eastern Europe in the 19th and 20th Centuries], (Budapest: Magvető, 1974), 48.

16 Hegedüs, *Adórendszerünk*, 115.

17 *Op. cit., Országgyűlés nyomatványai*, 13–25.

18 Pál Sándor's speech in *op. cit., Országgyűlés nyomtatványai. Képviselőház, Napoló* [House of Representatives, Minutes of Sessions], Vol. XXIII, 76–78.

19 *Országgyűlés nyomatatványai, Irományok*, Vol. XVIII, 4–12.

20 Béla Sarlós, *Közigazgatás és hatalompolitika a Dualizmus rendszerében* [Public Administration and Power Politics under the System of Dualism], (Budapest: Akadémai Kiadó, 1976), 200–233.

21 Hegedüs, *Adórendszerünk*, 115.

22 *Országgyűlés nyomtatványai, Irományok*, Vol. XVIII, 13–25.

23 In particular, the white–collar government workers protested the "steep progressivity" of the personal income tax at the middle levels, the high rates of taxation of family houses and the "double

taxation" of credit unions. OL K255 1908. 2. tétel, 600. csomó.
No. 1432, 16.

[24] Szende, *OMKE*, 247.

[25] Országos Iparegyesület, *1908. évi jelentés* [1908 Annual Report of the OIe], (Budapest: Országos Iparegyesület, 1908), 46–47.

[26] *Magyar Ipar*, XXIX, No. 9 (1908), 238–40.

[27] Sarlós, *Közigazgatás*, 212–18.

[28] GyOSz, *1908. évi jel.*, 131–34; Szende, *OMKE*, 236–37; for grievances of Országos Iparegyesület, see *Magyar Ipar*, XXIX, No. 9 (1908), *Melléklet* [Supplement].

[29] Szende, *OMKE*, 247.

[30] GyOSz, *1908. évi jel.*, 129.

[31] Szende, *OMKE*, 237.

[32] *Országgyűlés nyomtatványai, Irományok*, Vol. XXXI, 68, passim.

[33] Szende, *OMKE*, 249; *Országgyű.és nyomtatványai, Képviselőházi Napoló*, Vol. XXIII (January 1909).

[34] GyOSz, *1909. évi jel.*, 30.

[35] István Dolmányos, "Lehet–e rehabilitálni a koalíció adótörvényeit?" [Can the Tax Laws of the Coalition be Rehabilitated?] *Történelmi Szemle*, 1976, 3, 496–98; Béla Sarlós, "Válasz Dolmányos István kritikai megjegyzéseire" [Reply to the Critical Remarks of István Dolmányos], *ibid.*, 499–503.

[36] Béla Jankovitch, "Orztrák és magyar index–számok, 1867–1909" [Austrian and Hungarian Indices, 1879–1909], in *A drágaság* [The Inflation], (Budapest: Magyar Közgazdasági Társaság, 1912), 315–33. For England the same index rose by only 23 percent.

[37] Magyar Királyi Központi Statisztikai Hivatal, *Árstatisztika* [Price Statistics], Magyar Statisztikai Közlemények, Vol. 44, New Series, (Budapest: Központi Statisztikai Hivatal, 1913), 406–07.

[38] For the most serious contemporary analyses, see *A drágaság*; for the more popular views, Gyula Zachár and Béla Bálint, *A drágaság okai Budapestern és elhárításának módjai* [The Causes of the High Cost of Living in Budapest and the Means of Its Elimination], (Budapest: Országos Iparegyesület, 1910); anti–Austrian, Independence Party viewpoint in *Pesti Hírlap*, 1906, No. 247, 4–5.

[39] *Árstatisztika*, 18.

[40] Hanák *Magyarország története, 1890–1918*, 621–23, 774–76.

[41] For the views of Austrian industry on Balkan trade, see Bernard Michel, *Banques et banquiers en Austriche au debut du 20ᵉ siècle*,

(Paris: Presses de la Fondation Nationale des Sciences Politiques, 1976), 261–80.

42 GyOSz, *1909. évi jel.*, 132–34.

43 *Népszava*, Vol. 35, No. 300 (1907), 1–2.

44 GyOSz, *Közlemények*, No. 48 (1909), 11; see also Szende, *OMKE*, 80–81.

45 "Az ébredezö burzsoázia" [The Awakening Bourgeoisie], *Népszava*, 1908, No. 266, 3.

46 GyOSz, *Közlemények*, No. 48 (1909), 6.

47 József Szterényi, *Régmúlt idők emlékei*, 50.

48 Hanák, *Magyarország története, 1890–1918*, II, 767, 778–79.

49 Bernard Michel, *Banques et banquiers*, 229.

50 Hanák, *Magyarország története, 1890–1918*, II, 766–70, 776–84.

Notes to Chapter 7

1 Ferenc Pölëskei, *Kormányzati politika és parlamenti ellenzék, 1910–1914* [Government Policies and Parliamentary Opposition, 1910–1914], (Budapest: Akadémiai Kiadó, 1970). Pölöskei emphasizes only the conservative nature of the Party. Yet, he presents material that supports the interpretation I have indicated. See also, Béla Sarlós, *Közigazgatás és hatalompolitika a Dualizmus rendszerében* [Public Administration and Power Politics under the System of Dualism], (Budapest: Akadémai Kiadó, 1976), 235–38, for attempts of Party of National Work to gain support of urban middle classes.

2 Gusztáv Gratz, *A Dualizmus kora, Magyarország története, 1867–1918* [The Age of Dualism, The History of Hungary, 1867–1918], (2 vols.; Budapest: Magyar Szemle Társaság, 1934), II, 254–55.

3 GyOSz, *1910. évi jel.*, 128–29; Mór Gelléri, *Újabb napi kérdések a Magyar Ipar köréből* [Newer Actual Questions from the Circle of the Magyar Ipar], (Budapest: Singer és Wolfner, 1914), 241.

4 Lóránt Hegedüs, *Ady és Tisza* [Ady and Tisza], (Budapest: Nyugat, n.d., 48.

5 Péter Hanák, (ed.), *Magyarország története, 1849–1918, Az Abszolutizmus és Dualizmus kora* [History of Hungary, 1849–1918, The Age of Absolutism and Dualism], (2nd edition; Budapest: Tankönyvkiadó, 1967), 477.

6 GyOSz, *1911. évi jel.*, 118.

7 *Magyar Gyáripar*, II, No. 13 (1912), 3.

8 GyOSz, *1912*. *èvi jel.*, 205–06; *Magyar Gyáripar*, II, No. 8 (1912), 7; *ibid.*, No. 24, 11; GyOSz, *1914*. *èvi jel.*, 175. On beginnings of depression, see Iván Berend and György Ránki, *Magyarország gyáripara, 1900–1914* [Hungarian Industry, 1900–1914], (Budapest: Szikra, 1955), 358.

9 GyOSz, *1913*. *évi jel.*, 38–39.

10 Pölöskei, 34–35; *Magyar Gyáripar*, II, No. 1 (1912), 2.

11 Endre Scheiber, "A Gy.O.Sz., a kormány és az összeférhetetlenség" [The GyOSz, the Government and the Law of Incompatibility] *Magyar Ipar*, II, No. 2 (1912), 3.

12 Hegedüs, *Ady és Tisza*, 48.

13 Pölöskei, 138–40.

14 GyOSz, *1911*. *évi jel.*, 170.

15 *Magyar Gyáripar*, III, No. 1 (1913), 1–2; GyOSz, *1913*. *évi jel.*, 164–72.

16 *Magyar Gyáripar*, II, No. 3 (1912), 7.

17 GyOSz, *1913.évi jel.*, 171–72.

18 Gyula Rácz, "A választójogi törvényjavaslat és a városi polgárság" [The Suffrage Reform Bill and the Bourgeoisie], *Városi Szemle*, 1913, 90.

19 Hanák, *Magarország története, 1849–1918*, 484–85.

20 *Magyar Gyáripar*, II, No. 11 (1912), 2.

21 *Ibid.*, III, No. 2 (1913), 1–2, 9.

22 *Ibid.*, III, No. 1 (1913), 2.

23 *Magyar Gyáripar*, III, No. 2, 3–9.

24 *Magyar Gyáripar*, III, No. 7 (1913), 3–4.

25 *Ibid.*, 3; see also *Magyar Tövénytár* 1913, Law XIV; Pölöskei, 148.

26 Pölëski, 139–41, 241.

27 Péter Hanák, (ed.), *Magyarország története, 1890–1918* [History of Hungary, 1890–1918], (2 vols.; Budapest: Akadémiai Kiadó, 1978), II, 841–42.

28 For views of Hegedüs (echoing those of Gratz in *A Dualizmus kora*), see *Ady és Tisza*, 76.

29 For its opposition to increased military spending after the second Balkan War, see *Magyar Gyáripar*, III, No. 20 (1913), 2; for government contracts, see Berend and Ránki, *Magyarország gyáripara, 1900–1914*, 288–93.

Notes to Conclusion

1 Siegfried Mielke, *Der Hansa-Bund für Gewerbe, Handel und Industrie, 1909-1914,* (Göttingen: Vandenhoeck u. Ruprecht, 1976); Hartmut Kaelble, *Industrielle Interessénpolitik in der Wilhelmischen Gesellschaft,* (Berlin: Walter de Gruyter, 1967); Hans–Peter Ullmann, *Der Bund der Industriellen. Organisation, Einfluss und Politik klein- und mittelbetrieblicher Industrieller im deutschen Kaiserreich, 1895-1914,* (Göttingen: Vanderhoeck u. Ruprecht, 1967).

2 *Protokollen des Zentralverband der Industriellen Österreichs,* (Vienna: 1905), 68; *ibid.,* (1906), 28; *Rechenschafts-Bericht des Ausschusses und Protokoll der I. Jahresversammlung des "Wiener Industriellenverband" am 14. April 1907,* (Vienna), 9-10; Wiener Industrieller Klub, *Mitteillungen,* 1906, No. 72 (November 20, 1906), 3.

Notes to Epilogue

1 "Vállalkozói közgyülés' [General Meeting of Entrepreneurs], *Heti Világgazdaság,* Budapest, March 11, 1989, 50; and February 11, 1989, 52.

INDEX